❖ 'HER GAZE WENT
ROUND THE LADEN
SHELVES, THE STORED
HERBS DANGLING,
THE BRAZIER AND THE
POTS AND FLASKS,
INTERESTED AND CURIOUS,
BUT IN NO WAY
AWED BY CADFAEL OR
HIS MYSTERIES.'

THE PILGRIM OF HATE

BROTHER CADFAEL'S HERB GARDEN

An Illustrated Companion to
Medieval Plants and their Uses

Text by Robin Whiteman • Photographs by Rob Talbot

A Bulfinch Press Book
Little, Brown and Company
BOSTON NEW YORK TORONTO LONDON

First United States Edition

Based upon the books *The Brother Cadfael
Chronicles* by Ellis Peters, and the television
series produced by Carlton UK Television

ISBN 0-8212-2387-9

Library of Congress Catalog Card Number 96–78402

Bulfinch Press is an imprint and trademark of
Little, Brown and Company (Inc.)

Designed by Janet James
Specially commissioned artwork by Nadine Wickenden

PRINTED IN ITALY

THE CADFAEL CHRONICLES

BY ELLIS PETERS

All the Chronicles (except numbers 10–13)
are published in the USA by The
Mysterious Press/Warner Books Inc.,
A Time Warner Company.
Numbers 10–13 are published by William
Morrow & Co., Inc.

Contents

INTRODUCTION

❖ Quotations from
The Cadfael Chronicles

❖ Other quotations

❖ 'BROTHER CADFAEL HAD COME LATE TO THE MONASTIC LIFE, LIKE A BATTERED SHIP SETTLING AT LAST FOR A QUIET HARBOUR. HE WAS WELL AWARE THAT IN THE FIRST YEARS OF HIS VOWS THE NOVICES AND LAY SERVANTS HAD BEEN WONT TO POINT OUT TO ONE ANOTHER WITH AWED WHISPERINGS. "SEE THAT BROTHER WORKING IN THE GARDEN THERE? THE THICKSET FELLOW WHO ROLLS FROM ONE LEG TO THE OTHER LIKE A SAILOR? YOU WOULDN'T THINK TO LOOK AT HIM, WOULD YOU, THAT HE WENT ON CRUSADE WHEN HE WAS YOUNG? HE WAS WITH GODFREY DE BOUILLON AT ANTIOCH, WHEN THE SARACENS SURRENDERED IT. AND HE TOOK TO THE SEAS AS A CAPTAIN WHEN THE KING OF JERUSALEM RULED ALL THE COAST OF THE HOLY LAND, AND SERVED AGAINST THE CORSAIRS TEN YEARS! HARD TO BELIEVE IT NOW, EH?"'

CADFAEL'S SKILLS OF HERBALIST, apothecary and healer were mostly learned, without formal training, in the Holy Land from both Saracen and Syrian physicians. Yet almost from the moment he became a novice in Shrewsbury abbey at the age of forty, he began to improve and refine his medicinal expertise in the use of plants and herbs, 'by experience, by trial and study, accumulating knowledge over the years, until some preferred his ministrations to those of the acknowledged physicians.'

There can be little doubt that the abbey at Shrewsbury – which, like all Benedictine monasteries in England, placed great emphasis on study and learning – contained and preserved books, laboriously copied by hand and often beautifully illuminated, on subjects ranging from classical philosophy and science to canon law and the history and lives of the saints. Indeed, within *The Cadfael Chronicles* are a number of references to specific authors: St Augustine of Hippo (354–430), 'of whom Cadfael was not as fond as he might have been'; St Anselm (c.1033–1109); St Benedict of Nursia (c.480–547), father of Western monasticism and originator of the Rule which demanded from monks in the Benedictine Order a life-long vow of poverty, chastity, obedience and stability; Archbishop Lanfranc of Canterbury (c.1005–89), whose reasonings led Abbot Radulfus to cease accepting child oblates into the abbey until they were 'able to consider for themselves what manner of life they desire'; and Origen (c.185–254), the great Christian writer, scholar and head of the Catechetical School in Alexandria, 'who held that in the end everyone would find salvation. Even the fallen angels would return to their fealty, even the devil would repent and make his way back to God.'

Yet only two authors of works on plants or gardening are mentioned in the

❖ 'Distantly this springtime snow stirred his memory of other Springs, and later blossoms, like but unlike this, when the hawthorns came into heady, drunken sweetness, drowning the senses.'

THE HOLY THIEF

Chronicles: Palladius (c.365–425), famous for his history of early monasticism, who also wrote a book on agriculture, *Palladius de Agricultura*, with hints on what to do each month throughout the gardening year; and Aelfric (c.955–1010), also known as 'the Grammarian', a Benedictine monk of Cerne Abbas and also of Winchester, who was considered to be the greatest prose writer of his time. Among the latter's numerous works, written in both Latin and Old English, was *Colloquy (Nominum Herbarum)*, compiled in 995 and comprising a list of over 200 herbs and trees, several of which are no longer identifiable. The ambiguity contained in Aelfric's vocabulary is touched on in *The Devil's Novice*, set in late 1140. Cadfael had 'got hold of a copy of Aelfric's list of herbs and trees from the England of a century and a half earlier, and wanted peace and quiet in which to study it.' 'Within minutes he was absorbed in the problem of whether the "dittanders" of Aelfric was, or was not, the same as his own "dittany".' The uncertainty, however, was not because Cadfael – a 'practical man of hand and brain' – found reading difficult. On the contrary, the *Chronicles* clearly state that in addition to speaking fluent Welsh (it was, after all, his 'first, best language') Cadfael was literate in English. Furthermore, he had 'mastered' Latin 'laboriously in maturity', though 'it remained unfamiliar, an alien tongue.' Being 'endlessly curious', Cadfael would almost certainly have combed every cupboard and carrel within the abbey [†] in search of herbal mysteries, and to discover more about the science he had devoted himself to study in his cloistered retirement as gardener and apothecary of Shrewsbury. Indeed, Hugh Beringar was so impressed by Cadfael's arts in *One Corpse Too Many* that he accused him of being an 'alchemist' and even a 'wizard'.

"'In the forest . . . in the dark? We'll get through!'"

THE LEPER OF SAINT GILES

One book that Cadfael may very well have consulted was the Latin poem *De virtutibus herbarum*, compiled in France in the first half of the eleventh century and widely copied by hand throughout Europe. Interestingly, at Naples in 1477 it became the first herbal ever to be printed in the Western world. Being a Welshman, Cadfael may also have heard of the 'Physicians of Myddfai', a remarkable group of herbal doctors (probably all belonging to the same family) who passed their healing knowledge down from generation to generation for

[†] It was not until the fifteenth century that a single room was set aside in monasteries for collections of books. The number of books at Shrewsbury would probably only have totalled a few hundred.

many hundreds of years. Myddfai, formerly a manor of the Princes of south Wales, is a small village situated amidst wooded hills above the Afon Tywi (Tywi river), three miles south of Llandovery. Although some of the secrets of the physicians were written down in the twelfth or thirteenth century, the manuscripts were not translated from Welsh into English until the mid-nineteenth century. In addition to being a valuable source of information on Druidic herbal traditions, the writings also reveal that the Welsh physicians had a knowledge of Greek, Roman and Arabic plant and healing lore.

The history of herbal medicine dates back to the dawn of time, when our earliest ancestors began to realize that certain plants had a particular affect on their health and well-being. Unlike animals, which instinctively avoid eating anything that is poisonous, humans had to learn by trial and error. Some plants may well have proved harmful, even deadly, but others were found to soothe, to smell sweetly, to yield a coloured dye or to be good to eat; a few, when ingested, produced a curious effect on the human body or mind. Little wonder, therefore, that plants were deemed to possess inner 'powers', either for good or for evil, and in themselves became objects of veneration and worship: trees especially, as they lived far longer than the span of a single human lifetime. Most of the plants regarded as magical were used for medicine rather than for food. Corn was one exception, for reputedly within the corn plant lived a spirit or goddess who had to be kept alive over winter, from the end of the harvest to the sowing of the next year's crop. In ancient Greece this goddess was known as Demeter, and in Rome, Ceres.

As magic and religion, biology and medicine, botany and philosophy all originally coexisted side by side (rather than being separate and distinct sciences), elaborate rituals grew up around the gathering and use of plants and herbs. To be most efficacious they had to be picked and prepared at specific times of the day or year. The Druids, for example, cut oak mistletoe at the new moon with a golden sickle, making sure that it did not touch the ground, for the earth would rob it of its magical powers. Some of these 'magical' plants venerated by pagans were later Christianized by a simple name change: ragwort, for example, became *Herba Sancti Jacobi* or the 'herb of Saint James'.

Although references to herbs, including spells and prescriptions, have been preserved from the civilizations of ancient Egypt, Mesopotamia, India and China, it was the classical works of the Greeks and Romans that dominated European science and medicine up to and throughout the medieval period.

The Greek physician Hippocrates (c.460–370 BC), may be traditionally regarded as the father of medicine, but the standard medical texts in Europe and western Asia until the Renaissance were by another Greek physician, Galen (AD c.130–199). Relying heavily on the teachings of Hippocrates, Galen brought together all the best knowledge of the Greek medical schools (while striving to remove ritual and superstition), classified herbs by their essential qualities of hot or cold, dry or moist, and strongly supported the theory of the four humours – blood, phlegm, black bile and yellow bile. These humours, on which Galen based many of his treatments, were also linked with the four seasons of the year, and the four elements of earth, air, fire and water. It was at Alexandria in Egypt, the great centre of learning in which Galen practised for a time, that the Greeks developed the idea that the astrological signs of the zodiac influenced parts of the body – a notion supported by Nicholas Culpeper (1616–54), author of the popular *The Complete Herbal and English Physician*, and for which he was much ridiculed and maligned by his contemporaries.

After Hippocrates and Galen, the most important classical writer on medicine is Pedanius Dioscorides, a Sicilian of Greek extraction who was reputed to have been a doctor in the Roman army during the reign of the Emperor Nero (AD 54–68). His *De Materia Medica*, written in about AD 64 and dealing with over 500 plants, was the principal and most influential source of Western herbal knowledge for over 1,500 years. The earliest surviving copy of Dioscorides' authoritative herbal, usually called the *Codex Vindobonensis*, was written and illustrated at Constantinople for Juliana Anicia, daughter of the Emperor Flavius, in about AD 512. In addition to being a milestone in botanical art, it is the earliest surviving illustrated herbal in the Western world. Arising out of the writings of Dioscorides came the 'Doctrine of Signatures', the theory that the appearance or outward sign of a plant resembled the part of the human body that it could help to heal or cure.

The botanical works of Theophrastus (c.372–287 BC), the Greek philosopher who succeeded Aristotle as the head of the Peripatetic School at Athens, were not translated into Latin until the fifteenth century, yet they were an important source of reference for many medieval herbalists and apothecaries. To a lesser degree, so were the writings of the Roman author known as Pliny the Elder (AD 23–79), whose *Natural History* was described by *The Oxford Companion to English Literature* (1986) as 'an encyclopaedic rag-bag of popular science.' As his writings were uncritical and his findings unverified, coupled with the fact that he lacked a first-hand knowledge of the sciences, his work is considered to have little importance today. The letters of his nephew, Pliny the Younger (AD 62–c.112) provide valuable information on plants and the layout of Roman gardens.

Although the Romans introduced many plants and herbs into Britain, it was the Emperor Charlemagne (c.742–814) who actively encouraged the spread of Mediterranean herbs and spices throughout Europe. Impressed by the health-giving beauty and usefulness of the herbarium at the Benedictine monastery of St Gall, near Lake Constance in Switzerland, Charlemagne decreed that each city within his empire should have a garden planted with 'all herbs'. In his famous 'Decree concerning Towns', there is a list of over eighty plants and fruit-bearing trees, at the head of which are the rose and the lily. It is not known who advised the emperor on which plants to include in the list, but among the possible candidates are Alcuin, a former pupil at the cathedral school of York and eventually abbot of the monastery of St Martin at Tours in France, and the great gardener Benedict, abbot of the monastery at Aniane in the south of France.

Charlemagne's edicts, however, did not stretch as far as Britain, and therefore during the so-called Dark Ages it was left to the monasteries to preserve and augment the legacy of herbal knowledge abandoned by the Romans. The earliest surviving Anglo-Saxon manuscript dealing with the virtues of herbs is the *Leech Book of Bald*, written in the vernacular by a Saxon doctor or 'leech' in the early tenth century, and embodying beliefs that date back to primitive and mysterious times, long before Christianity, and indeed the Romans, invaded English shores. The oldest illustrated herbal to have been preserved from Anglo-Saxon times is a translation of the Latin *Herbarium of Apuleius*, originally compiled in the fifth century. The Anglo-Saxon translation of this herbal was produced between 1000 and 1050, and seems to have been copied from a manuscript that originated in southern Italy. One of the illustrations depicts a mandrake being pulled out of the ground by a lead attached to a dog. Clearly, many of the plants represented have been copied from older illustrations, and many are species not native to Britain. The *Lacnunga*, an Anglo-Saxon manuscript thought to have been written in the tenth century, contains an alliterative lay or charm in praise of the

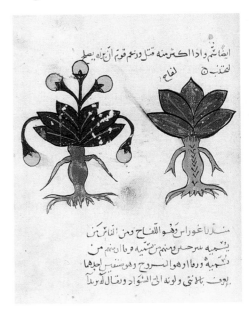

nine sacred herbs of the Nordic god Woden. These nine herbs, which 'have power against nine magic outcasts, against nine venoms, and against nine flying things, against the loathed things that over land rove' were mugwort, waybroad (plantain), stime (watercress), maythen (chamomile), wergulu (nettle), chervil, fennel, crab-apple and the unidentified 'atterlothe'.

Although the Anglo-Saxons were very interested in herbs, the main research and development in herbal medicine after the collapse of the Roman Empire was carried out by Arab physicians, who based much of their learning on the writings of the ancient Greeks. Avicenna (980–1037), known as the 'Prince of Physicians', for example, frequently acknowledged the teachings of Galen and Aristotle in his *Canon of Medicine*. The work was not only highly regarded in the Arab world, but was a key teaching text in European medical schools for some 600 years.

After the Norman conquest of England in 1066 (just fourteen years before Cadfael was born at Trefriw in north Wales) many Anglo-Saxon manuscripts were destroyed and replaced with books written exclusively in Latin. Among the Latin works concerning plants may have been: Macer's herbal poem *De virtutibus herbarum*; Isidore of Seville's celebrated encyclopaedia *Etymologiae*, compiled in the seventh century and containing a section on botany; and Walafrid Strabo's ninth-century gardening poem *Hortulus*. In addition to the works listed above, the only other major botanical sources to have been written in Europe before or during Cadfael's lifetime were *De Simplicibus Medicinis*, usually known as 'Circa Instans', composed in about 1150 by either Johannes or Matthaeus Platearius, and *Liber subtilitatum diversarum naturarum creaturarum*, written by Hildegard of Bingen between 1151 and 1158, which names about 140 herbs, as well as describing their medicinal uses.

Most of the herbals that appeared between the middle of the twelfth century and the middle of the fifteenth century, when the first, mechanically printed book appeared, were copies of earlier works. The only original treatise on herbs written in England during this period was the seventeenth book of the nineteen-volume *De Proprietatibus Rerum*, written in Latin by Bartholomaeus Anglicus in about 1250, and translated into English in 1398. Although there is no record of Bartholomaeus being a gardener, his writings reveal an instinctive love of plants and of the countryside:

'The spring spate from the mountains was over now, the river showed a bland face.'

THE SANCTUARY SPARROW

❖ 'SPRINGING TIME IS THE TIME OF GLADNESS AND OF LOVE; FOR IN SPRINGING TIME ALL THINGS SEEMETH GLAD; FOR THE EARTH WAXETH GREEN, TREES BURGEON AND SPREAD, MEADOWS BRING FORTH FLOWERS, HEAVEN SHINETH, THE SEA RESTETH AND IS QUIET, FOWLS SING AND MAKE THEIR NESTS, AND ALL THINGS THAT SEEMED DEAD IN WINTER AND WITHERED, [HAVE] BEEN RENEWED, IN SPRINGING TIME.'

The first printed English herbal, commonly known as *Banckes's Herbal*, is an anonymous compilation from various sources. Published in 1525 by Richard Banckes, it also contained a copy of the famous discourse on the virtues of rosemary, sent by the Countess of Hainault to her daughter Queen Philippa, wife of Edward I. The first Englishman to study plants scientifically was William Turner, whose *A New Herball*, published in three parts 1551–68, marked the beginning of the science of botany in England. *The Herball or Generall Historie of Plantes*, by the herbalist and superintendent of Lord Burghley's gardens, John Gerard, was published in 1597. This work is celebrated throughout the English-speaking world for its delightful descriptions and matchless Elizabethan prose. In his dedication to Lord Burghley Gerard wrote:

❖ 'WHAT GREATER DELIGHT IS THERE THAN TO BEHOLD THE EARTH APPARELLED WITH PLANTS, AS WITH A ROBE OF EMBROIDERED WORK, SET WITH ORIENT PEARLS, AND GARNISHED WITH GREAT DIVERSITY OF RARE AND COSTLY JEWELS? ... BUT THESE DELIGHTS ARE IN THE OUTWARD SENSES: THE PRINCIPAL DELIGHT IS IN THE MIND, SINGULARLY ENRICHED WITH THE KNOWLEDGE OF VISIBLE THINGS, SETTING FORTH TO US THE INVISIBLE WISDOM AND ADMIRABLE WORKMANSHIP OF ALMIGHTY GOD.'

At the Dissolution of the Monasteries 1536–41, some valuable books and manuscripts found their way into private libraries. Owen and Blakeway, in *A History of Shrewsbury* (1825), listed fifty books belonging to Henry Langley, 'knight, of Shropshire', which were inherited from his great-great-grandfather, 'the original purchaser' of Shrewsbury abbey from the Crown. Among these were *Petri Abaelardi Doctrina, Alcuinus Levita, Vita Sanctae Hildegardis, Augustini Sermones in Dominicis et quam plurima alia, Bedae Sermones in Dominicis, Isidor de Origine rerum, de summo bono, de Illustribus Viris, Rob. Talbot in partem Antonini, Palladius de Agricultura* and *Petrarcha de Remediis.*

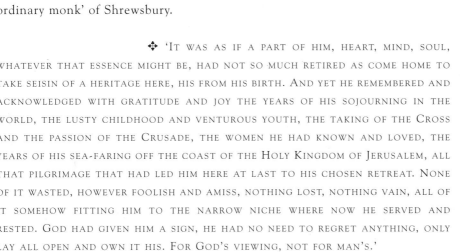

The authors then go on to reveal the wilful destruction of many books in monastic libraries:

✣ 'If these actually belonged to our abbey, the first lay proprietor, Langley, must have been an honourable exception to the great body of such purchasers, who generally sold them to grocers and chandlers. Whole shiploads, we are told, were sent abroad to the book-binders, that vellum or parchment might be cut up in their trade. Covers were torn off for their brass bosses and clasps: and their contents served the ignorant and careless for waste paper. In this manner English history sustained irreparable losses; and it is more than probable that some of the works of classical antiquity perished in the indiscriminate and extensive destruction.'

Like many herbalists and gardeners, Cadfael possessed a great love of plants and a deep reverence for the natural world, for which he was humbly thankful, and from which he gained an enormous amount of pleasure and satisfaction. In his roving youth he not only visited Italy, Greece and Arabia, the ancient cradle of European herbal medicine, but he brought back to England with him 'many exotic plants' which he carefully raised and cross-bred in his own monastic herb-garden. Yet despite having been 'forty years about the world, and from end to end of it' before he took the cowl, Cadfael was perfectly content with his 'green, sweet ending' as an 'elderly and ordinary monk' of Shrewsbury.

❖ 'It was as if a part of him, heart, mind, soul, whatever that essence might be, had not so much retired as come home to take seisin of a heritage here, his from his birth. And yet he remembered and acknowledged with gratitude and joy the years of his sojourning in the world, the lusty childhood and venturous youth, the taking of the Cross and the passion of the Crusade, the women he had known and loved, the years of his sea-faring off the coast of the Holy Kingdom of Jerusalem, all that pilgrimage that had led him here at last to his chosen retreat. None of it wasted, however foolish and amiss, nothing lost, nothing vain, all of it somehow fitting him to the narrow niche where now he served and rested. God had given him a sign, he had no need to regret anything, only lay all open and own it his. For God's viewing, not for man's.'

CHAPTER

I

❖ 'THE SUMMER
SEASON WAS AT
ITS HEIGHT,
AND PROMISING
RICH HARVEST.'

SAINT PETER'S FAIR

THE MONASTIC GARDEN

THE MONASTIC GARDENS at Shrewsbury, dating from the foundation of the abbey of St Peter and St Paul by Earl Roger de Montgomery in 1083, lay within and without the high boundary wall of the religious enclave. The abbey itself occupied a spur of high, dry land on the far east bank of the river Severn, beyond the eastern gate of the fortified town of Shrewsbury. Within the enclave, the abbey grounds – which embraced Cadfael's herb-garden – were hemmed to the south by the waters of the Meole brook.

❖ 'THIS SAME WATER, DRAWN OFF MUCH HIGHER IN ITS COURSE, SUPPLIED THE MONASTERY FISH-PONDS, THE HATCHERY, AND THE MILL AND MILLPOND BEYOND, AND WAS FED BACK INTO THE BROOK JUST BEFORE IT ENTERED THE SEVERN.'

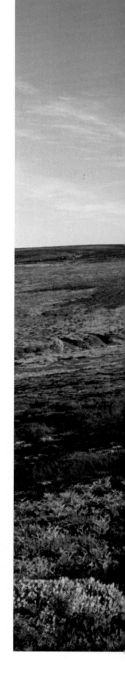

Forming a formidable and silent barrier to the west, the Severn almost encircled the town wall and hill of Shrewsbury on its long, meandering progress from the mountains of central Wales to the Bristol Channel and the Atlantic Ocean. To the east of the abbey precinct stood the wide triangular area of open ground known as the Horse-Fair, and beyond, the fields and copses that led to the leper hospital of St Giles, barely half a mile distant. To the north, across the bustling high road of the Abbey Foregate, and outside the monastic walls, lay the lush level land of the Gaye, together with the abbey's main orchards and vegetable gardens.

❖ 'CADFAEL BEGAN THE DESCENT TO THE GAYE. THIS PATH WAS TRODDEN REGULARLY, AND BARE OF GRASS, AND THE LANDWARD BUSHES THAT FRINGED IT DREW GRADUALLY BACK FROM ITS EDGE, LEAVING THE LEVEL, CULTIVATED GROUND OPEN. ON THE RIVER SIDE THEY GREW THICKLY, ALL DOWN THE SLOPE TO THE WATER, AND UNDER THE FIRST ARCH OF THE BRIDGE, WHERE ONCE A BOAT-MILL HAD BEEN MOORED TO MAKE USE OF THE FORCE OF THE CURRENT. CLOSE TO THE WATERSIDE A FOOTPATH LED OFF DOWNSTREAM, AND BESIDE IT THE ABBEY'S GARDENS LAY NEATLY ARRAYED ALL ALONG THE RICH PLAIN, AND THREE OR FOUR BROTHERS WERE PRICKING OUT PLANTS OF CABBAGE AND COLEWORT. FURTHER ALONG CAME THE ORCHARDS, APPLE AND PEAR AND PLUM, THE SWEET CHERRY, THE TWO BIG WALNUT TREES, AND THE LOW BUSHES OF LITTLE SOUR GOOSEBERRIES THAT WERE ONLY JUST BEGINNING TO FLUSH INTO COLOUR. THERE WAS ANOTHER DISUSED MILL AT THE END OF THE LEVEL, AND THE FINAL ABBEY GROUND WAS A FIELD OF CORN. THEN RIDGES OF WOODLAND CAME DOWN AND OVERHUNG THE WATER, AND THE CURLING EDDIES ATE AWAY THE BANK BENEATH THEIR ROOTS.'

On the opposite bank of the Severn, overlooking the orchards of the Gaye, and occupying the steep green slope, directly under and outside the town wall of Shrewsbury, were the abbot's vineyards.

In the twelfth century, the period in which the *Chronicles* are set, much of the countryside around Shrewsbury was covered in forest, especially the region to the south. The great belt of woodland known as the Long Forest, for instance, stretched westward from the southern outskirts of the town almost into Wales. Roads led north from the castle to the 'wilderness of dark-brown pools and quaking mosses and tangled bushes' bordering Shropshire and Cheshire; east from the English Bridge to the hospital of St Giles, from where one fork led to Lichfield and another to London; south from the Abbey

'In the north of the
shire the land was
flatter, with less
forest but wide
expanses of heath.
moorland and scrub.'

THE DEVIL'S NOVICE

Foregate to the heather-clad hills and windswept heights of the Long Mynd, Wenlock Edge and the Clee Hills; and west from the Western Bridge to either Welshpool or Oswestry, both routes leading past Offa's massive earthwork dyke and into Cadfael's native Wales. Fugitives often escaped English justice by fleeing west into Welsh territory: some seeking a permanent sanctuary, and others safe passage by sea to Ireland or Normandy.

Unrest along the border was rife. In *The Devil's Novice*, set in the autumn of 1140, the sheriff of Shropshire, Gilbert Prestcote, and Hugh Beringar, then his deputy, had held:

❖ 'THE COUNTY STAUNCH AND WELL-DEFENDED, REASONABLY FREE FROM THE DISORDERS THAT RACKED MOST OF THE COUNTRY, AND THE ABBEY HAD GOOD CAUSE TO BE GRATEFUL TO THEM, FOR MANY OF ITS SISTER HOUSES ALONG THE WELSH MARCHES HAD BEEN SACKED, PILLAGED, EVACUATED, TURNED INTO FORTRESSES FOR WAR, SOME MORE THAN ONCE, AND NO REMEDY OFFERED. WORSE THAN THE ARMIES OF KING STEPHEN ON THE ONE HAND AND HIS COUSIN THE EMPRESS ON THE OTHER — AND IN ALL CONSCIENCE THEY WERE BAD ENOUGH — THE LAND WAS CRAWLING WITH PRIVATE ARMIES, PREDATORS LARGE AND SMALL, DEVOURING EVERYTHING, WHEREVER THEY WERE SAFE FROM ANY FORCE OF LAW STRONG ENOUGH TO CONTAIN THEM. IN SHROPSHIRE THE LAW HAD BEEN STRONG ENOUGH, THUS FAR, AND LOYAL ENOUGH TO CARE FOR ITS OWN.'

During the unsettled period of the *Chronicles*, 1137–45, the abbey at Shrewsbury suffered from only two major physical upheavals, both of which could have been far more damaging: the siege of Shrewsbury by the army of King Stephen in the summer of 1138; and the great flood of February 1145, which invaded much of the abbey enclave, including the nave of the church. In *The Holy Thief*, incidentally, it is stated that similar flooding 'had happened twice since Cadfael entered the Order.' Although the Welsh made frequent forays into Shropshire and, for eight years from 1149, ruled over the Lordship of Oswestry, which they seized from the Normans, it was not until 1215, under Llywelyn the Great, that they besieged and captured Shrewsbury, if only for a while. It is unreasonable to suppose that the abbey gardens remained unaffected by these historical or fictional disturbances, especially during the occasions when the town was under attack, and bands of armed men roamed the countryside scavenging for food as well as for plunder. Within the protective walls of the enclave the monks may well have been able to maintain the cloistered routine and ordered discipline of the house. But outside, their lands and possessions would have been extremely vulnerable. Indeed, in *One Corpse Too Many*, the abbey mill at the far end of the Gaye was abandoned because of the siege of 1138 'and had suffered damage which would keep it out of use until repairs could be undertaken.' The same Chronicle further stated, with fatalistic optimism: 'Blessedly, the Flemings were not likely to ransack the gardens until they had looted stables and barns and stores.'

From the departure of the Romans (whose gardens were designed for leisure and entertainment as well as for usefulness) until the arrival of the Normans, there is scanty information on monastic horticultural practice in Britain. The Venerable Bede (673–735), in his *Ecclesiastical History of the English People*, recorded that the island was 'rich in crops and in trees, has good pasturage for cattle and beasts of burden, and also produces vines in certain districts.' Yet considering that gardening was second only to prayer in the monastic regime, his writings reveal very little about the cultivation of plants during the Anglo-Saxon period. As the followers of the Benedictine Rule had a Christian duty to care for the sick and needy, 'before all things and above all things', plants were grown with special emphasis on their medicinal and healing virtues. In order to be as self-sufficient as possible, the monks also grew their own vegetables and flowers. Until the development of the medieval pleasure garden, such as that described by Albertus Magnus in his treatise on vegetables and plants, *De Vegetabilibus et Plantis*, of about 1260[†], aesthetic beauty and sensual delight in the monastic garden were an incidental bonus.

[†] Quoted by John Harvey in *Medieval Gardens* (1981)

A copy of a ninth-century plan for the ideal monastery and its associated gardens was fortunately preserved at the Benedictine abbey of St Gall in Switzerland. Thought to have been drawn up by Abbot Haito of Reichenau, an island monastery in Lake Constance, it was addressed to Gozbert, abbot of St Gall from 816 to 836. The design, incidentally, displays similarities to the layout of Roman villas, and the first monasteries were built along these lines. In addition to outlining the position of all the principal buildings, the plan

shows, east of the church, three main gardens running from north to south: a medicinal or physic garden, next to the house of the physician and near the blood-letting room; an orchard, with fruit and blossom trees planted and arranged amidst the graves of the monks, and around a central cross; and a kitchen garden, beside the gardener's workshop and toolshed. Clearly, the gardens have been carefully sited: the medicinal herbs are by the infirmary; the orchards make attractive use of the cemetery; and the vegetables benefit from being in close proximity to an endless source of nitrogen-rich fertilizer from the poultry yards, as well as from the monks' latrines.

The square physic garden, or *herbularius*, has sixteen beds, one for each variety of named herb, among which are cumin, fennel, mint, lovage, sage, rue, savory, flag iris, pennyroyal, rosemary, and the lily and the rose. The much larger kitchen garden, or *hortus*, has eighteen beds, divided by a path into two equal rows of nine, and contains plants ranging from onions, garlic and leeks to coriander, chervil, poppy and dill. The enclosed cloister-garth, south of the church, would also have been laid out as a garden, with grass, flowers, intersecting paths, and possibly statues of saints or the Holy Family. At both ends of the church, east and west, is a semi-circular area for prayer and meditation. Open to the sky and planted with flowers, these small enclosures were known as 'paradises'.

In addition to being cultivated in monastic gardens, herbs were also gathered from the wild. Sometimes flowers were grown because they had some religious significance, rather than for beauty, perfume or decoration. Produce for the refectory tables came not just from the kitchen garden but from the abbey's arable fields, granaries, mills and fish ponds. Alcoholic drinks such as ale, wine and liqueurs, the monks brewed and distilled for themselves. Although their diet was mainly vegetarian – for the Rule of St Benedict said (though it was not always strictly followed), 'let everyone, except the sick, who are very weak, abstain entirely from eating the meat of four-footed animals' – the brothers in the *Chronicles* were sometimes offered treats:

❖ 'WITH THE APPROACH OF CHRISTMAS IT WAS QUITE USUAL FOR MANY OF THE MERCHANTS OF SHREWSBURY, AND THE LORDS OF MANY SMALL MANORS CLOSE BY, TO GIVE A GUILTY THOUGHT TO THE WELFARE OF THEIR

'Birds skimmed the bushes of the headland and flickered among the trees of the crest, and the uneasy memory of man was gone.'

THE POTTER'S FIELD

SOULS, AND THEIR STANDING AS DEVOUT AND OSTENTATIOUS CHRISTIANS, AND TO
SEE SMALL WAYS OF ACQUIRING MERIT, PREFERABLY AS ECONOMICALLY AS POSSIBLE.
THE CONVENTUAL FARE OF PULSE, BEANS, FISH, AND OCCASIONAL AND MEAGRE MEAT,
BENEFITED BY SUDDEN GIFTS OF FLESH AND FOWL TO PROVIDE TREATS FOR THE MONKS
OF ST PETER'S. HONEY-BAKED CAKES APPEARED, AND DRIED FRUITS AND CHICKENS,
AND EVEN, SOMETIMES, A HAUNCH OF VENISON, ALL DEVOTED TO THE PITTANCES
THAT TURNED A DEVOTIONAL SACRAMENT INTO A RARE INDULGENCE, A HOLY DAY
INTO A HOLIDAY.'

From the time when Earl Roger granted the abbey certain privileges, including
the exclusive right to grind the town's corn (a right confirmed by Henry I),
there was an uneasy friction between the citizens of Shrewsbury and the mill-
owning monks. Eventually, the townspeople erected their own mills in
violation of the charters. In 1267, on a visit to Shrewsbury, Henry III decreed
that the mills in the suburbs should be destroyed, while those within the town
walls should be jointly owned and the profits shared. It was not until 1328 that
the townspeople were able to grind their corn in complete independence from
the abbey. Nevertheless, during the reign of Edward I (1272–1307), according
to Owen and Blakeway's *A History of Shrewsbury* (1825), the monks were
forced to cede three of their four islands in the Severn to the burgesses of the
town.

❖ 'THESE ISLANDS WERE LARGE ENOUGH TO BEAR TREES
UPON THEM: YET THEY HAVE NOW NEARLY DISAPPEARED. IT IS PROBABLE THAT THE
FIRST THING THE BURGESSES DID WHEN THEY GOT THEM INTO THEIR POWER, WAS TO
TO DESTROY THEM: FOR THEY MUST MOST MATERIALLY HAVE OBSTRUCTED THE
NAVIGATION OF THE RIVER.'

During the period of the *Chronicles*, however, despite disagreements:

❖ 'RELATIONS BETWEEN THE TOWN OF SHREWSBURY ON
ONE SIDE OF THE RIVER AND THE ABBEY ON THE OTHER, IF NEVER EXACTLY CORDIAL
– THAT WAS TOO MUCH TO EXPECT, WHERE THEIR INTERESTS SO OFTEN COLLIDED –
WERE ALWAYS CORRECT, AND THEIR SKIRMISHES CONDUCTED WITH WARY COURTESY.'

Surplus produce from the abbey's fields, orchards and vegetable gardens was
sold at the abbey markets and fairs. Among his endowments, Earl Roger had

granted the abbot of Shrewsbury the right to hold an annual three-day fair at Lammas, the first day of August, a day known to the monks as St Peter ad Vincula, and an occasion of 'solemn and profitable importance to the house'. Held in 'the great triangle of the horse-fair, and all along the Foregate from the bridge to the corner of the enclosure, where the road veered right to Saint Giles, and the king's highway to London', the great festive event attracted people from far and wide, by river, by road and by foot.

❖ 'TRADERS OF ALL KINDS BEGAN TO MAKE THEIR WAY TO SHREWSBURY. AND INTO THE GREAT COURT OF THE ABBEY FLOCKED ALL THE GENTRY OF THE SHIRE, AND OF NEIGHBOURING SHIRES, TOO, LORDLINGS, KNIGHTS, YEOMEN, WITH THEIR WIVES AND DAUGHTERS, TO TAKE UP RESIDENCE IN THE OVERFLOWING GUEST-HALLS FOR THE THREE DAYS OF THE ANNUAL FAIR. SUBSISTENCE GOODS THEY GREW, OR BRED, OR BREWED, OR WOVE, OR SPAN FOR THEMSELVES, THE YEAR ROUND, BUT ONCE A YEAR THEY CAME TO BUY THE LUXURY CLOTHS, THE FINE WINES, THE RARE PRESERVED FRUITS, THE GOLD AND SILVER WORK, ALL THE TREASURES THAT APPEARED ON THE FEAST OF SAINT PETER AD VINCULA, AND VANISHED THREE DAYS AFTER. TO THESE GREAT FAIRS CAME MERCHANTS EVEN FROM FLANDERS AND GERMANY, SHIPPERS WITH FRENCH WINES, SHEARERS WITH THE WOOLCLIP FROM WALES, AND CLOTHIERS WITH THE FINISHED GOODS, GOWNS, JERKINS, HOSE, TOWN FASHIONS COME TO THE COUNTRY.'

As the Welsh were present at such festivals in great numbers, Cadfael sometimes found himself being called upon to act as interpreter. His main concern, however, was obviously the care and maintenance of the abbey's gardens, especially the herbarium, that 'pale-flowered, fragrant inner kingdom', where he ruled unchallenged. The wooden workshop in which he brewed his mysteries stood within the herb-garden, on the southern side of the church, beyond the monastic buildings and near the fish-ponds.

❖ 'IN THE HALF-HOUR BEFORE HIGH MASS AT TEN, CADFAEL BETOOK HIMSELF VERY THOUGHTFULLY TO HIS WORKSHOP IN THE HERB-GARDENS, TO TEND A FEW SPECIFICS HE HAD BREWING. THE ENCLOSURE, THICKLY HEDGED AND WELL TRIMMED, WAS BEGINNING NOW TO LOOK BLEACHED AND DRY WITH THE FIRST MODERATE COLD, ALL THE LEAVES GROWN ELDERLY AND LEAN AND BROWN, THE TENDEREST PLANTS WITHDRAWING INTO THE WARMTH OF THE EARTH; BUT THE AIR STILL BORE A LINGERING, AROMATIC FRAGRANCE COMPOUNDED OF ALL

THE GHOSTLY SCENTS OF SUMMER, AND INSIDE THE HUT THE SPICY SWEETNESS MADE THE SENSES SWIM. CADFAEL REGULARLY TOOK HIS PONDERINGS THERE FOR PRIVACY. HE WAS SO USED TO THE DRUNKEN, HEADY AIR WITHIN THAT HE BARELY NOTICED IT, BUT AT NEED HE COULD DISTINGUISH EVERY INGREDIENT THAT CONTRIBUTED TO IT, AND TRACE ITS SOURCE.'

Beyond his workshop and herb-garden, in the outer levels running down to the Meole brook, Cadfael 'grew food crops, beans and cabbages and pulse, and fields of pease.' In *A History of Shrewsbury*, one of Ellis Peters' main reference sources for the Chronicles, Owen and Blakeway wrote:

❖ 'THE MONKS WERE FOND OF HORTICULTURE. ITS GENTLE EXERCISE AND PLACID RECREATION SUITED THEIR HABITS. THEY PLANTED THE BEST FRUIT-TREES, FLOWERS, AND HERBS, WHICH THOSE AGES COULD FURNISH. THEY WERE PARTICULARLY PLEASED WITH ARBOURS AND SHADY WALKS. IT WAS NOT UNCOMMON FOR THEM TO HAVE EACH A PECULIAR GARDEN, DIVIDED BY A LOW WALL, AND LAID OUT IN BEDS OF FLOWERS.'

After the Conquest, the Normans revolutionized horticulture in Britain, introducing many new plants from the Continent, laying out gardens, and encouraging the planting of vineyards and orchards. Large tracts of the countryside were also turned into royal hunting 'forests', reserved for the exclusive recreation of the king and his followers and protected by laws that were particularly harsh and cruel. In *A Light on the Road to Woodstock* in *A Rare Benedictine* Cadfael visited Henry I's court at the palace of Woodstock, where the king hunted in the royal forest, and kept his beasts, 'lions and leopards – even camels.' The importance of hunting to the king is made apparent in part of Alard the Clerk's conversation with Cadfael: 'He makes his forest lodges the hub of his kingdom, there's more statecraft talked at Woodstock, so they say, than ever at Westminster.'

Monastic gardens were not simply places in which to toil, to grow plants, and to dispel idleness, 'the enemy of the soul': they were also secluded open-air temples in which to celebrate and worship the Creator, and a daily reminder of the mortality of all living things in which God may be glorified. Celtic Christianity maintained that God was experienced through nature, especially through the cultivation of a garden. As Cadfael's roots were deeply embedded in the Celtic traditions and beliefs of his Welsh ancestry, perhaps –

as a man of unquestioning faith – he can be forgiven for straying from strict adherence to the form of Christianity practised by the Roman Church, and conveniently freeing himself for service as a physician of both body and soul. The problem was knowing which 'brews', human or herbal, to stir and which to let alone. As Cadfael said himself in *Saint Peter's Fair*: 'I know my herbs. They have fixed properties, and follow sacred rules. Human creatures do not so. And I cannot even wish they did.'

God may resolve all in time, but Cadfael had 'the uncomfortable feeling that God, nevertheless, required a little help from men, and what he got was hindrance.' Yet, by his personal affirmation of the omniscience of God, Cadfael had to 'admit the inadequacy of human effort.' In *Welsh Angel in Fallen England: Ellis Peters' Brother Cadfael (Mysterium and Mystery: The Clerical Crime Novel)*, William David Spencer suggests that, as far greater insight can be gained by experience rather than by contemplation, Cadfael had to create his own 'eclectic theology'.

❖ 'PARGETER'S HERO DOES NOT FOLLOW A RELIGION THAT TAKES THE WORSHIPPER OUT OF THE WORLD, THAT NEGATES IMAGES AND GIFTS TO ARRIVE AT LAST IN UNION WITH THAT IMAGED, THE GREAT GIVER. HER IDEAL IS INSTEAD THE INTEGRATED WORSHIPPER WHO INVITES THROUGH ACTIVITY THE REIGN OF GOD INTO THE WORLD, WHO DOES NOT INVEST ARDUOUS HOURS IN MEDITATION BUT RATHER FINDS GOD IN THE GROWING OF HERBS, THE HEALING OF SADDENED HEARTS, THE CHAMPIONING OF TRUTH AND THE FERRETING OUT AND ROUTING OF EVIL.'

In her Introduction to *A Rare Benedictine*, Ellis Peters defined exactly how far Cadfael was prepared to stray from his monastic obligations: 'On occasions and for what he feels to be good reasons, he may break the rules. He will never transgress against the Rule, and never abandon it.'

On New Year's Day 1142 – the day Father Ailnoth, the 'Raven in the Foregate' was buried – Cadfael was in a reflective mood.

❖ '"TALK OF FALLING INTO SIN," SAID CADFAEL LATER, WHEN HE AND HUGH WERE SITTING EASY TOGETHER IN THE WORKSHOP IN THE HERB GARDEN, "FORCES ME TO EXAMINE MY OWN CONSCIENCE. I ENJOY SOME PRIVILEGES, BY REASON OF BEING CALLED ON TO ATTEND SICK PEOPLE OUTSIDE THE ENCLAVE, AND ALSO BY VIRTUE OF HAVING A GODSON TO VISIT. BUT I OUGHT NOT TO TAKE

'He waded the bushes towards the arch, and the last of the dew darkened his sandals and the skirt of his habit.'

THE ROSE RENT

26

advantage of that permission for my own ends. Which I have done shamelessly on three or four occasions since Christmas. Indeed, Father Abbot must be well aware that I went out from the precinct this very morning without leave, but he's said no word about it."

"No doubt he takes it for granted you'll be making proper confession voluntarily, at chapter tomorrow," said Hugh, straight-faced.

"That I doubt! He'd hardly welcome it I should have to explain the reason, and I know his mind by now. There are old hawks like Radulfus and myself in here, who can stand the gales, but there are also innocents who will not benefit by too stormy a wind blowing through the dovecote.'"

Outside the dim, sheltered warmth and well-oiled timbers of Cadfael's sweet-scented workshop, the monastic gardens at Shrewsbury had sunk deep into their winter sleep, all growth having ceased in the cold. Everything was neat and clean, the beds dug and manured, the spent herbage cleared, the harvested produce secured in barn and loft and store. Yet, with the clarion call of spring, there would be a new beginning, and all those plants – all those 'drowsy minor manifestations of God' that had grown old and tired – would grow young and vigorous again. Miraculously, the monastic garden would be renewed.

❖ 'WITH AUTUMN
NOW WELL ADVANCED,
THE PEOPLE OF THE
ROADS WOULD
BE THINKING AHEAD
TO THE
WINTER WEATHER ...'

THE POTTER'S FIELD

CADFAEL'S HERBAL KINGDOM

 HE FIRST *Chronicle of Brother Cadfael, A Morbid Taste for Bones*, opens on a 'fine, bright morning in early May' in the year 1137, to find Cadfael – seventeen years tonsured and approaching sixty – working among the vegetables in the enclosed gardens of Shrewsbury abbey.

❖ 'BROTHER CADFAEL HAD BEEN UP LONG BEFORE PRIME, PRICKING OUT CABBAGE SEEDINGS BEFORE THE DAY WAS AIRED, AND HIS THOUGHTS WERE ALL ON BIRTH, GROWTH AND FERTILITY.'

Begrudging 'the necessity to take himself indoors for Mass, and the succeeding half hour of chapter', Cadfael found satisfaction in pursuing more congenial labours among the herbs and plants entrusted to his patient care. But there was no evading his duty.

❖ 'HE HAD, AFTER ALL, CHOSEN THIS CLOISTERED LIFE WITH HIS EYES OPEN, HE COULD NOT COMPLAIN EVEN OF THOSE PARTS OF IT HE FOUND UNATTRACTIVE, WHEN THE WHOLE SUITED HIM VERY WELL.'

Right from the outset the *Chronicles* place particular emphasis on Cadfael's monastic vocation as a gardener, stressing also that he had come to this stasis after a wide-ranging career that had taken him across much of the Christian and Muslim world. Yet, consciously or not, Cadfael must have sensed that one day he would exchange his sword for a spade, not only to raise plants, but to make especial use of them for the benefit of others. For amid those unregretted experiences of battle and adventure and love, he had made a positive effort to collect the seeds of exotic medicinal plants such as the opium poppy, which he brought back to England with him, and ultimately raised and perfected in his own garden at Shrewsbury.

❖ 'HE DOUBTED IF THERE WAS A FINER BENEDICTINE GARDEN IN THE WHOLE KINGDOM, OR ONE BETTER SUPPLIED WITH HERBS BOTH GOOD FOR SPICING MEATS, AND ALSO INVALUABLE AS MEDICINE. THE MAIN ORCHARDS AND LANDS OF THE SHREWSBURY ABBEY OF SAINT PETER AND SAINT PAUL LAY ON THE NORTHERN SIDE OF THE ROAD, OUTSIDE THE MONASTIC ENCLAVE, BUT HERE, IN THE ENCLOSED GARDEN WITHIN THE WALLS, CLOSE TO THE ABBOT'S FISH-PONDS AND THE BROOK THAT WORKED THE ABBEY MILL, BROTHER CADFAEL RULED UNCHALLENGED. THE HERB GARDEN IN PARTICULAR WAS HIS KINGDOM, FOR HE HAD BUILT IT UP GRADUALLY THROUGH FIFTEEN YEARS OF LABOUR, AND ADDED TO IT MANY EXOTIC PLANTS OF HIS OWN CAREFUL RAISING, COLLECTED IN A ROVING YOUTH THAT HAD TAKEN HIM AS FAR AFIELD AS VENICE, AND CYPRUS AND THE HOLY LAND.'

Indeed, Cadfael himself felt that 'in such a garden a man could believe in peace, fruitfulness and amity.'

Despite the fact that each *Chronicle* stands as a story in its own right, the entire sequence, totalling twenty, proceeds steadily year by year, season by season, in an unbroken tension that skilfully interweaves historical fact with derived fiction. Cadfael, the fictional protagonist, is an ordinary, non-ordained monk, a lay brother, having 'no official function', and ranking too low in the monastic hierarchy to be invited to the abbot's table when there were important guests.

'The brightness of the morning, opening like a rose as the gossamer cloud parted, seemed instead to darken the promising day.'

THE HERETIC'S APPRENTICE

❖ 'Since he held no troublesome parchment office, he was unlikely to be called upon to speak in chapter upon the various businesses of the house, and when the matter in hand was dull into the bargain it was his habit to employ the time to good account by sleeping, which from long usage he could do bolt upright and undetected in his shadowy corner. He had a sixth sense which alerted him at need, and brought him awake instantly and plausibly. He had even been known to answer a question pat, when it was certain he had been asleep when it was put to him.'

Retiring to the privacy of his workshop in the herbarium was 'always a convenient excuse for not being where according to the horarium he should have been.'

❖ 'Within the Benedictine rule, and in genial companionship with it, he had perfected a daily discipline of his own, that suited his needs admirably.'

More often than not, he was up before dawn, before the first office of the monastic day, to put in an hour's work in his herbarium.

❖ 'BROTHER CADFAEL ROSE WELL BEFORE PRIME TO GO
TO HIS WORKSHOP, WHERE HE HAD LEFT A BATCH OF TROCHES DRYING OVERNIGHT.
THE BUSHES IN THE GARDEN, THE HERBS IN THE ENCLOSED HERBARIUM, ALL
GLIMMERED SOFTLY WITH THE LINGERING DEW OF A BRIEF SHOWER, AND REFLECTED
BACK THE DAWN SUNLIGHT FROM THOUSANDS OF TINY FACETS OF SILVER. ANOTHER
FINE, FRESH DAY BEGINNING. EXCELLENT FOR PLANTING, MOIST, MILD, THE SOIL
FINELY CRUMBLED AFTER THE INTENSE FROSTS OF THE HARD WINTER. THERE COULD BE
NO BETTER AUGURIES FOR GERMINATION AND GROWTH.'

Sometimes he left the enclave altogether in order to collect certain plants
fresh from the surrounding countryside.

❖ 'IT WAS A PLEASURE TO WALK ALONG THE TRODDEN
PATH THAT WAS ONLY A PALER LINE IN THE TURF, FOLLOWING THE FAST, QUIET FLOOD
DOWNSTREAM. CADFAEL WENT WITH HIS EYES ON THE HALF-TURGID, HALF-CLEAR
EDDIES THAT SPAN AND MURMURED UNDER THE LIP OF GREEN, A STRONG CURRENT
HERE HUGGING THIS SHORE. ACROSS THE STREAM, SO SILENT AND SO FAST, THE
WALLS OF SHREWSBURY LOOMED, AT THE CREST OF A STEEP GREEN SLOPE OF GARDENS,
ORCHARDS AND VINEYARD, AND FURTHER DOWNSTREAM FUSED INTO THE SOLID BULK
OF THE KING'S CASTLE, GUARDING THE NARROW NECK OF LAND THAT BROKE
SHREWSBURY'S GIRDLE OF WATER.'

By the riverside, in due season, beyond the orchards and vegetable gardens of
the Gaye and past the abbey's wheatfields and abandoned mill, Cadfael
collected 'juicy water betony', and the roots and leaves of marsh mallow and
comfrey. Along the bushy edges of the pease-fields and the shore of the mill-
pond, he gathered the white blossoms of blackthorn. In the flowering meadows
of the Severn plain he found archangel, poppy, daisy and centaury. Under
tangled hedgerows and sheltering trees he picked woundwort and cleavers, and
among the rough stones of crumbling walls, toadflax, stonecrop and selfheal.
    Within the walls of the abbey enclave Cadfael nurtured a wide variety of
produce, ranging from fruit and vegetables for the kitchen, herbs for the
infirmary, and flowers for the church. During the active part of the gardening
year, he was accustomed to having two assistants allotted to him:

❖ 'FOR HE GREW OTHER THINGS IN HIS WALLED GARDEN BESIDES THE ENCLOSURE OF HERBS, THOUGH THE MAIN KITCHEN GARDENS OF THE ABBEY WERE OUTSIDE THE ENCLAVE, ACROSS THE MAIN HIGHWAY AND ALONG THE FIELDS BY THE RIVER, THE LUSH LEVEL CALLED THE GAYE. THE WATERS OF SEVERN REGULARLY MOISTENED IT IN THE FLOOD SEASON, AND ITS SOIL WAS RICH AND BORE WELL. HERE WITHIN THE WALLS HE HAD MADE, VIRTUALLY SINGLE-HANDED, THIS CLOSED GARDEN FOR THE SMALL AND PRECIOUS THINGS, AND IN THE OUTER LEVELS, RUNNING DOWN TO THE MEOLE BROOK THAT FED THE MILL, HE GREW FOOD CROPS, BEANS AND CABBAGES AND PULSE, AND FIELDS OF PEASE.'

In spite of the climate of anarchy and unrest generated by King Stephen and the Empress Maud in their long and fratricidal struggle for the crown of England, the horarium of the abbey at Shrewsbury progressed almost as steadily and imperturbably as the cycle of the seasons, 'two enduring rhythms in the desperately variable fortunes of mankind.' Cadfael, however, seemed to be more in harmony with the latter. After all: 'The seasons kept their even pace. Only men came and went, acted and refrained, untimely'.

According to the monastic horarium, the day began at dawn with Prime. Terce followed at about nine, Sext at about noon, None at about three, and Vespers in the late afternoon. The last office of the day, held at about eight-thirty in summer and about seven-thirty in winter, was Compline, 'the completion, the perfecting of the day's worship.' Just before midnight, however, the monks were awoken for the long service of Matins, 'the celebration of God made flesh, virgin-born and wonderful'. Between one and two in the morning, after the short office of Lauds which immediately followed Matins, the monks returned to their beds in the dortoir.

Once Prime was over, at about eight-thirty, the Morning Mass, or Lady Mass, was held for the servants and manual workers. Whilst this mass was in progress, the monks assembled in the chapter-house to discuss the dull, routine business of the monastery. It was during these sessions, known as Chapter, that Cadfael often dozed 'in his chosen corner, well to the rear and poorly lit, half-concealed behind one of the stone pillars.'

The principal mass of the day, High Mass, took place at about ten in the morning and lasted about an hour. Collations, held in the chapter-house after supper, involved a short formal reading on the monastic life, usually taken from the *Lives of the Saints*. In between these daylight offices – some of which he often conveniently excused himself from – Cadfael found time to labour in

the abbey gardens, as well as brew herbal mysteries in his workshop, or probe into those, more complex and human, in the cloistered and uncloistered world outside.

❖ '"I HAVE TRANSGRESSED AGAINST MY VOCATION,"SAID CADFAEL [TO HIS FRIEND HUGH BERINGAR], AT ONCE SOLACED AND SADDENED BY THE SEASON AND THE HOUR. "I KNOW IT. I UNDERTOOK THE MONASTIC LIFE, BUT NOW I AM NOT SURE I COULD SUPPORT IT WITHOUT YOU, WITHOUT THESE STOLEN EXCURSIONS OUTSIDE THE WALLS. FOR SO THEY ARE. TRUE, I AM OFTEN SENT UPON LEGITIMATE LABOURS HERE WITHOUT, BUT I ALSO STEAL, I TAKE MORE THAN IS MY DUE BY RIGHT. WORSE, HUGH, I DO NOT REPENT ME! DO YOU SUPPOSE THERE IS ROOM WITHIN THE BOUNDS OF GRACE FOR ONE WHO HAS SET HIS HAND TO THE PLOUGH, AND EVERY LITTLE WHILE ABANDONS HIS FURROW TO TURN BACK AMONG THE SHEEP AND LAMBS?"'

Cadfael may have done 'penance by biding dutifully within the walls through the winter', but with the first stirrings of spring, there also stirred 'somewhere deep within him, a morsel of the *vagus* who had roamed the world from Wales to Jerusalem and back to Normandy for forty years before committing himself to stability in the cloister, and an expedition sanctioned, even ordered by authority could be welcomed as blessed, stead of evaded as a temptation.'

Despite the horarium of the house, which regulated prayer, work and study from day to day, manual work in the gardens and fields was entirely dependent on time, weather and season, especially for Brother Cadfael.

In January, when 'every clod was as solid as stone' and the earth slept 'snugly under the rime', he might be found 'picking over stored trays of apples and pears in the loft of the abbot's barn, discarding the few decayed specimens before they could infect their neighbours.' Or feeding the brazier in his workshop 'with a few judiciously placed turves, to keep it burning with a slow and tempered heat.' 'All the winter he kept it thus turfed overnight, to be ready at short notice if needed, the rest of the year he let it out, since it could easily be rekindled.' Alternatively, he might be 'breaking the ice on the fish ponds, to let air through to the denizens below.'

February could find him 'busy about replenishing his stock of winter cordials in his workshop in the herb-garden.' In March 'there was already work to be done in field and garden,' like 'digging and clearing the fresh half of his mint-bed, to give it space to proliferate new and young and green, rid of the old and debilitated.' Perhaps Cadfael might decide to deliver herbs and medicines in person to someone outside the enclave, taking 'advantage of the opportunity as much as to satisfy his curiosity as to enjoy the walk and the fresh air on a fine, if blustery day.' Depending upon the severity of the winter, the 'blessed works of spring' could begin late or early. In 1145, for instance, March came in 'more lamb than lion, there were windflowers in the woods, and the first primroses, unburned by frost, undashed and unmired by further rain, were just opening.' Conversely, in 1142:

❖ 'BY REASON OF THE PROLONGED COLD, WHICH LINGERED FAR INTO APRIL, AND HAD SCARCELY MELLOWED WHEN THE MONTH OF MAY BEGAN, EVERYTHING BECAME LAGGARD AND RELUCTANT. THE BIRDS KEPT CLOSE ABOUT THE ROOFS, FINDING WARMER PLACES TO ROOST. THE BEES SLEPT LATE, DEPLETED THEIR STORES, AND HAD TO BE FED, BUT NEITHER WAS THERE ANY EARLY BURST OF BLOSSOM FOR THEM TO MAKE PLENTIFUL. IN THE GARDENS THERE WAS NO POINT IN PLANTING SEED THAT WOULD ROT OR BE EATEN IN SOIL TOO CHILLY TO ENGENDER LIFE.'

Yet despite being four weeks behind that year, the seasons somehow found a way of catching up: 'Spring was not far away when the spiny mounds of the blackthorn along the headlands of the fields turned from black to white, like drifts of snow.'

May 1140 found the orchards in flower and the lay brothers planting out seedlings and 'sowing a later field of pease for succession, to follow when those by the Meole brook were harvested.' Cadfael busied himself pricking out early lettuces, digging ground for the planting of kale, and bringing on flowers for the festival of St Winifred. Spring was 'so sweetful and hopeful a time.'

❖ 'WILLOW WITHIES SHONE GOLD AND SILVER WITH THE FUR-SOFT FLOWERS ... HEDGES OF HAZEL AND MAY-BLOSSOM SHED SILVER PETALS AND DANGLED PALE, SILVER GREEN CATKINS ROUND THE ENCLOSURE..., COWSLIPS WERE REARING IN THE GRASS OF THE MEADOWS BEYOND, AND IRISES WERE IN TIGHT, THRUSTING BUD. EVEN THE ROSES SHOWED A HARVEST OF BUDS, ERECT AND READY TO BREAK AND DISPLAY THE FIRST COLOUR.'

June might find Brother Cadfael in the abbot's garden, trimming off dead roses.

❖ 'IT WAS A TASK ABBOT RADULFUS KEPT JEALOUSLY FOR HIMSELF IN THE ORDINARY WAY, FOR HE WAS PROUD OF HIS ROSES, AND VALUED THE BRIEF MOMENTS HE COULD SPEND WITH THEM, BUT IN THREE MORE DAYS THE HOUSE WOULD BE CELEBRATING THE ANNIVERSARY OF THE TRANSLATION OF SAINT WINIFRED TO HER SHRINE IN THE CHURCH, AND THE PREPARATIONS FOR THE ANNUAL INFLUX OF PILGRIMS AND PATRONS WERE OCCUPYING ALL HIS TIME, AND KEEPING ALL HIS OBEDIENTIARIES BUSY INTO THE BARGAIN. BROTHER CADFAEL, WHO HAD NO OFFICIAL FUNCTION, WAS FOR ONCE ALLOWED TO TAKE OVER THE DEAD-HEADING IN HIS PLACE, THE ONLY BROTHER PRIVILEGED TO BE TRUSTED WITH THE ABBATIAL BLOSSOMS, WHICH MUST BE IMMACULATE AND BRIGHT FOR THE SAINT'S FESTIVAL, LIKE EVERYTHING ELSE WITHIN THE ENCLAVE.'

St Winifred's festival, held on the twenty-second of June, brought many visitors to the abbey, including Brother Adam of Reading – 'Benedictine, gardener and herbalist.' Having heard tell of Cadfael, even as far south as his own house, Brother Adam made a point of seeking him out.

❖ '"NOW COME," [SAID CADFAEL] "I'LL SHOW YOU WHATEVER WE HAVE HERE TO SHOW, FOR THE MAIN GARDEN IS ON THE FAR SIDE OF THE FOREGATE, ALONG THE BANK OF THE RIVER. BUT HERE I KEEP MY OWN HERBER. AND IF THERE SHOULD BE ANYTHING HERE THAT CAN BE SAFELY CARRIED TO READING, YOU MAY TAKE CUTTINGS MOST GLADLY BEFORE YOU LEAVE US."
THEY FELL INTO A VERY PLEASANT AND VOLUBLE DISCUSSION, PERAMBULATING ALL THE WALKS OF THE CLOSED GARDEN, AND COMPARING EXPERIENCES IN CULTIVATION AND USE. BROTHER ADAM OF READING HAD A SHARP EYE FOR RARITIES, AND WAS LIKELY TO GO HOME LADEN WITH SPOILS. HE ADMIRED THE NEATNESS AND ORDER OF CADFAEL'S WORKSHOP, THE COLLECTION OF RUSTLING BUNCHES OF DRIED HERBS HUNG FROM THE ROOF-BEAMS AND UNDER THE EAVES, AND THE ARRAY OF BOTTLES, JARS AND FLAGONS ALONG THE SHELVES. HE HAD HINTS AND TIPS OF HIS OWN TO PROPOUND, TOO, AND THE AMIABLE CONTEST KEPT THEM HAPPY ALL THE AFTERNOON.'

Left once again to himself, 'Cadfael went about the regular duties of his day, divided between church and herbarium, but with an interested eye open.' Weeding 'the close-planted beds of mint and thyme and sage' was 'a tedious, meticulous labour in the ripeness of a favourable June after spring sun and shower had been nicely balanced, and growth was a green battlefield.'

August was not one of Cadfael's busiest times in the gardens, but, in 1138:

❖ 'THERE WAS MORE THAN ENOUGH FOR ONE MAN TO DO PROPERLY, AND THE ONLY RELIEF THEY HAD TO OFFER HIM WAS BROTHER ATHANASIUS, WHO WAS DEAF, HALF-SENILE, AND NOT TO BE RELIED UPON TO KNOW A USEFUL HERB FROM A WEED, AND THE OFFER HAD BEEN FIRMLY DECLINED. BETTER BY FAR MANAGE ALONE. THERE WAS A BED TO BE PREPARED FOR PLANTING OUT LATE CABBAGES FOR SUCCESSION, AND FRESH SEED TO BE SOWN FOR THE KIND THAT CAN WEATHER THE WINTER, AS WELL AS PEASE TO BE GATHERED, AND THE DEAD, DRIED HAULMS OF THE EARLY CROP TO BE CLEARED AWAY FOR FODDER AND LITTER. AND IN HIS WOODEN WORK-SHED IN THE HERBARIUM, HIS OWN PARTICULAR PRIDE, HE HAD HALF A DOZEN PREPARATIONS WORKING IN GLASS VESSELS AND MORTARS ON THE SHELVES, ALL OF THEM NEEDING ATTENTION AT LEAST ONCE A DAY, BESIDES THE HERB WINES THAT BUBBLED BUSILY ON THEIR OWN AT THIS STAGE. IT WAS HIGH HARVEST TIME AMONG THE HERBS, AND ALL THE MEDICINES FOR THE WINTER DEMANDING HIS CARE.'

August brought harvest time in the cornfields, and by September with luck the abbey barns were full, the well-dried straw bound and stacked, and the early fruit from the orchards picked and stored, if not already eaten. For Cadfael and his assistants, the chief challenge of autumn was rough digging, 'to make the cleared ground ready for the operation of the frosts to come.' The ploughing of larger fields was carried out with 'the heavy, high-wheeled plough,' drawn by the abbey's team of six oxen. The apples and pears in the orchard, when ready, had to be gathered while it was dry, a task for which all hands were mustered, 'choir monks and servants, and all the novices except the schoolboys.' In his workshop Cadfael might be found busy sorting beans for next year's seed, or in his garden subjecting the box hedge to a second clipping to remove 'the straggling shoots that come late in summer.'

The autumn of 1142 proved mild and prolonged, but Cadfael knew it 'could not last much longer, the weather-wise were beginning to sniff the air and foretell the first hard frost, and plentiful snow to come in December.'

The closing of the year and the imminent arrival of winter brings the entire sequence of Chronicles to a close. In the very last novel, *Brother Cadfael's Penance*, set at the end of 1145, Cadfael is found 'standing motionless in the middle of his small, beloved kingdom, staring rather within his own mind than at the straggling, autumnal growth about him.'

Fathoms deep, in some secret place at the centre of his being, Cadfael was pondering the circular nature of human life, and the seasons of the year, and the hours of the day.

❖ 'ALL THE APPLES WERE IN THE LOFT, ALL THE CORN MILLED, THE HAY LONG STACKED, THE SHEEP TURNED INTO THE STUBBLE FIELDS. A TIME TO PAUSE, TO LOOK ROUND, TO MAKE SURE NOTHING HAD BEEN NEGLECTED, NO FENCE UNREPAIRED, AGAINST THE WINTER.'

Inevitably, his thoughts turn from birth to death, from the dimness and mystery in which the world and man both began, to 'a new seed-time and a new generation' about to begin.

❖ 'OLD MEN, THOUGHT CADFAEL, BELIEVE IN THAT NEW BEGINNING, BUT EXPERIENCE ONLY THE ENDING. IT MAY BE THAT GOD IS REMINDING ME THAT I AM APPROACHING MY NOVEMBER. WELL, WHY REGRET IT? NOVEMBER HAS BEAUTY, HAS SEEN THE HARVEST INTO THE BARNS, EVEN LAID BY NEXT YEAR'S SEED. NO NEED TO FRET ABOUT NOT BEING ALLOWED TO STAY AND SOW IT, SOMEONE ELSE WILL DO THAT. SO GO CONTENTEDLY INTO THE EARTH WITH THE MOIST, GENTLE, SKELETAL LEAVES, WORN TO COBWEB FRAGILITY, LIKE THE SKINS OF VERY OLD MEN, THAT BRUISE AND STAIN AT THE MERE BRUSHING OF THE BREEZE, AND FLOWER INTO BROWN BLOTCHES AS THE LEAVES INTO ROTTING GOLD. THE COLOURS OF LATE AUTUMN ARE THE COLOURS OF THE SUNSET: THE FAREWELL OF THE YEAR AND THE FAREWELL OF THE DAY. AND OF THE LIFE OF MAN? WELL, IF IT ENDS IN A FLOURISH OF GOLD, THAT IS NO BAD ENDING.'

Shortly after, Cadfael suddenly abandons, not only his vows, but twenty-five years of labour and love in his herbal kingdom, all forsaken to go in search of his son, Olivier de Bretagne, who had been imprisoned in some unknown location.

That he returned to the abbey of St Peter and St Paul at Shrewsbury, was received back into the Order and resumed his work in the monastic gardens is certain. Beyond that, there is silence. The *Chronicles* end.

Yet, the cycle – like those of worship, season and lifetime – is somehow satisfyingly complete.

'His mood was contemplative, in keeping with the autumn air and the falling leaves.'
THE POTTER'S FIELD

CADFAEL: HERBALIST AND HEALER

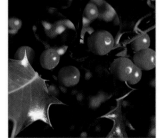

UNDER THE absolute rule of the abbot, the father of all the monks, the Benedictine monastery of St Peter and St Paul at Shrewsbury was run by a number of departmental officials, known as obedientiaries. The most important of these officers was the cellarer, whose responsibility covered everything from the purchase of all the community's basic requirements, such as food, drink and fuel, to looking after the monastery's estates and granges, as well as its brewhouse, bakery and mills. Although in charge of the abbey's gardens, the cellarer was far too busy to cultivate them himself and, in consequence, relied heavily on the assistance of others, from both within and without the enclave.

Throughout all twenty of the *Chronicles* responsibility for the abbey gardens appears to have been delegated to Brother Cadfael. Although the novels do not specifically define the limits of his herbal kingdom, they do suggest that the area of his responsibilities – as an ordinary monk, having 'no official function' – extended over much of the abbey grounds, including the vegetable gardens and orchards of the Gaye. In *Saint Peter's Fair*, set in 1139, Ellis Peters stated categorically that Cadfael had 'supervised the herbarium and the manufactory derived from it, for sixteen years.'

It therefore follows that, in 1123, only three years after embracing the cloistered life, Cadfael was given charge of at least a part of the abbey gardens, notably that part often referred to 'as his own small kingdom'. To him the walled herbarium, or herb-garden, was 'a sanctuary within a sanctuary', and its associated workshop 'a home within a home'. The one garden that seems to have lain outside Cadfael's particular rule was the small garden that belonged to the abbot and sheltered the abbot's lodging. Although Cadfael occasionally helped out in the abbot's garden, his presence there is rarely mentioned.

Clearly, Cadfael and his one or two named assistants were not the only monk- or novice-gardeners at Shrewsbury. For, according to *Saint Peter's Fair*: 'The brothers were great gardeners, and valued food crops for good reason, but they had time also for roses.' And in *The Leper of Saint Giles it* states: 'Benedictine nuns, like Benedictine monks, think well of manual labour, and are expected to expend their energies as generously in cultivation as in prayer.'

In addition to the cellarer, many other monastic officials relied heavily on produce from the abbey gardens. The infirmarer, who had a duty to care for the sick and infirm, required a regular supply of herbal medicines. The kitchener needed fruit, vegetables and culinary spices. The almoner had to find food and sometimes medicine to distribute to the needy. The sacristan required wine for the altar, perfumed oil for the lamps, incense for the burners and flowers for the shrines. Others, like the fraterer and the chamberlain, needed herbs and flowers to sweeten the air, repel insects, or strew on hard, cold floors.

Although Brother Cadfael supplied many of these officials with produce from his gardens, most of his time and energy was expended on the raising and cross-breeding of plants for medicine and healing. Indeed, even Prior Robert, who disapproved of the amount of freedom granted to Cadfael, considered him to be 'the abbey's most skilled herbalist and apothecary.'

In *The Devil's Novice*, when asked by Meriet Aspley what he did in the monastery, Cadfael summed up his own vocation:

❖ '"I grow herbs, and dry them, and make remedies for all the ills that visit us. I physic a great many souls besides those of us within."

"And that satisfies you?" It was a muted cry of protest; it would not have satisfied him.

"To heal men, after years of injuring them? What could be more fitting? A man does what he must do," said Cadfael thoughtfully, "whether the duty he has taken on himself is to fight, or to salvage poor souls from the fighting, to kill, to die or to heal. There are many will claim to tell you what is due from you, but only one who can shear through the many, and reach the truth. And that is you, by what light falls for you to show the way. Do you know what is hardest for me here of all I have vowed? Obedience. And I am old."

And have had my fling, and a wild one, was implied.'

Despite finding the vow of obedience the hardest of all his vows to keep, Cadfael's prevalent sin was being endlessly curious. Yet, as he admitted himself, it was a sin that, once confessed, was 'well worth a penance.' Adding, by way of justification: 'As long as man is curious about his fellowman, that appetite alone will keep him alive.'

During the years of his sojourning in Europe and the Holy Land, Cadfael not only collected many exotic plants, but gained valuable medicinal experience from both Saracen and Syrian physicians. He also helped treat the wounded on the fields of battle, where he 'had seen death in many shapes.' Yet, despite everything:

❖ 'BROTHER CADFAEL FOUND NOTHING STRANGE IN HIS WIDE-RANGING CAREER, AND HAD FORGOTTEN NOTHING AND REGRETTED NOTHING. HE SAW NO CONTRADICTION IN THE DELIGHT HE HAD TAKEN IN BATTLE AND ADVENTURE, AND THE KEEN PLEASURE HE NOW FOUND IN QUIETUDE. SPICED, TO BE TRUTHFUL, WITH MORE THAN A LITTLE MISCHIEF WHEN HE COULD GET IT, AS HE LIKED HIS VICTUALS WELL-FLAVOURED, BUT QUIETUDE ALL THE SAME, A SHIP BECALMED AND ENJOYING IT.'

As a herbalist and healer, Cadfael had not only an unrivalled knowledge of plants and a deep understanding of human nature, but an unquestioning belief in God, an inward conviction of grace, an unswerving trust that justice will always prevail, and, as Ellis Peters said in her Introduction to *A Rare Benedictine*, 'an inexhaustible fund of resigned tolerance for the human condition'. He also rejected the notion that being a Christian made one a better person.

❖ 'HE HAD SEEN BATTLES, TOO, IN HIS TIME IN THE WORLD, AS FAR AFIELD AS ACRE AND ASCALON AND JERUSALEM IN THE FIRST CRUSADE, AND WITNESSED DEATH CRUELLER THAN DISEASE, AND HEATHEN KINDER THAN CHRISTIANS, AND HE KNEW OF LEPROSIES OF THE HEART AND ULCERS OF THE SOUL WORSE THAN ANY OF THESE HE POULTICED AND LANCED WITH HIS HERBAL MEDICINES.'

Or, in Cadfael's own words:

❖ '"THERE ARE AS HOLY PERSONS OUTSIDE ORDERS AS EVER THERE ARE IN, AND NOT TO TRIFLE WITH TRUTH, AS GOOD MEN OUT OF THE CHRISTIAN CHURCH AS MOST I'VE MET WITHIN IT. IN THE HOLY LAND I'VE KNOWN SARACENS I'D TRUST BEFORE THE COMMON RUN OF THE CRUSADERS, MEN HONOURABLE, GENEROUS AND COURTEOUS, WHO WOULD HAVE SCORNED TO HAGGLE AND JOSTLE FOR PLACE AND TRADE AS SOME OF OUR ALLIES DID. MEET EVERY MAN AS YOU FIND HIM, FOR WE'RE ALL MADE THE SAME UNDER HABIT OR ROBE OR RAGS. SOME BETTER MADE THAN OTHERS, AND SOME BETTER CARED FOR, BUT ON THE SAME PATTERN ALL."'

'Cadfael went down to the banks of the Meole Brook, the westward boundary of the enclave.'

THE PILGRIM OF HATE

And, after abandoning his arms for the cowl, it was to caring for *all* those in need, spiritually as well as bodily, that Cadfael devoted the rest of his long and active life. Indeed: 'With or without love, such service as he pledged, that he would provide.'

When he was not visiting the town or gallivanting about the countryside on one of his many excursions, sanctioned or otherwise, Cadfael could usually be found between offices in his workshop in the herb-garden. Within the warm interior and beneath the bunches of dried herbs that hung from the roof-beams, Cadfael brewed his draughts, rolled his pills, stirred his rubbing oils, and pounded his poultices 'to medicine not only the brothers, but many who came for help in their troubles from the town and the Foregate, sometimes even from the scattered villages beyond.'

The shelves were full of bottles, jars and flagons, some containing oils, lotions and hog's fat, and others maturing wines of Cadfael's own making, 'distilled with herbs, good for the blood and heart.' Ready to hand on the little shelf near the door Cadfael kept his lamp and little box with tinder and flint. Arrayed along the benches were stoneware pots, clay dishes and saucers, pestles and mortars, brass scales, jars of gently-bubbling wine, little wooden bowls of medicinal roots, 'and a batch of small white lozenges drying on a marble slab.' When moulded and dried, the tablets, lozenges and pastilles were stored away in 'a little wooden box, almost black in colour.' All around were oils for rubbing aching joints, mixtures for coughs and colds, salves for bed-sores, syrups for sore throats, balsams for the chests of the old, lotions for cleansing broken bruises, ointments for soothing frost-nipped hands, rolls of linen for dressing wounds, troches (lozenges) for queasy stomachs, pastes and poultices for fighting malignant ulcers, and the clear syrup, made from eastern poppies, which Cadfael used to relieve pain, 'the chief enemy of man.'

'Pain, and the absence of sleep, which is the most beneficent remedy for pain.' Cadfael's various concoctions were brewed on the brazier in the centre of the workshop and when ready, left to cool on the stone slab beside it, or on the beaten earth of the floor.

❖ 'ALL THE WINTER HE KEPT HIS BRAZIER TURFED OVERNIGHT, TO BE READY AT SHORT NOTICE IF NEEDED, THE REST OF THE YEAR HE LET IT OUT, SINCE IT COULD EASILY BE REKINDLED. NONE OF HIS BREWS WITHIN HERE REQUIRED POSITIVE WARMTH, BUT THERE WERE MANY AMONG THEM THAT WOULD NOT TAKE KINDLY TO FROST.'

As a further precaution against medicines freezing and bottles bursting, Cadfael kept blankets in his workshop 'for swathing some of his jars and bottles against frost.'

Within the abbey enclave one of Cadfael's duties was to replenish the medicine cupboard in the infirmary. Sometimes Brother Edmund, the infirmarer, came to Cadfael's hut to collect certain medicines himself. In the winter of 1138 he had had to isolate several young victims of a sneezing rheum to stop it spreading to the rest of his inmates, some of whom were old men 'waiting peacefully for their end.'

'The smell of growth and greenness was already in the air, elusive but constant.'

THE HOLY THIEF

❖ '"ALL THE LADS NEED IS A FEW DAYS IN THE WARM,
AND THEY'LL CURE THEMSELVES WELL ENOUGH," SAID CADFAEL, STIRRING AND
POURING A LARGE FLASK INTO A SMALLER ONE, A BROWN MIXTURE THAT SMELLED
HOT AND AROMATIC AND SWEET. "BUT NO NEED TO ENDURE DISCOMFORT, EVEN FOR
A FEW DAYS. LET THEM DRINK A DOSE OF THIS, TWO OR THREE TIMES IN THE DAY AND
AT NIGHT, AS MUCH AS WILL FILL A SMALL SPOON, AND THEY'LL BE EASIER FOR IT."
"WHAT IS IT?" ASKED BROTHER EDMUND CURIOUSLY. MANY OF BROTHER CADFAEL'S
PREPARATIONS HE ALREADY KNEW, BUT THERE WERE CONSTANTLY NEW
DEVELOPMENTS. SOMETIMES HE WONDERED IF CADFAEL TRIED THEM ALL OUT ON
HIMSELF.
"THERE'S ROSEMARY, AND HOREHOUND, AND SAXIFRAGE, MASHED INTO A LITTLE OIL
PRESSED FROM FLAX SEEDS, AND THE BODY IS A RED WINE I MADE FROM CHERRIES AND
THEIR STONES. YOU'LL FIND THEY'LL DO WELL ON IT, ANY THAT HAVE THE RHEUM IN
THEIR EYES OR HEADS, AND EVEN FOR FOR THE COUGH IT SERVES TOO."'

A few of the ingredients in Cadfael's medicines were extremely poisonous if swallowed, and occasionally preparations, 'meant to bring comfort and relief from pain', were used to bring death. Monk's-hood oil, for example, worked wonders when rubbed well into creaking old joints, but, taken internally, even a little could kill a person. 'So can many things,' said Cadfael, 'used wrongly, or used in excess. Even wine, if you take enough of it. Even wholesome food, if you devour it beyond reason.'

Monk's-hood was so deadly that when Gervase Bonel was poisoned with the oil in his messuage at Shrewsbury, even Cadfael's considerable doctoring skills were unable to save him.

Every two or three weeks, 'more often in times of increased habitation and need', Cadfael made his way from the abbey of St Peter and St Paul to its chapel and hospital of St Giles, 'half a mile away at the very rim of the town.' Beyond the hospice hall, 'which was used for eating and for sleeping, except for those too sick to be left among their more healthier fellows,' there was a large locked cupboard, 'to which Cadfael had his own key, and its shelves within were full of jars, flasks, bottles, wooden boxes for tablets, ointments, syrups, lotions, all products of Cadfael's workshop.'

Indeed, Cadfael's herbal remedies were in heavy demand at St Giles for their application 'soothed and placated the mind as well as the skin'. From his crusading years in the east, Cadfael had first-hand experience of lepers and leprosy. He had also served a voluntary year or more at St Giles – where 'it was not unknown that the attendant should become attended' – and was of the opinion that some of the inmates, although labelled lepers, did not have the 'true' bacterial disease. Many of the ills they treated at the hospital:

❖ 'THOUGH THEY CARRIED THE SAME BANISHMENT AND WERE CALLED BY THE SAME NAME, WERE NOT TRUE LEPROSY. ANY MAN WHO BROKE OUT IN NODES THAT TURNED TO ULCERS, OR PALLID, SCALY ERUPTIONS OF THE SKIN, OR RUNNING SORES, WAS SET DOWN AS A LEPER, THOUGH CADFAEL HAD HIS SUSPICIONS THAT MANY SUCH CASES AROSE FROM UNCLEANLINESS, AND MANY OTHERS FROM TOO LITTLE AND TOO WRETCHED FOOD.'

In addition to the brothers and those in their care, Cadfael was often called upon to tend the inhabitants of both town and Foregate. Indeed, there were few people within the walls of Shrewsbury and in the parish of Holy Cross that he did not know.

❖ 'HE HAD TREATED MANY OF THEM, OR THEIR CHILDREN, AT SOME TIME IN THESE HIS CLOISTERED YEARS; EVEN, SOMETIMES, THEIR BEASTS, FOR HE WHO LEARNS ABOUT SICKNESS OF MEN CANNOT BUT PICK UP, HERE AND THERE, SOME KNOWLEDGE OF THE SICKNESSES OF THEIR ANIMALS, CREATURES WITH AS GREAT A CAPACITY FOR SUFFERING AS THEIR MASTERS, AND MUCH LESS

MEANS OF COMPLAINING, TOGETHER WITH FAR LESS INCLINATION TO COMPLAIN. CADFAEL HAD OFTEN WISHED THAT MEN WOULD USE THEIR BEASTS BETTER, AND TRIED TO SHOW THEM THAT IT WOULD BE GOOD HUSBANDRY. THE HORSES OF WAR HAD BEEN PART OF THAT CURIOUS, SLOW PROCESS WITHIN HIM THAT HAD TURNED HIM AT LENGTH FROM TRADE IN ARMS INTO THE CLOISTER.

NOT THAT ALL ABBOTS AND PRIORS USED THEIR MULES AND STOCK BEASTS WELL, EITHER. BUT AT LEAST THE BEST AND WISEST OF THEM RECOGNISED IT FOR GOOD POLICY, AS WELL AS GOOD CHRISTIANITY.'

Despite being bound by the Rule of St Benedict in the abbey of St Peter and St Paul at Shrewsbury, Cadfael: 'had, within reason, authority to come and go as he thought fit, even to absent himself from services if his aid was required elsewhere.'

Sometimes, when Cadfael's healing skills proved inadequate, the sufferer was healed by a miracle, but only very rarely, and 'as frequently on the undeserving as on the deserving.' In *The Pilgrim of Hate*, set in 1141, the crippled right leg of sixteen-year-old Rhun was miraculously straightened before the altar of St Winifred, and the pain he had endured from a child immediately relieved. Cadfael had tried massaging and manipulating the misshapen leg, to no avail. He had even given the boy a draught of his poppy syrup to ease his pain and help him sleep, but Rhun had decided not to take it. Instead, as he had nothing else to give to the saint on the day of her festival, Rhun had chosen to humbly offer up his 'lameness and pain freely, not as a price for favour.'

❖ 'THERE COULD HARDLY BE, THOUGHT CADFAEL, AMONG ALL HER DEVOTEES, A MORE COSTLY OBLATION. HE HAS GONE FAR ALONG A DIFFICULT ROAD WHO HAS COME TO THE POINT OF SEEING THAT DEPRIVATION, PAIN AND DISABILITY ARE OF NO CONSEQUENCE AT ALL, BESIDE THE INWARD CONVICTION OF GRACE, AND THE SECRET PEACE OF THE SOUL. AN ACCEPTANCE WHICH CAN ONLY BE MADE FOR A MAN'S OWN SELF, NEVER FOR ANY OTHER. ANOTHER'S GRIEF IS NOT TO BE TOLERATED, IF THERE CAN BE ANYTHING DONE TO ALLEVIATE IT.'

In lifelong gratitude to the saint, the boy asked to be allowed to take the cowl at Shrewsbury. After his request had been granted, Brother Rhun devoted himself to St Winifred – 'or whatever represented her there in the sealed and secret place' – making himself the custodian of her altar, her page and her squire.

Cadfael, being a Welshman, felt very close to the Welsh saint, having 'an almost family affection' for her. He had, after all, secretly put her slender bones back in her grave at Gwytherin, rather than, as the rest of his party believed, sealed them inside the reliquary bound for Shrewsbury. A deception for which she had long forgiven him, and shown him 'humouring kindness.' If Cadfael had need to speak to her in actual words, 'he found himself addressing her in Welsh, but usually he relied on her to know all the preoccupations of his mind without words.'

❖ 'CADFAEL HAD RETURNED TO THE CHURCH AFTER PRIME TO REPLENISH THE PERFUMED OIL IN THE LAMP ON SAINT WINIFRED'S ALTAR. THE INQUISITIVE SKILLS WHICH MIGHT HAVE BEEN FROWNED UPON IF THEY HAD BEEN EMPLOYED TO MAKE SCENTS FOR WOMEN'S VANITY BECAME PERMISSIBLE AND EVEN PRAISEWORTHY WHEN USED AS AN ACT OF WORSHIP, AND HE TOOK PLEASURE IN TRYING OUT ALL MANNER OF FRAGRANT HERBS AND FLOWERS IN MANY DIFFERENT COMBINATIONS, PLYING THE SWEETS OF ROSE AND LILY, VIOLET AND CLOVER AGAINST THE SEARCHING AROMATIC RICHES OF RUE AND SAGE AND WORMWOOD. IT PLEASED HIM TO THINK THAT THE LADY MUST TAKE DELIGHT IN BEING SO SERVED, FOR VIRGIN SAINT THOUGH SHE MIGHT BE, SHE WAS A WOMAN, AND IN HER YOUTH HAD BEEN A BEAUTIFUL AND DESIRABLE ONE.'

When Cadfael finally returned to his cloistered home at Shrewsbury in *Brother Cadfael's Penance*, having discarded his vocation to go in search of his son, Olivier de Bretagne, he could not, or would not, go to St Winifred's altar within the choir, unabsolved as he was:

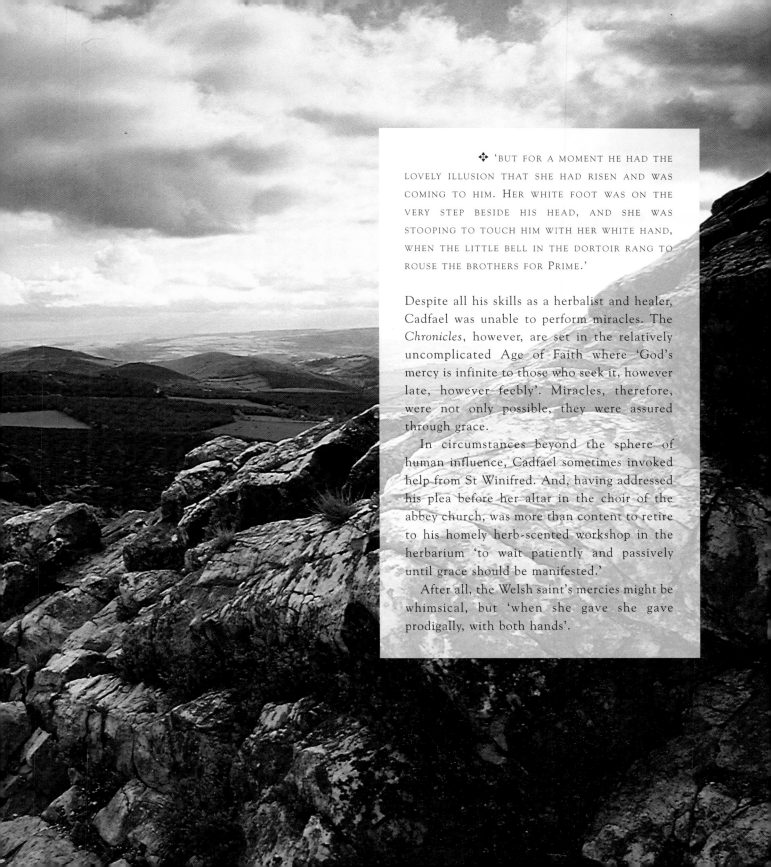

❖ 'BUT FOR A MOMENT HE HAD THE
LOVELY ILLUSION THAT SHE HAD RISEN AND WAS
COMING TO HIM. HER WHITE FOOT WAS ON THE
VERY STEP BESIDE HIS HEAD, AND SHE WAS
STOOPING TO TOUCH HIM WITH HER WHITE HAND,
WHEN THE LITTLE BELL IN THE DORTOIR RANG TO
ROUSE THE BROTHERS FOR PRIME.'

Despite all his skills as a herbalist and healer,
Cadfael was unable to perform miracles. The
Chronicles, however, are set in the relatively
uncomplicated Age of Faith where 'God's
mercy is infinite to those who seek it, however
late, however feebly'. Miracles, therefore,
were not only possible, they were assured
through grace.

In circumstances beyond the sphere of
human influence, Cadfael sometimes invoked
help from St Winifred. And, having addressed
his plea before her altar in the choir of the
abbey church, was more than content to retire
to his homely herb-scented workshop in the
herbarium 'to wait patiently and passively
until grace should be manifested.'

After all, the Welsh saint's mercies might be
whimsical, but 'when she gave she gave
prodigally, with both hands'.

A-Z OF MEDIEVAL PLANTS AND HERBS

THE FOLLOWING LIST of plants and herbs, in alphabetical order, have been derived from the *Chronicles of Brother Cadfael*, plus the three short stories in *A Rare Benedictine*. Selected information from Culpeper's *Herbal* has been included because it was one of Ellis Peters' key sources of reference. Peters' own version, in her own words, was a 'dilapidated copy published by Joseph Smith, High Holborn, too early to bear a date, but certainly earlier than 1838 when my great-grandfather wrote his name and date of ownership in it.' All 'Culpeper' quotations in the list are from Culpeper's *Complete Herbal and English Physician* (published by J. Gleave and Son, Deansgate, 1826), or from Culpeper's *Complete Herbal* (published by W. Foulsham & Co. Ltd., Slough, no date). Culpeper specified the astrological aspect of a particular herb. Peters incorporated this information in the Chronicles, and, therefore, where known, the appropriate ruling planet has been included under each entry. Like modern astrologers the early herbalists believed that the sun, moon, the known planets and the constellations of the zodiac affected everything on earth, including plants and human beings.

Other references are as follows: 'Aelfric': *Colloquy (Nominum Herbarum)*, 995 – Cadfael obtained a copy of Aelfric's list of herbs and trees in September 1140 (*The Devil's Novice*); 'Harvey': John Harvey, *Mediaeval Gardens*, 1981; 'Pliny': Pliny the Elder, *Natural History*, completed in AD 77; 'Gerard': John Gerard, *The Herball or Generall Historie of Plantes*, 1633; Julius Caesar, *The Conquest of Gaul*, c 52 BC; *Banckes's Herbal* : first printed English herbal, published by Richard Banckes in 1525; 'Turner': William Turner, *A New Herball*, 1551-68; 'Parkinson': John Parkinson, *Paradisus Terrestris*, 1629, & *Theatrum Botanicum*, 1640.

It should be noted that the photographs and illustrations may not represent the exact variety or species of plant listed. Through special breeding and cultivation, many medieval plants and herbs have been superseded by much-improved modern varieties.

ADDER'S TONGUE

Ophioglossum vulgatum
also known as Serpent's Tongue
or Christ's Spear
CHRONICLES: XI AN EXCELLENT MYSTERY

Used for cleansing and as an astringent, adder's tongue was good for old, ulcerated wounds. It was found growing wild in the hedgerows and meadows around Shrewsbury Abbey and along the banks of the Meole brook. Cadfael used the herb, both fresh and from store, to 'draw out the evil' from the wound that Godfrid Marescot (later Brother Humilis) had received in battle in the Holy Land. The injury, which refused to heal, had left Marescot half disembowelled and unable to father children.

Ruling Planet: Moon in Cancer

USES

Medicinal: Highly valued for the treatment of wounds, the juice from both the roots and leaves of adder's tongue fern was used in healing ointments and salves. Culpeper recommended the juice, mixed with the distilled water of horsetail (*Equisetum arvense*), for internal wounds, bruises and vomiting. Added to bath-water, it was ideal for washing sensitive skin.

Miscellaneous: The name is derived from the distinctive shape of the fern's leaves, the tongue being a single spike issuing from a round, hollow rootstock crown. The plant is found in moist meadows and pastures.

ALDER

Alnus glutinosa
CHRONICLES: VII THE SANCTUARY SPARROW; XVI
THE HERETIC'S APPRENTICE

❖ 'The alders leaned over the shallows lissome and rosy with catkins.'   THE SANCTUARY SPARROW

Alders not only screened the Aurifaber drying-ground at Shrewsbury, they also clustered in many places along the banks of the river Severn. To establish the place where Baldwin Peche was murdered, 'smothered. Held down somewhere in the shallows, with his face pressed into the mud. And set afloat in the river afterwards' Cadfael searched for a spot where 'crowfoot and alder and fox-stones all grow together.'

Ruling Planet: Venus

USES

Medicinal: Alder bark was used externally as a gargle for sore throats and mouth infections; the fresh, sticky leaves as a poultice to ease swellings, inflammations and rheumatic pain.

Miscellaneous: Grains of pollen, found in peat, confirm that the alder has been established in Britain for thousands of years. Because the wood is tinged a yellowish-red like blood when freshly cut, it used to be feared to contain evil, or be unlucky. As it likes wet ground, the alder is often found growing by water and in damp woods. Various coloured dyes can be obtained from the bark, fruit and leaves. The branches produced excellent charcoal. Culpeper stated that the leaves, 'gathered while the morning dew is on them', will rid beds of fleas.

Alkanet

Alkanna tinctoria

also known as Dyer's Bugloss

(*Culpeper: Anchusa tinctoria*)

Chronicles: V The Leper of Saint Giles

❖ "'A wedding," said Cadfael seriously, stacking away jars of salves and bottles of lotion made from alkanet, anemone, mint, figwort, and the grains of oats and barley, most of them herbs of Venus and the moon, "a wedding is the crux of two lives, and therefore no mean matter.'" The Leper of Saint Giles

Ruling Planet: Venus

USES

Medicinal: In an ointment, alkanet was used externally to treat wounds, ulcers, rashes, burns and bed-sores. Culpeper said that, made into a vinegar, it 'helps yellow jaundice, spleen, and gravel in the kidneys.'

Culinary: The flowers and young leaves of alkanet were eaten raw in salads or cooked like spinach.

Miscellaneous: In the Middle Ages alkanet was mainly grown for its root, from which was extracted a reddish dye. Powdered, it was also used cosmetically as a rouge. Harvey claimed that there is no evidence for the plant being cultivated in England before the late sixteenth century.

Almond

Prunus dulcis

also known as Greek Nuts

Chronicles: XII The Raven in the Foregate

❖ 'In the afternoon of the twenty-ninth of December, Cadfael was called out to the first sufferers from coughs and colds in the Foregate, and extended his visits to one elderly merchant in the town itself, a regular chest patient of his in the winter. He had left Ninian [Bachiler] sawing and splitting wood from the pruning of the trees, and keeping cautious watch on a pot of herbs in oil of almonds, which had to warm on the edge of the brazier without simmering, to make a lotion for the frost-nipped hands too tender to endure the hog's fat base of the ointment.' The Raven in the Foregate

Ruling Planet: Jupiter

USES

Medicinal: Oil extracted from almond seeds, or kernels, was mainly used in cough mixtures. Externally, it soothed and softened the skin; internally, it acted as a laxative. The ancients held that eating almonds prevented intoxication.

Culinary: Almond seeds were used in sweet and savoury dishes, or were eaten raw, blanched or roasted. They were also used to make a kind of butter.

Miscellaneous: Although the Romans may have introduced almonds into Britain from Mediterranean lands, the tree was not cultivated in England until much later (possibly the sixteenth century). Harvey, however, states that the tree had arrived 'by the mid-thirteenth century, at the latest'. What is certain is that it was mainly grown for its blossom, as the fruit seldom ripened fully because of the British climate. The tree was listed by Aelfric.

ANEMONE

Anemone nemorosa

also known as Windflower, Wood Anemone, Smell Fox or Wood Crowfoot

CHRONICLES: V THE LEPER OF SAINT GILES; VII THE SANCTUARY SPARROW; IX DEAD MAN'S RANSOM; X THE PILGRIM OF HATE; XVII THE POTTER'S FIELD; XIX THE HOLY THIEF

✢ 'The night was dark, clear and still young, so that light lingered in unexpected places, won from a smooth plane of the river, a house-front of pale stone, a flowering bush, or scattered stars of windflowers under the trees.'

THE SANCTUARY SPARROW

Windflowers – 'quivering in the grass' – were used as an ingredient in a bottle of unspecified lotion. Brother Rhun's eyelids were 'blue-veined like the petals of anemones'.

Ruling Planet: Mars

USES

Medicinal: During medieval times the juice of the anemone was prescribed externally for leprosy. Mixed with hog's grease, it was used as an ointment for scalds and ulcers. Modern research has revealed that the herb is potentially poisonous.

Miscellaneous: Pliny claimed that anemone flowers only opened when the wind blew, hence the name 'windflower'. Indeed, the name is derived from the Greek for wind. The Pasque flower (*Pulsatilla vulgaris*), another type of anemone also known as windflower, produces flowers of various colours, including white.

Angelica

Angelica archangelica
Wild Angelica: *Angelica sylvestris*
Chronicles: IV Saint Peter's Fair

❖ "'I finished making the balm for ulcers," said Brother Mark, making dutiful report, and happily aware of work well done. "And I have harvested all the poppy-heads that were ripe, but I have not yet broken out the seed. I thought they should dry in the sun a day or two yet."
Cadfael pressed one of the great heads between his fingers, and praised the judgement. "And the angelica water for the infirmary?"
"Brother Edmund sent for it half an hour ago. I had it ready.'"
Saint Peter's Fair

Although angelica water was used in the infirmary at Shrewsbury Abbey, its use was unspecified.

Ruling Planet: Sun in Leo

USES

Medicinal: Praised by Paracelsus (d. 1541) as a 'marvellous medicine', angelica was thought in ancient times to be a panacea for all ills. Every part of the plant had health-giving properties, including the seeds. Herbalists valued it as a tonic, and as a remedy for coughs and colds. Angelica tea stimulated the appetite, calmed digestive disorders and relieved flatulence, or 'corrupt air'. In large doses, however, it can over-stimulate the central nervous system, and even paralyse. Culpeper recommended that the powdered root be taken in angelica water to resist poison and the plague.

Culinary: Angelica has long been used for flavouring and confectionery: the candied green stems are still used for decorating cakes and puddings; the seed and roots for flavouring drinks, such as gin and liqueurs. The tender leaves and shoots were also used in salads; stewed with rhubarb and gooseberries, they reduce the tartness of the fruit.

Miscellaneous: An ancient herb which featured in pagan rituals, angelica was grown in England during the Anglo-Saxon period. As it was reputed to possess angelic, or heavenly, powers the herb was worn as a protection against evil spells and witchcraft. Its aromatic properties were exploited in perfumes and pot-pourri.

APPLE

Malus pumila, Pyrus malus,
or *Malus domestica*

❖ 'There was a fair crop of October apples that year in the orchards along the Gaye, and since the weather had briefly turned unpredictable, they had to take advantage of three fine days in succession that came in the middle of the week, and harvest the fruit while it was dry. Accordingly they mustered all hands to work, choir monks and servants, and all the novices except the schoolboys. Pleasant work enough, especially for the youngsters who were allowed to climb trees with approval, and kilt their habits to the knee, in a brief return to boyhood.'   THE DEVIL'S NOVICE

Apple trees – valued for their edible fruit, either cooked or raw, wrinkled or dried – were grown in the Gaye orchard at Shrewsbury Abbey. One of the branches of the tip-bearing variety of apple trees in the orchard broke under Brother Wolstan's heavy weight and he fell in 'a flurry of falling leaves and crackling twigs, straight on to the upturned blade of the sickle.' Cadfael had planted a couple of apple trees in the small plot of land next to his herb-garden. The apples were stored in trays in the lofts of various barns, including the great barn and the abbot's barn. The core of an apple and the heel of a loaf provided the sheriff's men with plain evidence that Joscelin Lucy had hidden in Bishop Roger de Clinton's hay-store at Shrewsbury.

Ruling Planet: Venus

USES

Medicinal: The popular rhyme 'an apple a day keeps the doctor away', echoes the ancient belief that the fruit was a cure-all. The bark was also used medicinally. The fruit was mainly used to alleviate constipation, reduce acidity of the stomach and assist in the digestion of other foods. Rotten apples were used as a poultice for sore eyes.

Culinary: A favourite medieval fruit, apples were chiefly used as a food, cooked or raw, and for making cider. They were also included in chutneys, sauces, jams and jellies.

Miscellaneous: Cultivated varieties of apple were probably introduced into England by the Romans. During medieval times, the monks increased the number of varieties by grafting scions (shoots), brought from other monasteries or imported from the Continent, on to established rootstocks.

ARCHANGEL, WHITE

Lamium album

also known as Deadnettle or Blind Nettle;
Yellow Archangel: *Lamiastrum galeobdolon*

CHRONICLES: VI THE VIRGIN IN THE ICE;
XVII THE POTTER'S FIELD

❖ 'The crop Haughmond had not found it worth its while to garner was bleaching into early autumn pallor, having ripened and seeded weeks earlier, and among the whitened standing stems all manner of meadow flowers still showed, harebell and archangel, poppy and daisy and centaury, with the fresh green shoots of new grass just breaking through the roots of the fading yield, and under the headland above tangles of bramble offered fruit just beginning to blacken from red.'

THE POTTER'S FIELD

Archangel was one of the meadow flowers found growing in the Potter's Field. Although the plants could have been cut and dried for bedding, it was decided to plough them back into the soil. Cadfael detected the smell of yellow mild nettle in the greenish salve that had been used to dress Evrard Boterel's knife wound at the manor of Ledwyche.

Ruling Planet: Venus

USES

Medicinal: Although valued for the treatment of internal disorders, particularly menstrual problems, archangel was also applied externally to open wounds to staunch bleeding and reduce inflammation. The dried leaves, made into a tea, promoted perspiration. Gerard said that the sugared flowers could make the 'heart merry' and 'refresh the vital spirits.'

Culinary: The young leaves of archangel were used in salads and soups, and cooked as a vegetable.

Miscellaneous: Although archangel resembles the stinging nettle (*Urtica dioica*), it is not related; the leaves do not sting. As it flowers around May 8 in the Julian calendar, the day dedicated to Michael the Archangel, it came to be known as archangel. The plant was listed by Aelfric.

ASH

Fraxinus excelsior

CHRONICLES: V THE LEPER OF SAINT GILES;
XIV THE HERMIT OF EYTON FOREST

❖ 'Cadfael knew the place, Eilmund's pride, the farmed part of Eyton forest, as neat and well-ditched a coppice as any in the shire, where the regular cutting of six- or seven-year-old wood let in the light at every cropping, so that the wealth of ground cover and wild flowers was always rich and varied. Some trees, like ash, spring anew from the stool of the original trunk, just below the cut. Some, like elm or aspen, from below the ground all round the stump. Some of the stools in Eilmund's care, several times cropped afresh, had grown into groves of their own, their open centres two good paces across.' THE HERMIT OF EYTON FOREST

A coppice-tree, ash was used for all manner of things, including fuel, charcoal and carpentry. As it was springy and supple the wood was ideal for making the curved felloes of the rim of a wheel.

Ruling Planet: Sun

USES

Medicinal: Ash bark was used to make a tonic for liver complaints and rheumatism. Before the discovery of quinine, obtained from Peruvian Bark (*Cinchona succirubra*), it was used to treat fever. The fruits, or keys, were eaten for flatulence; and the leaves used as a mild laxative.

Culinary: Ash keys were repeatedly boiled or soaked to remove the bitterness, then pickled.

Medicinal: In Norse mythology, the ash was considered a sacred tree: symbol of the life-force; and the 'Tree of the World' (Yggdrasil). Spears made of ash were believed to be invincible. The tree was listed by Aelfric, while Pliny praised it as a snake-repellant. Burning the logs was reputed to drive evil spirits away.

ASPEN

Populus tremula
CHRONICLES: XIV THE HERMIT OF
EYTON FOREST

The new growth of coppiced aspen emerged from below the ground all round the stump.

Ruling Planet: Saturn in Capricorn

USES

Medicinal: Aspen bark was used to lower fever and as a remedy for digestive problems. The sticky buds were made into a tea for coughs and sore throats, and into a salve, applied externally, for burns, inflammation, chapped skin and scratches.

Miscellaneous: The trembling of the leaves in the slightest breeze gave rise to the old saying 'to tremble like an aspen.' Many believed that the tree constantly quaked because it harboured some secret grief or guilt: some said, by way of explanation, that the wood was used for the cross on which Christ was crucified.

BARLEY

Hordeum vulgare

CHRONICLES: III MONK'S-HOOD;
V THE LEPER OF SAINT GILES;
XVII THE POTTER'S FIELD

❖ 'The field they had parted with, distant beyond Haughton, had been best left under stock, here they could very well take a crop of wheat or barley, and turn the stock from the lower pasture into the stubble afterwards, to manure the land for the next year.'   THE POTTER'S FIELD

Grains of barley were used to make gruel, and were also an ingredient in an unspecified bottle of lotion.

Ruling Planet: Saturn

USES

Medicinal: Barley was taken internally for digestive disorders and bronchitis. Barley water soothed gastro-intestinal inflammations. Cooked barley, applied externally in the form of a poultice, was used to treat skin sores.

Culinary: Ale, made of malted barley (seeds that have germinated), was a staple drink in English medieval monasteries. Pearl barley (seeds that have had the husk removed) was cooked in soups and stews. Malt extracts were also produced from barley.

Miscellaneous: Barley has been cultivated as a cereal crop as far back as Neolithic times. The grains have been discovered in ancient Egyptian remains, while the Greeks considered the seeds to be sacred.

Basil

Ocimum basilicum
also known as Sweet Basil
Chronicles: I A Morbid Taste for Bones;
III Monk's-Hood

The plant was grown in Cadfael's herb-garden and dried in bunches for culinary use. Richildis Bonel sent her manservant, Aelfric, to ask Cadfael for some basil to flavour a dish.

Ruling Planet: Mars in Scorpio

USES

Medicinal: Basil leaves were used in wine as a tonic for gastro-intestinal complaints and, although a stimulant, to soothe nerves. When crushed, they were used as a snuff to relieve headaches and nasal colds.

Culinary: Basil, preferably fresh, seasoned medieval sauces, soups and drinks. Although versatile, it is one of the few herbs that increases its flavour when cooked, and should be used sparingly.

Miscellaneous: Thought to be a native of southeast Asia, basil has been cultivated in Europe from at least Roman times. As it likes a warm Mediterranean climate, it is difficult to grow in Britain. Because it releases its scent when walked upon, basil was a useful herb for strewing on floors to cover offensive smells. It also, reputedly, repelled flies. The oil is not only used in medicine, but also for making perfumes and incense.

BAY

Laurus nobilus

also known as Sweet Laurel

CHRONICLES: XII THE RAVEN IN
THE FOREGATE; XIII THE ROSE RENT

B

❖ 'It was a large pot, and a goodly quantity of aromatic brown syrup bubbling gently in it. "A mixture for coughs and colds," said Cadfael. "We shall be needing it any day now, and plenty of it, too." "What goes into it?" "A great many things. Bay and mint, coltsfoot, horehound, mullein, mustard, poppy – good for the throat and the chest – and a small draught of the strong liquor I distil does no harm in such cases, either."'

THE RAVEN IN THE FOREGATE

Ruling Planet: Sun in Leo

USES

Medicinal: Oil from bay leaves, applied externally, was used for bruises and rheumatism; powdered berries improved the appetite and reduced fever. Added to bath-water, the leaves relieved aches and pains. Bay was also regarded as a potent antiseptic.

Culinary: Bay leaves were mainly used to flavour soups, stews and sauces. As an evergreen they can be used for cooking at any time of the year.

Miscellaneous: Native to the Mediterranean region, bay was dedicated to Apollo and to his son, Aesculapius, the god of medicine. In ancient Greece and Rome a crowning wreath of laurel leaves was used to honour heroes, as well as poets (hence the title 'poet laureate'). During the Middle Ages bay was used as a strewing herb, valued not only for its scent but also as an insect-repellant.

Bean

Vicia faba

also known as Broad Bean

CHRONICLES: III MONK'S-HOOD;
V THE LEPER OF SAINT GILES;
XIV THE HERMIT OF EYTON FOREST;
XVII THE POTTER'S FIELD;
XX BROTHER CADFAEL'S PENANCE

❖ 'Cadfael went out to the refectory, and his own dinner, which turned out to be boiled beef and beans as he had foreseen. No savoury intermissum here.' MONK'S-HOOD

A staple food at Shrewsbury Abbey, beans were grown in the fields running down to the Meole brook. Some, after being dried and sorted in Cadfael's workshop, were stored in a pottery jar for next year's seed. The rejected beans were added to the compost. Once the bean vines had been cleared the haulms, or stems, were dug back into the ground.

Ruling Planet: Venus

USES

Medicinal: Beans were used in the form of a poultice to reduce inflammation and swellings. Culpeper said that the 'water distilled from the green husks, is held to be very effectual against the stone, and to provoke urine.'

Culinary: A basic vegetable in medieval England, beans were used as a dried vegetable and to make a thick starchy soup, or pottage.

Miscellaneous: Although broad beans are not a true native of Britain, they were in use during the Iron Age, and possibly earlier.

BEECH

Fagus sylvatica

CHRONICLES: IV SAINT PETER'S FAIR;
VI THE VIRGIN IN THE ICE;
X THE PILGRIM OF HATE;
XIII THE ROSE RENT;
XIV THE HERMIT OF EYTON FOREST

B

❖ 'The woods were thick and well grown here, the ground so shadowed that herbal cover was scant, but the interlacing of boughs above shut out the sky. Sometimes the path emerged for a short way into more open upland where the trees thinned and clearings of heath appeared, for all this stretch of country was the northern fringe of the Long Forest, where men had encroached with their little assarts and their legal or illegal cutting of timber and pasturing of pigs on acorns and beech mast. But even here settlements were very few.'

THE ROSE RENT

❖ 'There were very old trees in their tract of forest, enormous beeches with trunks so gnarled and thick three men with arms outspread could hardly clip them.' THE PILGRIM OF HATE

Ruling Planet: Saturn

USES

Medicinal: The oil of beech seeds, or mast, was used as an antiseptic. The leaves were applied externally to alleviate swellings, and the tar to treat various skin diseases.

Culinary: The sap of the beech tree, tapped from the tree and fermented, was made into a wine and also an ale. Oil from the seeds was used for cooking, while the seeds were roasted.

Miscellaneous: Listed by Aelfric, the beech – one of the largest British trees – was established in England at least 1,000 years before Julius Caesar (d. 44 BC) wrongly stated that there were no beech trees in England. In medieval times the tree was valued for its timber, and was sometimes pollarded. In autumn pigs were often turned out into the woods to forage on the fallen beech mast. The word book is thought to be derived from beech, because northern Europeans used to write on blocks of the wood.

Beet

Beta

White Beet: *Beta vulgaris*;
Red Beet: *Beta hortensis*

Chronicles: III Monk's-Hood

❧ '"An easy year so far," said Brother Simon, viewing his leggy, tough hill-sheep with satisfaction. Sheep as Welsh as Brother Cadfael gazed towards the south-west, where the long ridge of Berwyn rose in the distance; long, haughty, inscrutable faces, and sharp ears, and knowing yellow eyes that could outstare a saint. "Plenty of good grazing still, what with the grass growing so late, and the good pickings they had in the stubble after harvest. And we have beet-tops, they make good fodder, too. There'll be better fleeces than most years, when next they're shorn, unless the winter turns cruel later on."'   Monk's-Hood

Ruling Planet: Jupiter (White Beet);
Saturn (Red Beet)

Uses

Medicinal: According to Culpeper, the juice of the white beet 'doth much loosen the belly, and is of a cleansing, digestive quality, and provoketh urine.' It was also recommended for headaches and giddiness. The red beet was said to 'stay the bloody flux, women's courses and to help yellow jaundice.'

Culinary: The leaves of white beet were used as spinach, added to porrays (a thick vegetable soup), and for flavouring. The roots, rich in sugar, were also a valuable food.

Miscellaneous: Beets have been cultivated in England since at least Anglo-Saxon times. In medieval times the tops of white beet were cut back to the root to encourage more leaves to grow.

BETONY

Stachys officinalis
also known as Woundwort
CHRONICLES: XI AN EXCELLENT MYSTERY;
XVI THE HERETIC'S APPRENTICE

❖ "'Tomorrow,' said Cadfael, "I'll gather the same herbs fresh, and bruise them for a green plaster, it works more strongly, it will draw out the evil. This has happened many times since you got the injury?"
"Not many times. But if I'm overworn, yes – it happens," said the bluish lips [of Brother Humilis], without complaint.
"Then you must not be allowed to overwear. But it has also healed before, and will again. This woundwort got its name by good right. Be ruled now, and lie still here for two days, or three, until it closes clean, for it you stand and go it will be longer healing."' AN EXCELLENT MYSTERY

Woundwort, like water betony, was an ingredient in Cadfael's healing creams and waxes. In a lotion it was used for cleansing wounds and grazes.

Ruling Planet: Jupiter

USES

Medicinal: Medieval herbalists highly valued the healing properties of betony, considering it a cure-all for all disorders, including migraine, indigestion and nervous complaints. The herb was also used for staunching bleeding and healing wounds, sores, ulcers and boils. According to the eleventh-century *Herbarium* of Apuleius, it was effective against 'monstrous nocturnal visions', and 'frightful visions and dreams'. All the species of betony listed here possess similar healing properties.

Culinary: The dried leaves of betony were used as a substitute for tea and to make a conserve.

Miscellaneous: Listed by Aelfric, betony was considered to possess magical powers by the Anglo-Saxons, and was worn as a charm against evil spirits. The fresh plant yields a yellow dye.

BETONY, WATER

Betonica aquatica
also known as Brown-Wort, or Water Figwort
CHRONICLES: XI AN EXCELLENT MYSTERY

❖ 'Edmund ran for soft cloths and warm water, Cadfael for draughts and ointments and decoctions from his workshop. Tomorrow he would pick the fresh, juicy water betony, and wintergreen and woundwort, more effective than the creams and waxes he made from them to keep in store. But for tonight these must do.' AN EXCELLENT MYSTERY

Water betony was an ingredient in the healing creams and waxes that Cadfael used to treat Godfrid Marescot's old battle injury. It was also used in a lotion to cleanse wounds and grazes.

Ruling Planet: Jupiter in Cancer

USES

Medicinal: Poultices, ointments and infusions were made with the leaves of the herb to treat wounds and speed up the healing process.

BETONY, WOOD

Betonica officinalis
also known as Common Betony
CHRONICLES: XI An Excellent Mystery;
XII The Raven in the Foregate

❖ 'Cadfael warmed water in a pan, and diluted a lotion of betony, comfrey and daisy to cleanse the broken bruise on her [Dame Diota Hammet's] forehead and the scored grazes in both palms, scratches that ran obliquely from the wrist to the root of the forefinger and thumb, torn by the frozen and rutted ground.' The Raven in the Foregate

Cadfael not only used betony as a diluted lotion but also in a paste for dressing wounds.

Ruling Planet: Jupiter in Aries

USES

Medicinal: Antonius Musa, the Emperor Augustus's physician, said that the herb 'preserved the liver and body of man from the danger of epidemical diseases, and also from witchcraft.' He also claimed that it cured forty-seven different disorders.

Miscellaneous: Although found growing wild throughout England, betony was commonly cultivated in monastic herb-gardens.

BINDWEED, GREATER

Calystegia sepium
also known as Hedge Bindweed or
Lady's Nightcap; Lesser Bindweed or
Cornbine: *Convolvulus arvensis*;
(Culpeper: Great White Bindweed, or
Scammony: *Convolvulus sepium*)
CHRONICLES: XIII The Rose Rent

❖ 'Oh, be sure I know that no rule of silence keeps news from spreading like bindweed.' The Rose Rent

Ruling Planet: Moon in Cancer

USES

Medicinal: In herbal medicines both bindweeds were used as a laxative and purgative. Applied externally as a poultice the fresh leaves of the greater bindweed were said to burst a boil within twenty-four hours.

Miscellaneous: Both bindweeds, which are difficult to eradicate because of their extensive and easily-broken root and stem system, twine in an anti-clockwise direction around other plants, often strangling them.

BIRCH, SILVER

Betula pendula

(Culpeper: *Betula alba*)

CHRONICLES: IV SAINT PETER'S FAIR;
VIII THE DEVIL'S NOVICE;
XVII THE POTTER'S FIELD

❖ 'From the sandy escarpment of the river bank the slope of grass rose gradually towards a natural headland of bush and thorn, and a filigree screen of birch trees against the sky.' THE POTTER'S FIELD

❖ 'Nor was there any doubt about the traces of blood, meagre though they were. The sliver of birch bark under the tree showed a thin crust, dried black. Careful search found one or two more spots, and a thin smear drawn downhill, where it seemed the dead man had been turned on his back to be hauled the more easily down to the water' SAINT PETER'S FAIR

Ruling Planet: Venus

USES

Medicinal: Culpeper recommended that birch sap, or juice from the leaves, be used as a mouthwash and also 'to break the stone in the kidneys and bladder.' Tar from the fresh wood was used in ointments for skin disorders, especially eczema. Birch tea, made from the leaves, was taken for gout, rheumatism and arthritis.

Culinary: The sap from silver birch – a major source of sugar in eastern Europe – was fermented to make wine, spirits or vinegar.

Miscellaneous: As birch is able to grow on thin rocky soil, it was one of the earliest colonizers of Britain after the last Ice Age. In ancient times, birch bark not only served as a writing material, but was also used for tanning. Revered as sacred by the Celts, the tree was believed to drive out evil spirits (hence the birching of wrongdoers and the insane). During medieval times, a bundle of birch rods carried before a magistrate on his way to court symbolized both his authority and a means of correction. Traditionally, the twigs were used to make broomsticks.

BLACKTHORN

Prunus spinosa

also known as Sloe

CHRONICLES: XIX THE HOLY THIEF

'Cadfael had been awake and afield more than an hour by then, for want of a quiet mind, and had filled in the time by ranging along the bushy edges of his pease-fields and the shore of the mill-pond to gather the white blossoms of the blackthorn, just out of the bud and at their best for infusing, to make a gentle purge for the old men in the infirmary, who could no longer take the strenuous exercise that had formerly kept their bodies in good trim. A very fine plant, the blackthorn, good for almost anything that ailed a man's insides, providing bud and flower and bitter black fruit were all taken at their best. Good in hedges, too, for keeping cattle and sheep out of planted places.' THE HOLY THIEF

Some petals and fragments of blackthorn fell from Cadfael's sleeve or hair and lodged in the spine of the Gospels to point out the line: 'And the brother shall deliver up the brother to death.' (Matthew 10:21)

Ruling Planet: Saturn

USES

Medicinal: Blackthorn flowers were used as a tonic and mild laxative; the leaves as a mouthwash and to stimulate appetite; the bark to reduce fever; and the fruit for bladder, kidney and digestive disorders. The shrub was held to be 'the regulator of the stomach' since its flowers loosened the bowels and its fruits bound them.

Culinary: The bitter fruit of blackthorn, or sloes, were made into jellies, syrups, jams, wines and verjuice (an acid liquor). They were also used to make sloe gin, and were an ingredient in fruit cheeses.

Miscellaneous: Archaeological research has established that sloes, common in the wild, were consumed in large quantities as far back as Neolithic times. The purple-black juice, obtained by stabbing the point of a pen into a raw sloe, was used as a marking ink on linen and cloth.

BLUEBELL

Hyacinthoides non-scripta

also known as Wild Hyacinth:
Endymion non-scriptus
(Culpeper: *Hyacinthus non scriptus*)

CHRONICLES: XII THE RAVEN IN THE FOREGATE

The mark on Dame Diota Hammet's 'temple was merely a hyacinth oval, the bruise all but gone.'

Ruling Planet: Venus in Libra

USES

Medicinal: The bluebell bulb, dried and powdered, was used to stem bleeding and increase the production and discharge of urine.

Miscellaneous: Although the bluebell was abundant in medieval woodlands, it is not mentioned in British herbals before the sixteenth century. The root, which was made into a paper glue for bookbinding, and a starch for stiffening collars, is poisonous when fresh.

BORAGE

Borago officinalis

also known as Star Flower

CHRONICLES: III MONK'S-HOOD

In addition to treating Brother Barnabas for his bad chest and throat, Cadfael gave him:

❖ 'A hot draught of wine mulled with spices and borage and other febrifuge herbs. The potion went down patiently and steadily with eased breathing and relaxing sinews. The patient slept fitfully and uneasily; but in the middle of the night the sweat broke like a storm of rain, drenching the bed. The two attentive nurses lifted the patient, when the worst was past, drew the blanket from under him and laid a fresh one, rolled him close in another, and covered him warmly again.
"Go and sleep," said Cadfael, content, "for he does very well. By dawn he'll be awake and hungry."'

MONK'S-HOOD

Ruling Planet: Jupiter in Leo

USES

Medicinal: Internally, borage was used to treat fevers, dry skin conditions and bronchial infections. The oil was prescribed for kidney, bladder and bowel complaints, arthritis, and nervous disorders. Externally, the herb was used in a poultice to soothe inflammation and bruises; and, in a lotion, for bathing sore eyes. Gerard recommended syrup from the flowers to 'comforteth the heart, purgeth melancholy, and quieteth the frenetic or lunatic person.'

Culinary: The young leaves of borage were cooked like spinach or added raw to salads. They also added a cucumber-like flavour to wine and cold drinks.

Miscellaneous: Valued in ancient times for its ability to dispel melancholy and impart courage, borage flowers were included in stirrup cups offered to Crusaders departing for the Holy Land. Modern research suggests that chemicals in the herb act upon the adrenal gland, the 'organ of courage'. Gerard quoted the old Latin verse: 'I Borage bring always courage.' As a native of the Mediterranean, the plant was known to Greek and Roman botanists. Pliny said that it 'makes men merry and joyful.'

BOX

Buxus sempervirens

also known as Boxwood

CHRONICLES: X THE PILGRIM OF HATE;
XI AN EXCELLENT MYSTERY;
XII THE RAVEN IN THE FOREGATE;
XIV THE HERMIT OF EYTON FOREST;
XVI THE HERETIC'S APPRENTICE;
XIX THE HOLY THIEF

❖ 'After dinner in the refectory Brother Cadfael made his way across the great court, rounded the thick, dark mass of the box hedge – grown straggly now, he noted, and ripe for a final clipping before growth ceased in the cold – and entered the moist flower gardens, where leggy roses balanced at a man's height on their thin, leafless stems, and still glowed with invincible light and life. Beyond lay his herb garden, walled and silent, all its small, square beds already falling asleep.'

THE RAVEN IN THE FOREGATE

A thick screen of box separated the gardens from the main courtyard at Shrewsbury Abbey.

Ruling Planet: Mars in Scorpio

USES

Medicinal: Although all parts of the tree are poisonous if taken internally (animals have died from eating the leaves) box, taken in small doses, was used as a substitute for quinine in the treatment of recurrent fevers, like malaria. The leaves were used to purify the blood, stimulate hair growth and, together with the bark, to treat rheumatism and dispel intestinal worms. The oil was used to relieve toothache and piles. Pliny recommended the berries for diarrhoea.

Miscellaneous: Listed by Aelfric, box is an attractive evergreen tree that can reach a height of some thirty or more feet (nine metres). It was used for hedging, topiary work and to shelter more tender plants. The slow-growing, dwarf variety (*Buxus sempervirens* 'suffruticosa') was close-clipped (a custom said to have originated with the Romans) to make decorative edgings to formal herb gardens. During medieval times the wood, very hard and close-grained, was used for making small boxes, printing blocks, engraving plates and musical instruments. Both wood and leaves yield an auburn hair dye, while the bark was used to make perfume.

BRACKEN

Pteridium aquilinum

also known as Brake

(Culpeper: *Pteris aquilina*)

CHRONICLES: VIII THE DEVIL'S NOVICE;
XI AN EXCELLENT MYSTERY;
XII THE RAVEN IN THE FOREGATE;
XVI THE HERETIC'S APPRENTICE

❖ 'The hood had slipped back a little from her head, and showed him a coiled braid of hair of an indefinable spring colour, like the young fronds of bracken when they are just unfolding, a soft light brown with tones of green in the shadows.'

THE RAVEN IN THE FOREGATE

Bracken, a large fern, was used to cover the logs in a charcoal-burner's hearth, thereby keeping out the final, sealing covering of earth and ash. Ferns were often represented in illuminated designs and engravings.

Ruling Planet: Mercury

USES

Medicinal: According to Culpeper, the roots of bracken were used to kill intestinal worms and reduce swellings; boiled in oil, or hog's grease, they made a very profitable ointment for healing wounds; while powdered they speeded the healing of foul ulcers. Despite recommending the green fronds for stomach complaints, he warned that they were 'dangerous for women with child to meddle with by reason they cause abortions.' Smoking the legs with bracken was said to relieve thigh aches (sciatica).

Culinary: The young, uncoiled fronds of bracken could be used as a vegetable or, as in Norway, in the brewing of a kind of beer.

Miscellaneous: The minute spores, or fern-seeds, of bracken, if gathered at midnight on Midsummer Eve (reputedly the only time when they could be seen), were said to confer invisibility on their possessor. Because the fern-seeds gleamed like gold when caught by the sun, they were also said to bring riches, or locate hidden treasure. The ashes of burned bracken were used in glassmaking, as a substitute for soap, and as a fertilizer. The young fronds yield a yellowish-green dye.

BRAMBLE

Rubus fruticosus

also known as Blackberry

❖ 'A little further on this course, and the close, dark woods began, tall top cover, heavy interweaving of middle growth, and a tangle of bush and bramble and ground-cover below. Undisturbed forest, though there were rare islands of tillage bright and open within it, every one an astonishment.' THE PILGRIM OF HATE

Brambles, wild flowers, grasses and weeds grew over St Winifred's grave at Gwytherin. In addition, the plant grew in the Long Forest, on the wasteland near Farewell Abbey, on the headland above the Potter's Field and in the forest near Ullesthorpe.

Ruling Planet: Venus in Aries

USES

Medicinal: Bramble leaves were used as an astringent and tonic; for dysentery, diarrhoea and haemorrhoids; as a poultice to treat burns, swellings and ulcers; and as an infusion for stomach disorders. Externally, they were used as a mouthwash, and as a gargle for sore throats and gum inflammations. Culpeper recommended the leaves be used in a lotion for sores 'in the secret parts'. The ancient Greeks prescribed bramble for gout. Crawling backwards, or being dragged through a bramble thicket was an ancient remedy for boils (clearly a case of the cure being worse, or almost as bad as, the affliction). Bleeding caused by the thorns could be stemmed by rubbing the freshly-crushed leaves on the scratches.

Culinary: The fruit of the bramble was eaten fresh or cooked, and made into jams, jellies, syrups, cordials, vinegar and wine (it was also used to improve grape wines). The leaves were added to herbal teas.

Miscellaneous: Blackberries have been eaten in England since at least Neolithic times. Although used in medieval monasteries, they were not cultivated as a garden plant because they have always grown profusely in the wild, and have vicious thorns. The fruit yields a blue-grey dye, and the root an orange dye.

BRIAR

Rosa canina

also known as Dog Rose or
Wild Rose

CHRONICLES:
IV SAINT PETER'S FAIR;
XIV THE HERMIT
OF EYTON FOREST;
XVII THE POTTER'S FIELD

✤ 'They sat down together in a corner where the evening breeze coiled about them very softly and gratefully, and the view into the garth was all emerald turf and pale grey stone, and azure sky melting into green, through a fretwork of briars blowsy with late, drunken-sweet roses.'

SAINT PETER'S FAIR

Briars were found growing wild on the headland above the Potter's Field and were also trained to climb fretwork in the gardens at Shrewsbury Abbey.

Ruling Planet: Jupiter

USES

Medicinal: Rose hips, rich in vitamin C, were made into syrup, which could be added to cough mixtures or used to flavour medicines. By itself, or in the form of tea, it was taken internally as a gentle tonic. The leaves were used as a mild laxative and, being astringent, for healing wounds. Rose water made a soothing antiseptic tonic for sore and sensitive skins.

Culinary: Dog rose petals were sprinkled in salads. Both petals and hips were made into syrup and jam. The hips were also traditionally used for making wine or vinegar. Puréed fruit, deseeded and mixed with wine and sugar, was served as a dessert.

Miscellaneous: The name 'dog rose' is said to have originated in ancient Greece, where the root was reputed to cure the bite from a rabid dog. Fossilized roses, dating back thousands of years, have been discovered throughout Europe, including Britain. The Greeks used the plant to make perfumes, cosmetics and medicines, while the Romans cultivated it in their gardens for sweet fragrance and beauty. It seems that the further north the dog rose grows, the richer the hips are in vitamin C; hence the content of those in Scotland is four times greater than those in southern England. (*see also* Eglantine and Rose)

BROOM, COMMON

Sarothamnus scoparius or
Cytisus scoparius
(Culpeper: *Orobanche major*)

CHRONICLES: V THE LEPER OF SAINT GILES; XVII
THE POTTER'S FIELD

❖ 'They had brought spades with them, a mattock to peel off, with care, the matted root-felt of long, undisturbed growth, and a sickle to cut back the overhanging broom that hampered their movements and had partially hidden this secret burial place.'   THE POTTER'S FIELD

Generys was buried under the clump of broom-bushes in the headland above the Potter's Field. Broom, with gromwell creeping through the branches, also grew in the Long Forest near Huon de Domville's hunting lodge.

Ruling Planet: Mars

USES

Medicinal: Broom was mainly prescribed for heart and circulatory disorders, but was also used for kidney and bladder complaints. Culpeper recommended it for 'dropsy, gout, sciatica and pains of the hips and joints.' The young branches boiled in oil were used to kill head and body lice. In large doses, broom is dangerous. It is also slightly narcotic.

Culinary: Broom flowers and buds were pickled and used for flavouring savoury sauces.

Miscellaneous: Geoffrey, Count of Anjou (1113–51), second husband of the Empress Maud and father of Henry II, was also known as Geoffrey Plantagenet because he wore a sprig of broom (*Planta genista*) in his hat. Thereafter, the shrub – listed by Aelfric – became the badge of the Plantagenet kings of England. The stalks and branches were used to make brooms. The leaves, used to tan leather, yield a green dye. The bark was used in the manufacture of paper and cloth.

BROOM, BUTCHER'S

Ruscus aculeatus
also known as Box Holly

Ruling Planet: Mars

USES

Medicinal: Dioscorides, and other ancient physicians, prescribed the roots and stems of broom for kidney stones. Both roots and young shoots were traditionally used to treat haemorrhoids, gout and jaundice. It reduced inflammation, increased perspiration and acted as a mild laxative.

Culinary: The young shoots of broom were eaten like asparagus, to which the plant is related.

Miscellaneous: The shrub, listed by Aelfric, was traditionally used by butchers to clean chopping blocks and to decorate meat on festive occasions, like Christmas, when broom bears red berries.

Bryony

Bryonia dioica

also known as White Bryony or Wild Vine
(Culpeper: *Bryonia alba*)

Chronicles: XI An Excellent Mystery

❖ 'Brother Humilis was in the herb-garden with Cadfael, sitting in the shade while Fidelis chose from among the array of plants a few sprigs and tendrils he wanted for an illuminated border, bryony and centaury and bugloss, and the coiled threads of vetches, infinitely adaptable for framing initial letters. The young man had grown interested in the herbs and their uses, and sometimes helped to make the remedies Cadfael used in the treatment of Humilis, tending them with passionate, still devotion, as though his love could add the final ingredient that would make them sovereign.'   An Excellent Mystery

Ruling Planet: Mars

USES

Medicinal: Although poisonous, bryony has been valued medicinally since ancient times. Internally, in small doses, the root was taken as a purgative, and for rheumatism, sciatica and chest complaints. Externally, it was used to treat leprosy, old sores, gangrene and other skin ailments. In medieval times the juice, mixed with deadly nightshade (*Atropa belladonna*), was used as an anaesthetic. Culpeper warned that 'the root of bryony purges the belly with great violence, troubling the stomach and burning the liver, and therefore not rashly to be taken.'

Miscellaneous: Listed by Aelfric, bryony grew wild in British hedgerows and was also cultivated in physic gardens. The roots (cunningly adapted) were sold by the unscrupulous as 'English mandrake', because the genuine root was rare and costly. Gerard was shown a root so large that it was the size and weight of a year-old child.

BUGLOSS

Lycopsis arvensis or *Anchusa arvensis*
CHRONICLES: XI AN EXCELLENT MYSTERY

Cadfael grew bugloss in his herb-garden.

Ruling Planet: Jupiter in Leo

USES

Medicinal: Being mild and insipid, bugloss was added to medieval medicines more as an inoffensive extra than for any specific healing property. Under its French name *langue de boeuf*, or 'ox-tongue', the herb was used to 'comfort the heart and drive away melancholy' (Culpeper).

Culinary: Medieval monks grew bugloss as a pot-herb, to be boiled with meat, or added to cordials. The young leaves and flowers were eaten in salads.

Miscellaneous: Culpeper placed bugloss (*Lycopsis arvensis*) under the same entry as borage (*Borago offinalis*); indeed, some herbalists state that bugloss is another name for borage. According to Gerard, wild bugloss was also known as alkanet. Alkanet and borage are members of the same family, *Boraginaceae*.

BURDOCK, LESSER

Arctium minus
also known as Sticky Buttons or
Beggar's Buttons;
Greater Burdock (*Arctium lappa*)
CHRONICLES: VII THE SANCTUARY SPARROW; VIII
THE DEVIL'S NOVICE

By the time Hugh Beringar had retrieved Peter Clemence's bay horse, found wandering loose on the desolate peat-mosses near Whitchurch, 'the burrs and the rubble of heather' had been removed from its coat.

Ruling Planet: Venus

USES

Medicinal: The dried roots of burdock were powered and taken as a blood purifier, to prevent colds and flu and to stimulate perspiration in fevers. During the Middle Ages burdock was used to treat leprosy, eczema, psoriasis, boils and other skin complaints. Fresh leaves were applied externally as a poultice to bruises, ulcers and swellings. Culpeper said that 'the seed being drunk in wine forty days together, doth wonderfully help sciatica.'

Culinary: The young and tender stems of burdock were eaten in salads, boiled as a vegetable, or candied like angelica. The roots, also cooked and eaten, were an ingredient in 'dandelion and burdock' cordials and beers.

Miscellaneous: The hooked burrs, or fruiting heads, catch on to clothes or animal fur, thereby dispersing the seeds. The herb was listed by Aelfric.

CABBAGE

Brassica oleracea capitata
CHRONICLES: I A MORBID TASTE FOR BONES;
II ONE CORPSE TOO MANY;
III MONK'S-HOOD; V THE LEPER OF
SAINT GILES; XI AN EXCELLENT MYSTERY;
XIII THE ROSE RENT;
XVI THE HERETIC'S APPRENTICE

❖ 'There was a bed to be prepared for planting out late cabbages for succession, and fresh seed to be sown for the kind that can weather the winter.'

ONE CORPSE TOO MANY

Cabbages, sown in spring or summer, were grown in the gardens of Shrewsbury Abbey. They were also grown by the leper hospital of St Giles and the nuns at Godric's Ford.

Ruling Planet: Moon

USES

Medicinal: Cabbage leaves were used to treat inflammations, heal sores and scabs, inhibit bacteria and detoxify the liver. Culpeper said that 'the juice thereof drunk in wine helpeth those that are bitten by an adder.'

Culinary: Cabbages were a staple food of the monks. Culpeper said: 'I am sure, cabbages are extremely windy whether you take them as meat or as medicine; yea, as windy meat as can be eaten, unless you eat bagpipes or bellows, and they are but seldom ate in our days.'

Miscellaneous: The cabbage of medieval times was a small, loose-leaved plant. Varieties of cabbage were certainly cultivated by the Romans and the Anglo-Saxons.

CARROT, WILD

Daucus carota
Garden Carrot: *Daucus carota sativus*
CHRONICLES: XIII THE ROSE RENT

❖ 'Brother Cadfael...continued to survey the vegetable patch outside the wall of his herb-garden, digging an experimental toe into soil grown darker and kinder after a mild morning shower. "By rights," he said thoughtfully, "carrots should have been in more than a month ago."'

THE ROSE RENT

Ruling Planet: Mercury

USES

Medicinal: Carrots were recommended for anaemia, kidney complaints, and liver and bowel disorders. The juice of the root was used to kill intestinal worms. Applied externally as a poultice, the pulped root soothed itchy skin and alleviated the pain of sores and ulcers. Eating carrots was traditionally said to be good for the eyes, especially for the improvement of night vision.

Culinary: The cultivated variety of carrot was used raw in salads or cooked as a vegetable. A drink was made from raw carrot juice.

Miscellaneous: Although carrots were eaten as a vegetable by the Greeks and the Romans, they were not cultivated in Britain until medieval times. Botanists have argued that medieval carrots were purple, or almost black, yet an illustration in the twelfth-century herbal of Bury St Edmunds Abbey depicts the vegetable with an orange root. Wild carrots, listed by Aelfric, are still found in the hedgerows of Britain.

CENTAURY, COMMON

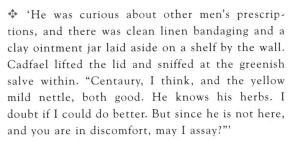

Centaureum erythraea

also known as Lesser Centaury or Feverwort)

(Culpeper: *Centaurea cyanus*)

CHRONICLES: VI THE VIRGIN IN THE ICE;
VII THE SANCTUARY SPARROW;
XI AN EXCELLENT MYSTERY;
XVII THE POTTER'S FIELD

❖ 'He was curious about other men's prescriptions, and there was clean linen bandaging and a clay ointment jar laid aside on a shelf by the wall. Cadfael lifted the lid and sniffed at the greenish salve within. "Centaury, I think, and the yellow mild nettle, both good. He knows his herbs. I doubt if I could do better. But since he is not here, and you are in discomfort, may I assay?"'

THE VIRGIN IN THE ICE

In addition to being found in Cadfael's herb-garden, centaury grew wild in the Potter's Field. It was an ingredient in a salve or ointment for wounds and, as such, was used to treat Liliwin, injured by a cudgel, and Evrard Boterel, knifed in the arm by Ermina Hugonin.

Ruling Planet: Sun

USES

Medicinal: The wound-healing and blood-staunching properties of centaury were known to the ancient Greeks, and in Europe it was traditionally used as a panacea for almost ever kind of ailment and disease, including malaria. Externally, in the form of a lotion, it was reputed to remove freckles and facial blemishes. Culpeper said that 'the herb is so safe you cannot fail in the using of it' adding, with reference to the herb's bitter taste, 'it is very wholesome, but not very toothsome.'

Culinary: Centaury was used to flavour herbal teas, wines and liqueurs.

Miscellaneous: Centaury is reputedly named after Chiron, the centaur of Greek mythology, who used the herb to heal himself of a wound contaminated by the blood of the many-headed serpent, Hydra. In *The Boke of Secretes of Albartus Magnus of the Vertues of Herbes, Stones, and Certain Beastes,* printed by William Copland in 1560, it was claimed that if centaury 'be joined with the blood of a female lapwing or black plover and be put with oil in a lamp, all they that compass it about shall believe themselves to be witches so that one shall believe of another that his head is in heaven and his feet on earth.' The plant was listed by Aelfric.

Cherry, Sweet

Prunus avium

also known as Wild Cherry or Gean
(Culpeper: *Prunus cerasus*, Morello Cherry)

Chronicles: III Monk's-Hood;
XIII The Rose Rent

Cadfael made a red wine from sweet cherries and their stones. Cherries were among the fruit trees grown in the Gaye orchards.

Ruling Planet: Venus

Uses

Medicinal: The fruit, bark and gum of cherry-trees were used to soothe irritating coughs, treat bronchial complaints and improve digestion. Crushed cherries, applied externally, were reputed to refresh tired skin and relieve migraines. Culpeper said that the gum, dissolved in wine, 'is good for a cold, cough, and hoarseness of the throat; mendeth the colour in the face, sharpeneth the eye-sight, provoketh appetite, and helpeth to break and expel the stone.'

Culinary: The fruit was cooked, eaten raw or (pulped with the stones) made into a wine. It was also used to make conserves and liqueur. In medieval times cherries were picked when they were wine-red, and eaten ultra-ripe.

Miscellaneous: Although the wild cherry, listed by Aelfric, is a native of Britain, it is thought that the Romans introduced the cultivated variety to England. Medieval monk-gardeners grafted more productive varieties on to the rootstock of the wild cherry. The fine-grained reddish-brown wood was highly suitable for wood-carving and turning.

CHERVIL

Anthriscus cerefolium
(Culpeper: *Chaerophyllum sativum*)
CHRONICLES: I A MORBID TASTE FOR BONES

Chervil was grown in Cadfael's herb-garden.

Ruling Planet: Jupiter

USES

Medicinal: Chervil was valued as a cleansing tonic, especially for liver, kidney and stomach complaints. Applied externally as a warm poultice, the leaves relieved aching joints, swellings and haemorrhoids. They were also used to treat conjunctivitis and sore eyes. The juice was taken to reduce fevers and treat jaundice and gout. The leaves eaten raw stimulated digestion. As a Lenten herb, chervil was traditionally taken for its restorative and blood-cleansing properties.

Culinary: The fresh leaves of chervil were added to salads, sauces and soups. Drying reduces the flavour. Gerard said that the roots were 'most excellent in a salad, if they be boiled and afterwards dressed as the cunning cook knoweth how better than myself.'

Miscellaneous: A native of the Middle East and eastern and southern Europe, chervil was almost certainly introduced into Britain by the Romans. It was listed by Aelfric.

CHESTNUT

Castanea sativa
also known as Sweet Chestnut
(Culpeper: *Castanea vesca*)
CHRONICLES: XI AN EXCELLENT MYSTERY;
XIII THE ROSE RENT;
XIV THE HERMIT OF EYTON FOREST;
XV THE CONFESSION OF BROTHER HALUIN;
XX BROTHER CADFAEL'S PENANCE

Brother Fidelis's hair was the 'colour of ripe chestnuts'.

Ruling Planet: Jupiter

USES

Medicinal: Chestnut leaves were used to control coughing and to reduce fevers and agues. Culpeper said that powdered fruits, or nuts, added to honey were an 'admirable remedy for the cough and spitting of blood.'

Chickweed Wintergreen

Trientalis europaea
Culpeper: *Pyrola minor*;
Common Wintergreen
CHRONICLES: XI AN EXCELLENT MYSTERY

Chickweed wintergreen was used by Cadfael in healing creams and waxes.

Ruling Planet: Moon

USES

Medicinal: During the Middle Ages chickweed wintergreen was reputed to heal wounds and cure blood poisoning. Culpeper said that the leaves of the common wintergreen 'are cooling and drying, and a good vulnerary both for inward and outward wounds and haemorrhages, ulcers in the kidneys or bladder.'

Miscellaneous: The name stems from the plant's use as food for birds and domestic fowls. Chickweed wintergreen, however, is not related to winter greens or to chickweeds.

Culinary: The fruits were roasted, boiled as a vegetable, or used for chestnut stuffings, soups and puddings. The Romans made them into a kind of porridge, called 'pollenta'. They were also ground into a nutritional flour.

Miscellaneous: A native of Mediterranean regions, the sweet chestnut was introduced into Britain by the Romans; but the fruit seldom fully ripens because of the cool climate. The tree was listed by Aelfric. Chestnut timber was used for exterior fencing, and for interior beams and panelling. Nut meal was used to whiten linen and make starch.

CINQUEFOIL

Silverweed: *Potentilla anserina*;
Creeping Tormentil: *Potentilla reptans*
(Culpeper: *Potentilla*)

CHRONICLES: XIX THE HOLY THIEF

❖ 'She thanked him, but did not sit. The array of mysterious containers fascinated her. She continued to prowl and gaze, restless but silent, a feline presence at his back as he selected from among his flasks cinquefoil and horehound, mint and a trace of poppy, and measured them into a green glass bottle. Her hand, slender, and long fingered, stroked along the jars with their Latin inscriptions.'   THE HOLY THIEF

Kept in a flask in Cadfael's workshop, cinquefoil was an ingredient in the linctus used to relieve Rémy of Pertuis's sore throat.

Ruling Planet: Jupiter (Silverweed);
Sun (Tormentil)

USES

Medicinal: Externally, cinquefoil was applied to cuts and wounds, or used as a gargle for sore throats and mouth ulcers. Internally, it was used for diarrhoea and as an aid to digestion. Dioscorides recommended boiling 'Myriophyllon' (Silverweed) in salted water to treat haemorrhages. Culpeper said that it 'is an especial herb used in all inflammations and fevers, whether infectious or pestilential, or among other herbs to cool and temper the blood and humours in the body.' Tormentil has similar properties to silverweed, but is more astringent and should be taken internally with care.

Culinary: From prehistoric times until the introduction of the potato in the sixteenth century, the starchy roots of silverweed (*Potentilla anserina*) were eaten raw and cooked, or ground to make porridge and bread.

Miscellaneous: Cinquefoil was known to the Anglo-Saxons and listed by Aelfric. Its name is derived from the French for 'five leaves'. The roots of tormentil yield a red dye.

CLEAVERS
see Goose-Grass

CLOVE-PINK

Dianthus caryophyllus

also known as Gilly-Flower or Carnation
(Culpeper: July Flower:*Motthiala incona*)

CHRONICLES: I A MORBID TASTE FOR BONES;
II ONE CORPSE TOO MANY

❧ 'So now what mattered was to make certain that for the rest of the evening he led Beringar into pastures far apart from where Godith operated. What Cadfael did must be noted, what she did must go unseen and unsuspected. And that could not be secured by adhering faithfully to the evening routine . . . so it was essential that Beringar should continue to concentrate on Cadfael, even if he was doing nothing more exciting than trimming the dead flowers from the abbot's roses and clove-pinks.'
ONE CORPSE TOO MANY

Clove-pinks were grown in the abbot's own garden at Shrewsbury Abbey. Gilvers were grown in Cadfael's herb-garden.

Ruling Planet: Jupiter (Pink, or Stock); Moon (Wallflower)

USES

Medicinal: Culpeper recommended a tincture of the July Flower (*Mattiola incana*) as the 'best medicine' for 'faintings, headaches, and other nervous disorder.' He said that wallflowers (*Cheiranthus cheiri* and *Leucoium sylvestris*) were used for mouth ulcers, to cleanse the blood, relieve inflammations and as 'a singular remedy for the gout, and all aches and pains in the joints and sinews.' Pinks were also reputed to alleviate malignant fevers, promote perspiration and quench raging thirsts.

Culinary: The petals of pinks (without the bitter white heel) were used to flavour soups, sauces, jams, cordials, wines and vinegars, or to make a syrup. They were also crystallized.

Miscellaneous: Clove-pinks were grown in monastic gardens mainly for their beauty and fragrance. 'Dianthus', mentioned by Theophrastus in the fourth century BC, is derived from the Greek for divine flower. Both Greeks and Romans wove them into garlands (the words carnation and coronation have the same ancient origin). The names gilver, gillyvor or gilly-flower were variously used in medieval times to describe clove-pink (*Dianthus*), stock (*Mattiola*), or wallflower (*Cheiranthus*). The oil of pinks was used in soaps and perfumery.

CLOVER

Trifolium repens

also known as White Clover;
Red Clover: *Trifolium pratense*
(Culpeper: *Trifolium*;
Trefoil or Honey-Suckle)

CHRONICLES: II ONE CORPSE TOO MANY;
XI AN EXCELLENT MYSTERY;
XII THE RAVEN IN THE FOREGATE;
XVI THE HERETIC'S APPRENTICE;
XX BROTHER CADFAEL'S PENANCE

❖ "'Too late! There are things I want to know, now. How did Father and Son first become three? Who first wrote of them as three, to confuse us all? How can there be three, all equal, who are yet not three but one?"

"As the three lobes of the clover leaf are three and equal but united in one leaf," suggested Anselm.

"And the four-leaved clover, that brings luck? What is the fourth, humankind? Or are we the stem of the threesome, that binds all together?"

Anselm shook his head over him, but with unperturbed serenity and a tolerant grin. "Never write a book, son! You would certainly be made to burn it!'"

THE HERETIC'S APPRENTICE

Clover, found growing on the Horse-Fair at Shrewsbury, was dried and stored for fodder and used as a sweet, fragrant ingredient in perfumed oils in altar lamps.

Ruling Planet: Mercury (White Clover); Venus (Red Clover)

USES

Medicinal: Internally, clover was taken for skin complaints, especially eczema and psoriasis. Clover tea was said to stimulate liver and gall-bladder activity, improve appetite, and cure indigestion, bronchitis and whooping-cough. Externally, the herb was applied as a poultice to relieve inflammations, ease rheumatic aches and pains, and to treat cancerous growths. Culpeper said that made into an ointment the herb 'is good to apply to the bites of venomous creatures.' It was also used to heal wounds and sores.

Culinary: Clover was added to salads and soups. A wine was made from the flowers.

COLEWORT

Brassica oleracea

also known as Kale

❖ 'Close to the waterside a footpath led off downstream, and beside it the abbey's gardens lay neatly arrayed all along the rich plain, and three or four brothers were pricking out plants of cabbage and colewort.'   THE ROSE RENT

Colewort, or kale, was grown by Cadfael and the monks in Shrewsbury Abbey gardens.

Ruling Planet: Moon

USES

Medicinal: According to Culpeper, the twice-boiled leaves of colewort, drunk with broth, 'helpeth the pains, and the obstruction of the liver and spleen, and the stone in the kidneys.' Also, taken with honey, 'it recovereth hoarseness or loss of voice.' External use, in the form of a liquid or ointment, eased muscle aches, reduced swellings and helped heal painful eruptions of the skin.

Culinary: Coleworts, like cabbages, were an important pot vegetable, or 'porray', in the medieval kitchen. The standard method of cooking all greens was to boil them from morning to night until they had become a soggy pulp, or purée.

Miscellaneous: Cabbages and coleworts belong to the same family, *Cruciferae*, as Black Mustard (*Brassica nigra*), Brown Mustard (*Brassica juncea*) and White Mustard (*Brassica hirta*).

Miscellaneous: Pliny said that when clover leaves trembled and stood upright a storm or tempest was on its way. During medieval times clover was grown as a forage crop, or ploughed back into the ground to enrich the soil. The flowers were valued by bee-keepers, because their nectar made a superior honey. The herb's Latin name *Trifolium* refers to the three-lobed leaves. Traditionally, the leaves were a symbol of the Trinity and were worn to bring good luck, and as a protection against evil and witchcraft. The rare four-leaved clover was considered especially lucky (provided it was not given away) and was reputed to bestow on its owner clairvoyant powers. At sunset the leaves close as if in prayer.

COLTSFOOT

Tussilago farfara

also known as Coughwort,
Horsehoof, or Bullsfoot

CHRONICLES: XII THE RAVEN IN
THE FOREGATE

Ruling Planet: Venus

USES

Medicinal: Coltsfoot was anciently used to treat coughs and colds, hence the botanical name *Tussilago* is derived from the Latin for cough. Indeed, in classical times it was smoked as a cough remedy. Gerard said that 'the fume of the dried leaves taken through a funnel or tunnel, burned upon coals, effectually helpeth those that are troubled with the shortness of breath, and fetch their wind thick and often.' The herb was also applied externally to soothe irritation, reduce swellings and heal skin ulcers. In the form of a syrup it was recommended not only for colds, but for bronchitis, laryngitis and asthma. It was also taken as a tea, and in the form of lozenges.

Culinary: Coltsfoot was added to salads and soups, and cooked as a vegetable. The flowers were used to make wine.

Miscellaneous: Coltsfoot, so-called because of its hoof-shaped leaves, was listed by Aelfric. During the Middle Ages it was known as *filus ante patrem*, or 'the son before the father', because the flowers appear before the leaves. In France, a coltsfoot flower painted on a doorpost indicated an apothecary's shop. The white hairs on the underside of the leaves, scraped off and dried, were used for tinder, and also for stuffing pillows.

COLUMBINE

Aquilegia vulgaris

also known as Culverwort or
Granny's Bonnet
(Culpeper: *Aquilegia*)

CHRONICLES: I A MORBID TASTE FOR BONES

One of the flowers grown in Cadfael's herb-garden.

Ruling Planet: Venus

USES

Medicinal: Although poisonous (especially the seeds), columbine was used in an antiseptic and astringent lotion for sore mouths and throats. Externally, the root was used to treat ulcers and common skin diseases. The plant was also used as a sedative. During medieval times it was one of a few select herbs prescribed to treat the plague.

Miscellaneous: The botanical name *Aquilegia* is derived from the Latin for an eagle, because the spurs of the flower were said to resemble an eagle's talons. Likewise, 'columbine' is derived from the Latin for a dove, or pigeon, because the flowers were supposed to resemble the bird in flight. The Anglo-Saxon 'culverwort' means pigeon-plant. Like the dove, the columbine symbolized the Holy Spirit or Holy Ghost. The plant was grown in monastic gardens mainly for decoration. Gerard called it *Herba Leonis*, or 'the herb wherein the lion doth delight'.

COMFREY

Symphytum officinale

also known as Saracen's Root, Knitbone, Boneset or Bruisewort

CHRONICLES: XII THE RAVEN IN THE FOREGATE; XVI THE HERETIC'S APPRENTICE

✤ 'Cadfael wanted comfrey and marsh mallow, both the leaves and the roots, and knew exactly where they grew profusely. Freshly prepared root and leaf of comfrey to heal Elave's broken head, marsh mallow to soothe the surface soreness, were better than the ready-made ointments or the poultices from dried materia in his workshop.

Nature was a rich provider in summer. Stored medicines were for the winter.'

THE HERETIC'S APPRENTICE

Found growing wild along the banks of the river Severn, comfrey was an ingredient in a lotion, diluted for cleansing wounds and grazes. Soothing preparations were made from the roots and leaves.

Ruling Planet: Saturn in Capricorn

USES

Medicinal: The root and leaves of comfrey were used in numerous herbal preparations. Externally, in the form of a poultice, the herb was valued for its powers of healing bruises, wounds and sprains. The moistened, pulped root applied around a broken limb set like plaster, helping the bone to mend more quickly. Comfrey tea alleviated the symptoms of colds, bronchitis and stomach ulcers. Gerard noted that 'the slimy substance of the root made in a posset of ale, and given to drink against the pain in the back, gotten by any violent motion, as wrestling, or over much use of women, doth in four or five days perfectly cure the same.'

Culinary: Although the root of comfrey is edible, it was the leaves, picked young and fresh, that were mainly used as a vegetable, often eaten raw. When cooked the hairs on the leaves disappear. Recent research, however, suggests that excessive consumption of the herb may be dangerous.

Miscellaneous: A native of Europe and Asia, comfrey is said to have been brought to England by Crusaders returning from the Holy Land. In addition to growing wild, beside water and in damp meadows, the plant was grown in monastic herb-gardens. When boiled the leaves produce a yellow fabric dye and also make good compost and mulch.

CORN
see Wheat

CORNFLOWER

Centaurea cyanus
also known as Bluebottle or Hurt-Sickle
CHRONICLES: I A MORBID TASTE
FOR BONES; V THE LEPER OF SAINT GILES

❖ 'The eyes, now conning Cadfael rather warily over the rim of the cup, were as radiantly blue as Cadfael remembered them from Saint Giles, like cornflowers in a wheat-field. He [Joscelin Lucy] did not look like a deceiver or a seducer, rather like an overgrown schoolboy, honest, impatient, clever after his fashion, and probably unwise. Cleverness and wisdom are not inevitable yoke-fellows.' THE LEPER OF SAINT GILES

Ruling Planet: Saturn

USES

Medicinal: An infusion of cornflowers was used for digestive and gastric disorders. The flowers were also used to produce a lotion for sore and tired eyes. Culpeper said that 'the juice put into fresh or green wounds doth quickly solder up the lips of them together, and is very effectual to heal all ulcers and sores in the mouth.'

Culinary: Cornflower petals were used fresh in salads.

Miscellaneous: Cornflowers were so-called because they were common in cornfields. Culpeper supposed that the plant was called 'hurt-sickle' because the tough stems blunted 'the edges of the sickles that reap the corn.' The petals were used to colour ink, cosmetics and medicines.

COWSLIP

Primula veris
also known as Paigle, Palsywort or
Bunch of Keys
CHRONICLES: X THE PILGRIM OF HATE

Cowslips were found in the grass of the meadows around Shrewsbury Abbey.

Ruling Planet: Venus in Aries

USES

Medicinal: Cowslip leaves were used as a salve for healing wounds, and the flowers as a mild sedative. Cowslip tea was recommended for headaches, insomnia and nervous tension. The root was used to alleviate arthritis, hence in old herbals it was called *radix arthritica*. The root was also prescribed for whooping cough and bronchitis. The tradition that the herb cured palsy may have arisen from the trembling or nodding of the flowers. Indeed, Culpeper said that 'the leaves are good in wounds, and the flowers take away trembling.'

Culinary: Cowslip leaves and flowers were eaten in salads. The flowers were used to make cowslip wine, syrup, pickle, conserve, vinegar and mead. They were also crystallized or sugared.

Miscellaneous: Native to northern and central Europe, cowslips grew wild in meadows and chalk grassland. The name is thought to derive from the Old English for cow dung or cowpat, from which the plant was said to spring. Commenting on the herb's reputation as a wrinkle-removing cosmetic, Culpeper said that 'our city dames know well enough the ointment or distilled water of it adds to beauty, or at least restores it when it is lost.' The plant was listed by Aelfric.

CRAB-APPLE

Malus sylvestris

also known as Wild Apple

CHRONICLES: II ONE CORPSE TOO MANY

❖ 'It was a large, rough-cut gem stone, as big as a crab-apple, a deep-yellow topaz still gripped and half-enclosed by an eagle's talon of silver-gilt.'

ONE CORPSE TOO MANY

Ruling Planet: Venus

USES

Medicinal: Fermented crab-apple juice (or verjuice) was recommended for scalds and sprains, and for sore throats and mouth disorders (*see also* Apple). Gerard said that applied to scalds it kept them from blistering.

Culinary: The bitter fruit of crab-apple was made into jelly, jam and wine. Verjuice was added like lemon juice to various dishes.

Miscellaneous: A native of Britain, the crab-apple is the ancestor of all cultivated apples. Indeed, to produce new varieties, grafts are still made on to its rootstock. The wood was highly valued for fine carving and wood-engraving. The name crab is said to derive from the Norse word for scrubby; but it may refer to the crabby nature of the tree which produces disagreeably sour fruit. In folklore, apples were often associated with love and marriage. One old custom, for example, concerned the throwing of apples pips into a fire, while reciting the name of one's love: if the pip exploded then the love would last; if not, the love would fade, just as the pip burned quietly away.

Crowfoot, common water

Ranunculus aquatilis

CHRONICLES: VII THE SANCTUARY SPARROW; XVI THE HERETIC'S APPRENTICE

❖ 'This was the season when delicate rafts of crowfoot swayed and trembled wherever there were shallows or slower water.'

THE SANCTUARY SPARROW

Cadfael found a wisp of crowfoot amongst the thick slime of fine gravel silting the nostrils of Baldwin Peche's corpse. Tendrils of crowfoot also 'clung' in the dead man's 'large, crooked teeth' and 'deep in his throat', where 'it had been inhaled in the struggle for breath.' Little rafts of water crowfoot, delicately anchored, were found growing in the shallows of the river Severn.

Ruling Planet: Moon

USES

Miscellaneous: There are thirteen different species of water crowfoot in Britain, most of which bear white buttercup-like flowers. The crowfoot recorded by Culpeper was *Ranunculus auricomus* (*see* Buttercup). Gerard said of the water crowfoot: 'Most apothecaries and herbarists do erroneously name it *Hepatica aquatica*, and *Hepatica alba*; and with greater error they mix it in medicine instead of *Hepatica alba* or grass of Parnassus.'

DAISY

Bellis perennis

also known as Bruisewort
(Culpeper: *Bellis minor perennis*)
Ox-Eye Daisy: *Chrysanthemum leucanthemum*
or *Leucanthemum vulgare*

CHRONICLES: III MONK'S-HOOD;
IX DEAD MAN'S RANSOM;
XII THE RAVEN IN THE FOREGATE;
XIV THE HERMIT OF EYTON FOREST;
XVII THE POTTER'S FIELD

❖ "'And this ointment you can take with you and use as often as you choose. It helps take out the sting and lower the swelling.'"
Warin turned the little jar curiously in his hand, and touched a finger to his cheek. "What's in it, to work such healing?"
"Saint John's wort and the small daisy, both good for wounds.'"   THE HERMIT OF EYTON FOREST

Cadfael used daisies in a lotion or ointment for cleansing and healing wounds and grazes. It grew in the Potter's Field.

Ruling Planet: Venus in Cancer

USES

Medicinal: Although daisies were mainly used in ointments to help heal wounds and bruises, they were also prescribed for stiff necks, swellings, lumbago and all kinds of aches and pains. Taken internally, the herb was used to treat fevers, coughs, catarrh and inflammatory disorders of the liver. An infusion of the flowers was used as a skin tonic. Chewing the fresh leaves was reputed to cure mouth ulcers. Gerard said that the juice of the leaves and roots 'given to little dogs with milk, keepeth them from growing great.'

Culinary: The leaves of the daisy were added raw to salads, or cooked as a vegetable to be served with meat.

Miscellaneous: A symbol of innocence, the daisy was grown in gardens not only for its usefulness as a herb but for its beauty. The botanical name *Bellis* may derive from the Latin for pretty or beautiful; or from *bellum*, meaning war, a reference to its use on the battlefield as a wound herb. 'Daisy' is thought to derive from the Old English words for days and eye, or day's eye, possibly because the flower resembles a small sun, or because it opens during the day and closes at night. An old proverb states that 'it is not Spring until you can plant your foot upon twelve daisies.' A common method of measuring love was to pull off the flower petals one at a time, while saying: 'he (she) loves me'; 'he (she) loves me not'. The flowers were added to pot-pourri. The daisy was listed by Aelfric.

DAMSON

Prunus institia or *Prunus domestica*
also known as Bullace
CHRONICLES: I A MORBID TASTE FOR BONES

❖ 'Sioned's "face was oval and firm of feature, the hair that fell in wild waves about her shoulders was almost black, but black with a tint of dark and brilliant red in it where the light caught, and the large, black-lashed eyes that considered Brother Cadfael with such frank interest were almost the same colour, dark as damsons, bright as the sparkles of mica in the river pebbles."' A MORBID TASTE FOR BONES

Ruling Planet: Venus

USES

Medicinal: An infusion of damson flowers was prescribed as a mild purgative. The roots were used to check bleeding and lower fevers, while the gin prepared from the fruit, because of its astringency, was recommended for diarrhoea.

Culinary: The bitter fruits of damsons were stewed, bottled, and made into jams, jellies and preserves. They were also used to make bullace wine.

Miscellaneous: The damson derives its name from the city of Damascus in Syria, where tradition says that it was first cultivated. In England the tree was commonly found growing wild in woods, thickets and hedges. The wood being hard and attractively-coloured was ideal for turning and cabinet-making.

DILL

Anethum graveolens or
Peucedanum graveolens
also known as Dillweed or Dillseed
CHRONICLES: I A MORBID TASTE FOR BONES;
II ONE CORPSE TOO MANY;
XII THE RAVEN IN THE FOREGATE

❖ 'They had entered the walled garden, and were suddenly engulfed and drowned in all those sun-drenched fragrances, rosemary, thyme, fennel, dill, sage, lavender, a whole world of secret sweetness.' ONE CORPSE TOO MANY

A fragrant herb grown in Cadfael's walled garden, dill was used in a cordial to soothe the stomach of a baby with wind.

Ruling Planet: Mercury

USES

Medicinal: Dill seeds were used to make a cordial to relieve digestive problems, flatulence, stomach cramps, headaches and insomnia. Dill or gripe water was prescribed to alleviate colic in babies. Like the ancient Greeks, Culpeper recommended the herb to 'stayeth the hiccough, being boiled in wine'. During medieval times the seeds were chewed to freshen the breath, and to allay hunger pains (especially during long church services). The herb was also administered to nursing mothers to promote the flow of milk.

Culinary: Dill leaves and dried seeds were used for flavouring vinegars and cooked dishes, particularly fish. The leaves were added to salads and sauces, or used as a garnish. The herb was also used as pickling spice for cucumbers and gherkins. The seed is more pungent than the leaves.

Miscellaneous: A native of southern Europe and the eastern Mediterranean, dill was probably introduced into Britain by the Romans, and was listed by Aelfric. Its name is derived from the Norse *dilla*, or the Anglo-Saxon *dylle*, both meaning to lull, or soothe. During the Middle Ages the herb was added to love potions and to witches spells, or hung up in a house as protection against the 'evil eye'. It was also used to perfume soap and cosmetics.

DITTANY

Dictamnus albus
also known as Burning Bush,
White Dittany or Fraxinella
(Culpeper: Dittander: *Lepidium sativum*)
CHRONICLES: VIII THE DEVIL'S NOVICE

Reading Aelfric's list of plants, Cadfael pondered whether dittany, grown in his garden, was the same as 'dittanders'.

Ruling Planet: Venus

USES

Medicinal: Dittany was mainly prescribed for pains such as cramp, rheumatism and kidney stones. It was also used to treat fevers and nervous complaints. Culpeper said that 'the root is a sure remedy for epilepsies, and other diseases of the head, opening obstructions of the womb, and procuring the discharges of the terms.' Dittany of Crete (*Origanum dictamnus*) was an ancient wound herb.

Culinary: The leaves of dittany were used to produce a scented tea; the flowers and roots for flavouring liqueurs and wines.

Miscellaneous: Dittander was listed by Aelfric. In medieval England the names dittander and dittany often referred to the same plant, 'possibly native cress *Lepidium latifolium*' (Harvey). Like several other plants known as 'burning bush', dittany (*Dictamnus albus*) produces a volatile vapour that can be ignited. Dittany is a member of the *Rutaceae* family; Dittander, the *Cruciferae* family; and Dittany of Crete, the *Labiatae* family. Distilled dittany water was popularly used as a cosmetic.

Dock, common

Rumex obtusifolius

also known as Broad-leaved Dock or Butter
Dock; Yellow or Curled Dock:

Rumex crispus

Chronicles: X The Pilgrim of Hate

❖ 'He was busy bruising fresh leaves of dock and
mandrake in a mortar for a soothing ointment.'

The Pilgrim of Hate

Ruling Planet: Jupiter

USES

Medicinal: Both yellow and broad-leaved dock
were used for the same medicinal purposes, notably
to treat skin complaints, liver disorders and
respiratory problems. The roots were used as a
laxative, and for anaemia. Rubbing the fresh leaves
on nettle stings was supposed to lessen the hurt.

Culinary: The young leaves of dock, although
somewhat bitter, were cooked as a vegetable.
Culpeper said that 'all docks being boiled with
meat, make it boil the sooner', adding that they
were 'as wholesome a pot herb as any growing in a
garden.'

Miscellaneous: The plant was listed by Aelfric. In
country districts, the leaves were used to wrap
butter, hence the name 'butter-dock'. The roots of
broad-leaved dock yield a greenish-yellow dye. (*see
also* Sorrel)

EGLANTINE

Rosa rubiginosa or *Rosa eglanteria*
also known as Sweet Briar
CHRONICLES: XVI THE HERETIC'S APPRENTICE

❖ '"It is Irish miniscule, the insular script."
Anselm's voice grew more reverent and awed as he
turned page after page, into the ivory whiteness of
the main part of the book, where the script had
abandoned gold for a rich blue-black, and the
numerals and initials flowered in exquisite colours,
laced and bordered with all manner of meadow
flowers, climbing roses, little herbers no bigger
than a thumbnail, where birds sang in branches
hardly thicker than a hair, and shy animals leaned
out from the cover of blossoming bushes. Tiny,
perfect women sat reading on turfed seats under
bowers of eglantine. Golden fountains played into
ivory basins, swans sailed on crystal rivers, minute
ships ventured oceans
the size of a tear.'

THE HERETIC'S APPRENTICE

Ruling Planet: Jupiter

USES

Medicinal: The seed oil of eglantine was applied
externally to help regenerate skin and scar tissue,
and to heal burns and scalds. Culpeper said that
the 'hips, if made into a conserve, and eaten
occasionally, gently bind the belly, stop defluxions
of the head and stomach, help digestion, sharpen
the appetite, and dry up the moisture of cold
rheum and phlegm upon the stomach.' In the
Middle East eglantine was prescribed for colic and
diarrhoea.

Miscellaneous: A native of Britain, eglantine not
only grew in the wild, but was also cultivated to
trail over trellises and hedges for its delicate
beauty, and the apple-like fragrance of its leaves
(the flowers have little scent). During medieval
times the plant represented both pleasure and
pain, for the scent was sweet and the thorns sharp.
(*see also* Briar and Rose)

ELM, ENGLISH

Ulmus procera

CHRONICLES: V THE LEPER OF SAINT GILES;
XVI THE HERETIC'S APPRENTICE

❖ 'A new elm stock, already fully provided with spokes, lay star-like on the grass, and the wheelwright, a thickset fellow of about forty-five years, bearded and muscular, was working away with an adze on a length of well-curved ash for the felloes, shaping with the grain of the wood.'

THE LEPER OF SAINT GILES

A coppice-tree, elm sprung 'anew from the stool of the original trunk, just below the cut.' The wood was essential for the stock, or hub, of a wheel.

Ruling Planet: Saturn

USES

Medicinal: The leaves of elm were used in ointments for burns, wounds and haemorrhoids, and in a decoction for skin inflammations. Sap from the branches was reputed to combat baldness. Culpeper said 'the leaves or the bark used with vinegar, cure scurf and leprosy very effectually: the decoction of the leaves, bark and root, being bathed, heals broken bones.' The inner bark of Slippery or Red Elm (*Ulmus rubra*) was used as a laxative, and, as a convalescent drink, to soothe sore throats and intestinal upsets.

Miscellaneous: A native to Britain, the elm was common in England during medieval times. In the 1970s a large proportion of the population was destroyed by Dutch elm disease (which, according to pollen records, may have also killed large numbers of the trees some 6,000 years ago). The wych elm (*Ulmus glabra*) is not only the hardiest of the species, but also has a greater resistance to the disease. Because elm timber is durable, especially in a wet environment, it was used for underground water pipes, the bottoms of boats, coffins, and the piles of bridges, groynes and waterfronts. Being almost impossible to split, the wood was traditionally used for the hubs of cartwheels. In Norse mythology Embla, the first woman, was created from the elm.

FENNEL

Foeniculum vulgare
also known as Sweet Fennel
(Culpeper: *Arethum foeniculum*)

CHRONICLES: I A MORBID TASTE FOR BONES;
II ONE CORPSE TOO MANY;
XII THE RAVEN IN THE FOREGATE;
XVI THE HERETIC'S APPRENTICE

❖ 'Cadfael half-filled the little spoon, touched it gently to the baby's lower lip, and instantly her mouth opened, willing to suck in the offering. It went down fairly tidily, leaving only a gloss upon the relaxed lips . . . "Nothing amiss with her that need cause you any worry," said Cadfael, re-stoppering the bottle. "If she wakes and cries in the night, and is again in pain, you can give her a little of this in the spoon, as I did. But I think she'll sleep. Give her somewhat less food at a time than you've been giving, and put three or four drops of this in the milk, and we'll see how she fares in a few days more."

"What is in it?" asked the widow [Nest], looking curiously at the bottle in her hand.

"There's dill, fennel, mint, just a morsel of poppy-juice . . . and honey to make it agreeable to the taste."'   THE RAVEN IN THE FOREGATE

Grown in Cadfael's walled garden, the herb was used in a cordial for soothing the stomach of a baby with wind.

Ruling Planet: Mercury

USES

Medicinal: Oil from the crushed roots of fennel was used to relieve flatulence, stomach aches and constipation. It was also added to gripe water, and

prescribed as an eyewash to improve bad eyesight, as an aid to digestion, and as a mouth-wash or gargle for sore throats. The seeds were chewed to alleviate hunger on fasting days. Culpeper said that the whole plant was 'much used in drink or broth, to make people lean that are too fat.' He also recommended the herb as an antidote against poisonous herbs and mushrooms, and for 'those that are bit by serpents.' Old herbalists used fennel to improve memory, and to stimulate the milk flow in nursing mothers. It was also reputed to be an aphrodisiac.

Culinary: Fennel was included in herbal teas, added to salads, and used as a garnish on vegetables. It was also used in soups, stuffings and sauces (particularly for oily fish dishes), and as a pot herb in meat stews. The seeds added an aniseed-like flavour to pastries, bread, liqueurs and cucumbers.

Miscellaneous: Valued by the ancient Greeks and Romans, who believed it bestowed strength and courage and prolonged life, fennel was one of the nine herbs held sacred by the Anglo-Saxons. It was listed by Aelfric. In medieval monasteries and churches it was used as a strewing herb to sweeten the air. Hung over doors or inserted in keyholes, fennel was reputed to ward off evil spirits. A facial pack of fennel tea and honey was said to remove wrinkles. The herb was also used to scent soaps and perfumes. It yields a yellow dye.

FERN
see Bracken

FIG

Ficus carica

❖ 'Brother Adam's eye was roving, as he spoke, towards some of Cadfael's rarer treasures, the eastern poppies he had brought from the Holy Land and reared here with anxious care, the delicate fig that still contrived to thrive against the sheltering north wall, where the sun nursed it.'

THE PILGRIM OF HATE

Ruling Planet: Jupiter

USES

Medicinal: Figs were prescribed internally for sore throats, bronchial complaints and constipation; and externally for boils, small tumours and haemorrhoids. The acrid juice from the leaves and stems was used to remove warts. Culpeper said that 'an ointment made of the juice and hog's grease, is an excellent a remedy for the biting of mad dogs, or other venomous beasts, as most are.' Adding that a syrup, made of the leaves or green fruits, 'is very good for the dropsy and falling sickness.'

Culinary: Figs, fresh or dried, were eaten raw or stewed, and made into jam.

Miscellaneous: The fig tree was held sacred by the Romans because it sheltered the she-wolf that suckled Romulus and Remus, the legendary founders of Rome. Like the elder, the fig was said to be the tree on which Judas Iscariot hanged himself after betraying Christ. The fig was probably introduced into England by the Romans. Although listed by Aelfric, it may have died out completely in Anglo-Saxon times. Tradition says that Thomas à Becket planted the first fig tree on English soil after returning from Rome. It was certainly grown on sheltered walls in monastic gardens.

FIGWORT

Scrophularia nodosa

also known as Throatwort or Carpenter's Square

The herb was used by Cadfael in an unspecified bottle of lotion.

Ruling Planet: Moon

USES

Medicinal: Medieval herbalists used figwort to treat the 'king's evil', or scrofula, a tubercular disease of the lymph glands in the neck; hence its botanical name *Scrophularia*, and its common name throatwort. 'Figwort' refers to the herb's ancient use in the treatment of haemorrhoids or *ficus* (Latin for fig). It was also used as a mild laxative, a heart stimulant, a pain reliever and a blood cleansing tonic. Applied externally, figwort was used for sores, ulcers, scratches, minor wounds and skin diseases, including eczema and fungal infections.

Miscellaneous: Despite the unpleasant smell of the flowers, wasps are greatly attracted to figworts. The herb was commonly known as carpenter's square because of its four-cornered stem. In France the plant is known as *herbe de siège*, because during the year-long siege of La Rochelle by Cardinal Richelieu in 1628 it was said to be the only nourishment available to the Huguenot garrison.

FLAX

Linum usitatissimum

also known as Linseed

Chronicles: I A Morbid Taste for Bones;
II One Corpse Too Many;
III Monk's-Hood; IV Saint Peter's Fair;
VII The Sanctuary Sparrow;
IX Dead Man's Ransom;
XVIII The Summer of the Danes;
XIX The Holy Thief; A Rare Benedictine (The Price of Light)

❖ '"Where would Anion [ap Griffri] get hold of any such rich material? He can never have handled anything better than drab homespun and unbleached flax in his life."'   Dead Man's Ransom

Oil extracted from flax seeds was an ingredient in a medicinal preparation for coughs, or rheum in the eyes or head. Fibres from the stems were used for the making of linen.

Ruling Planet: Mercury

USES

Medicinal: The oil from flax seeds was prescribed for urinary infections, constipation, respiratory disorders and gallstones, and to soothe coughs and sore throats. Externally, the plant was used for swellings, burns, boils, abscesses and ulcers, and to relieve aches and pains. In the eighth century, Charlemagne demanded that his subjects ate flax seeds to maintain good health. Eating the seeds in quantity can be poisonous.

Culinary: Linseed oil was used in cooking, and the roasted seeds eaten as a food. The ancient Greeks and Romans made bread from corn mixed with flax seeds.

Miscellaneous: Fibres from the stems of flax, one of the world's oldest crop plants, were woven into linen by many ancient civilizations, including the Mesopotamians, Egyptians and Greeks. In Britain the plant has been cultivated since prehistoric times, and the fibres used to make

ropes, nets, sacks, sails and even bowstrings. Pliny said: 'What department is there to be found of active life in which flax is not employed? And in what production of the earth are there greater marvels to us than this?' Most religious houses in medieval England grew a patch of flax, from which they could make their own napkins, cloths and, in the case of nuns, wimples. The inferior flax fibres, known as tow, were used as lamp wicks, or as stuffing to prevent draughts. Linseed oil was used in the making of paint, varnish, printer's ink and soap, and to lubricate cartwheels. The waste left over from the pulped seed was fed to cattle.

FLEUR-DE-LUCE
see Iris

FOX-STONES
see Orchis

FUNGUS, BRACKET

Laetioporus sulphureus or
Ganoderma adspersum
Toadstool: possibly *Panaeolus sphinctrinus*
CHRONICLES: VIII THE DEVIL'S NOVICE

❖ 'The copse was open and airy, the trees had shed half their leaves, and let in light to a floor still green and fresh. There were brackets of orange fungus jutting from the tree-boles, and frail bluish toadstools in the turf.' THE DEVIL'S NOVICE

USES

Medicinal: Pliny said that certain fungi were used as 'a remedy for the fluxes of the belly, known as bowel catarrh, and for fleshy growths on the anus, which they reduce and eventually cause to disappear; likewise, they remove freckles and spots on women's faces.' They were also applied to rashes, sores and dog bites.

Culinary: Among the edible species of bracket fungi are *Laetioporus sulphureus*, and *Pleurotus ostreatus*, or the bluish-coloured oyster mushroom. If in doubt, all fungi should be left alone.

Miscellaneous: Both mushrooms and toadstools are fungi, and several thousand species grow wild in Britain and Europe. Although there is no scientific difference between them, the term mushroom is commonly restricted to certain edible species, while toadstools are inedible. Indeed, the word toadstool is derived from the German for 'stool of death'. (*see also* Mushroom)

GENTIAN

Spring Gentian: *Gentiana verna*
Several similar species grow in the Alps
(Culpeper: *Sivertia perennis*)
CHRONICLES: X THE PILGRIM OF HATE;
XIX THE HOLY THIEF

❖ 'Crossing the half of Europe overland, long ago, Cadfael had seen gentians in the grass of the mountain meadows, bluer than blue.'

THE HOLY THIEF

Ruling Planet: Mars

USES

Medicinal: All gentians were once regarded as a panacea. Pliny said that the herbs, which are extremely bitter-tasting, were effective against stomach complaints, digestive disorders, ulcers and skin complaints, including 'the hairy affection appearing on the breasts at child-birth.' The species most commonly used in medieval European medicine was the great yellow gentian (*Gentiana lutea*). In addition to Pliny's list, the roots of gentians were used to reduce fever, stimulate the appetite and promote the flow of digestive juices and bile. Externally the herb was used for cleansing wounds.

Culinary: Gentians were used in the production of bitter liqueurs and aperitifs.

Miscellaneous: Although known to the ancient Egyptians, gentians are reputedly named after Gentius, King of Illyria, who discovered their medicinal value in the second century BC. Certain species of gentian, all of which are native to mountain pastures in Europe and Asia, were cultivated in England during the Middle Ages.

GILVER

see Clove-Pink

GINGER

Zingiber officinale
(Culpeper: *Asarum europaeum*; Asarabacca,
Hazelwort or European Wild Ginger)
CHRONICLES: I A MORBID TASTE FOR BONES

A plant grown in Cadfael's herb garden.

Ruling Planet: Mars

USES

Medicinal: As a hot, dry herb, the root of ginger was prescribed to warm the stomach, promote perspiration, treat colds, flu and lung infections, and improve blood circulation to peripheral parts of the body suffering from cold. It was also used to stimulate digestion, improve liver function, relax muscle spasms, and ease flatulence, colic and nausea. As a massage oil, ginger was used to stimulate circulation, and to relieve muscular and rheumatic aches and pains. Modern research has found that eating ginger is effective in reducing travel, or motion sickness.

Culinary: The aromatic roots of ginger were used fresh, dried, pickled, and preserved in syrup; while the stems were crystallized. Dried and ground into powder, the rhizomes were added as a spice to cakes, confectionery, gingerbread and ginger beer. 'Green ginger' refers to the root before it is dried.

Miscellaneous: A native of tropical Asia, ginger, or zingiber, was widely used by the Greeks, as well as by the Romans who brought it to Britain. Although grown in gardens in medieval England, Gerard remarked that it 'is most impatient of the coldness of these our northern regions', and 'as soon as it hath been touched with the first sharp blast of winter, it hath perished both blade and root.' Ginger was also used in perfumes.

GOOSE-GRASS

Galium aparine
also known as Cleavers, Clivers or Catchweed
CHRONICLES: II ONE CORPSE TOO MANY;
IV SAINT PETER'S FAIR;
VII THE SANCTUARY SPARROW;
X THE PILGRIM OF HATE;
XVI THE HERETIC'S APPRENTICE

❖ 'The dry grass was well laced with small herbs now rustling and dead but still fragrant, and there was a liberal admixture of hooky, clinging goose-grass in it. That reminded him not only of the shred of stem dragged deep into Nick Faintree's throat by the ligature that killed him, but also of Torold [Blund]'s ugly shoulder wound. He needed goose-grass to make a dressing for it, he would look along the fringe of the fields, it must be plentiful here. God's even-handed justice, that called attention to one friend's murder with a dry stem of last year's crop, might well, by the same token, design to soothe and heal the other friend's injuries by gift of this year's.' ONE CORPSE TOO MANY

Cadfael used goose-grass as the principal ingredient in a 'smooth green salve', ointment or unguent for healing grazes and wounds that are stubborn to knit.

Ruling Planet: Moon

USES

Medicinal: Goose-grass was used as a general cleansing tonic, and for treating glandular and urinary problems, skin disorders and lymphatic swellings. Applied externally, the herb was prescribed for burns, ulcers, skin inflammations, grazes, wounds and sores, and to staunch bleeding. Culpeper said that 'it is a good remedy in the spring, eaten (being first chopped small and boiled well) in water gruel, to cleanse the blood and strengthen the liver, thereby to keep the body in health, and fitting it for that change of season that is coming.' He also said that 'it is familiarly taken in broth, to keep them lean and lank that are apt to grow fat.'

Culinary: The young shoots of goose-grass were cooked as a vegetable, and added to soups. The seeds were a coffee substitute.

Miscellaneous: A native of Britain and considered a straggling weed, goose-grass supports itself amongst surrounding plants by means of the tiny hooked bristles that cover the stems and leaves. Similar burrs on the little round seeds enable them to cling, or 'cleave', to clothing and animal hair (hence the name cleavers). Its botanical name *aparine* derives from the Greek for to seize. Because of its clinging habit, it was also called sweethearts. Goose-grass is so-called because it was a favourite food of geese. In ancient Greece, shepherds were said to have used the stems and leaves for straining the hair out of milk. In medieval times, lacemakers pushed their pins through the hard round seeds to make a larger head. The root of the plant yields a red dye.

GOOSEBERRY

Ribes uva-crispa
(Culpeper: *Ribes grossularia*)
CHRONICLES: XIII THE ROSE RENT

✤ 'As so often in a late season, nature had set out to make good the weeks that had been lost to the spring cold, and contrived to bring on, almost at the usual time, both strawberries and the first of the little hard gooseberries on their thorny bushes.'
THE ROSE RENT

'Low bushes of little sour gooseberries' grew in the Gaye orchards.

Ruling Planet: Venus

USES

Medicinal: Culpeper said that the fruit of the gooseberry was 'cooling and astringent, creating an appetite, and quenching thirst'; while 'a decoction of the leaves cool hot swellings and inflammations.' The leaves were also prescribed for breaking up stones and gravel in the kidneys or bladder, and, applied externally as a dressing, to heal wounds. According to an old custom, pricking a sty or wart with a gooseberry thorn will cause it to disappear.

Culinary: The sharp and savoury fruits of the gooseberry were bottled, stewed, used to flavour wine, and made into jellies, jams, pickles and sauces. Gerard said that 'the fruit is much used in dinners, sauces for meats and used in broth instead of verjuice.'

Miscellaneous: Although a native to Britain, the gooseberry was rarely grown in medieval English gardens.

GORSE

Ulex europaeus

also known as Furze or Whin

❖ 'The first few green and sunny miles gave way to a rising track that kept company with a little tributary river, mounting steeply until the trees fell behind, and they emerged gradually into a lofty world of moorland, furze and heather, open and naked to the sky. No plough had ever broken the soil here, there was no visible movement but the ruffling of the sudden wind among the gorse and low bushes, no inhabitants but the birds that shot up from behind the foremost riders, and the hawks that hung almost motionless, high in the air.'

THE SUMMER OF THE DANES

Ruling Planet: Mars

USES

Medicinal: A decoction made from gorse flowers was prescribed for jaundice and kidney problems.

Culinary: Gorse buds were pickled, or made into a substitute tea. The flowers were used to make gorse wine.

Miscellaneous: A native to Britain, gorse was listed by Aelfric. Its name is derived from the Old English for a 'waste place', probably because it flourishes on the light soil of wild and exposed heathland. Gorse was used for fuel, as a hedging plant to protect livestock from predators, and for hanging washing over (the dense thorns stopped it from blowing away). In folklore, gorse was considered unlucky, and if allowed into the house it was believed to bring death or similar misfortune. The fact that the gorse is in bloom almost all the year round gave rise to the sayings: 'while the gorse is in flower Britain will never be conquered' and 'when the gorse is out of bloom, kissing's out of fashion.' The bark and flowers yield a yellow dye.

Grapevine

Vitis vinifera

also known as Vine

❖ 'August pursued its unshadowed course, without a cloud, and the harvest filled the barns . . . The grapes trained along the north wall of the enclosed garden swelled and changed colour.'

An Excellent Mystery

Vines were trained to grow along the north wall of the enclosed garden at Shrewsbury Abbey. The abbot's vineyard lay between the town wall and the river Severn, opposite the Gaye orchards.

An old, crabbed vine grew in Niall Bronzesmith's garden. Yves Hugonin entered La Musarderie by climbing the great vine which grew against the eastern wall of the castle. Grapes and vine-leaves were often represented in illuminated designs, carvings and engravings. Wine was produced from fermented grape-juice.

Ruling Planet: Sun

Uses

Medicinal: Pliny praised God for 'bestowing healing powers on the vine, not being satisfied with having richly supplied it with delicious flavours, perfumes, and unguents.' The plant's numerous healing properties that he then listed included the use of the leaves and the shoots to relieve headaches, inflammations, heartburn and diseases of the joints; the bark and dried leaves to staunch bleeding and heal wounds; the seeds to settle the stomach; and the fruit to 'check looseness of the bowels' and 'benefit those that spit blood.' Culpeper said that 'it is the most gallant tree of the Sun, very sympathetic with the body; that is the reason why spirit of wine is the greatest cordial among vegetables.'

Culinary: There are many species and hundreds of varieties of vine, the fruit of which was grown for specific usage: to be eaten raw; dried into currants, raisins and sultanas; pressed for juice; made into jelly; or fermented into drinking, cooking or ritual wines. Medieval vineyards produced both wine and verjuice (grape vinegar).

Miscellaneous: *Vitis vinifera*, the oldest cultivated species of vine, probably originated in north-west Asia. It was grown by the Egyptians at least 6,000 years ago, and was introduced into Britain by the Romans. During Anglo-Saxon times south-east England was famous for its vineyards. The plant was listed by Aelfric. In the twelfth century, Gerard of Wales said that the Vale of Gloucester was 'more densely covered with vines than any other part of England, and they have more fleshy produce and a more delicious taste, for the wine itself does not cause the mouths of its drinkers to twist ruefully at its bitterness, and indeed yields nothing to French wines in sweetness.'

GROMWELL, BLUE

Lithospermum purpurocaeruleum
also known as Creeping Gromwell;
Common Gromwell: *Lithospermum officinale*
CHRONICLES: V THE LEPER OF SAINT GILES

❖ 'Somewhere in his nocturnal ride Huon de Domville had added to his adornments a little bunch of frail, straight stems bearing long, fine leaves and starry flowers of a heavenly blue, even now, when they had lain all day neglected. Cadfael drew the posy out of the folds, and marvelled at it, for though it had commoner cousins, this plant was a rarity.

He knew it well, though it was seldom to be found even in shady places in Wales where he had occasionally seen it. He knew of no place here in England where it had ever, to his knowledge, been discovered. When he wanted seed to make powders or infusions against colic or stone, he had to be content with the poor relatives of this rarity. Now what, he wondered, viewing its very late and now somewhat jaded flowers, is a bunch of the blue creeping gromwell doing in these parts? Certainly Domville had not had it when he left the abbey.'

THE LEPER OF SAINT GILES

Blue creeping gromwell, exceedingly rare in England, grew only on chalk or limestone outcrops. The plant was found growing amidst the branches of a broom at Huon de Domville's hunting lodge in the Long Forest.

USES

Medicinal: In England, the crushed seeds of gromwell were used for urinary disorders, colic and kidney stones. In other parts of the world, several species of gromwell were used as an oral contraceptive, and to relieve irritant skin conditions.

Miscellaneous: 'Gromwell' may be derived from the French for grey millet, referring to the colour of its seeds; or possibly crane's millet. The hardness of the seeds is referred to in the plant's botanical name, *Lithospermum*, meaning stone seed. The roots of the herb yield a red colouring agent.

GROUNDSEL, COMMON

Senecio vulgaris
also known as Ground Glutton
CHRONICLES: XVII THE POTTER'S FIELD

Groundsel grew wild in the crevices of the flooring of Brother Ruald's derelict cottage.

Ruling Planet: Venus

USES

Medicinal: Although a common weed, groundsel has been valued as a healing herb since at least Roman times. Pliny said that 'if one touched a painful tooth with the plant three times, spitting after each touch, then replaced the plant back into the ground so as to allow it to continue growing, the tooth would never cause pain again.' In Anglo-Saxon and medieval times groundsel was used as a poultice for inflammation, haemorrhoids and gout. It was also widely used for menstruation problems, and to staunch bleeding. Culpeper said that 'the juice also provokes urine, and expels the gravel in the reins and kidneys, when taken in wine.' Taken in large doses groundsel can damage the liver.

Miscellaneous: A native of Britain, groundsel was listed by Aelfric. The head of white hairs (which appear after flowering to carry the seeds aloft on the slightest breeze) gave the plant its botanical name *Senecio*, from the Latin *senex*, old man. Its common name 'ground glutton' (derived from the Old English *grondeswyle*, ground swallower) refers to the weed's ability to spread widely and rapidly over the ground.

HAREBELL

Campanula rotundifolia
also known as Scottish Bluebell
CHRONICLES: V THE LEPER OF SAINT GILES;
XII THE RAVEN IN THE FOREGATE;
XV THE CONFESSION OF BROTHER HALUIN;
XVII THE POTTER'S FIELD

Harebells were found growing wild amongst the unreaped grass in the Potter's Field. Joscelin Lucy's eyelids were 'veined like harebells'.

Ruling Planet: Venus

USES

Medicinal: Harebell roots were applied as a compress to heal wounds, staunch bleeding and reduce inflammations.

Miscellaneous: In folklore the harebell was best avoided as it was believed to belong to the Devil, hence its common name 'old man's bells'. It was also associated with witches (who were said to transform themselves into hares), fairies, goblins and other supernatural beings.

HAWTHORN

Crataegus monogyna
also known as May or Quickthorn
(Culpeper: *Mespilus oxyacantha*)
CHRONICLES: I A MORBID TASTE FOR BONES;
VI THE VIRGIN IN THE ICE;
X THE PILGRIM OF HATE;
XIII THE ROSE RENT;
XVII THE POTTER'S FIELD;
XIX THE HOLY THIEF;
XX BROTHER CADFAEL'S PENANCE

❖ 'Long coils of bramble had found their way in at the vacant window from the bushes outside, and a branch of hawthorn nodded in over his shoulder, half its leaves shed, but starred with red berries.'
THE POTTER'S FIELD

Cadfael scattered white may-blossom in St Winifred's chapel at Gwytherin to suggest that Columbanus's disappearance was by miraculous means. After bathing his eyes in a distillation of the very same may-blossom, a blind man threw away his stick and went home seeing. Hawthorns were also found growing along the banks of the river Severn at Shrewsbury, and at Ruald's croft.

Ruling Planet: Mars

USES

Medicinal: Hawthorn fruits were mainly used to treat heart and circulatory disorders. Culpeper said that 'the seeds in the berries beaten to powder being drunk in wine, are good against the stone and dropsy. The distilled water of the flowers stays the lax. The seeds cleared of the down and bruised, being boiled in wine, are good for inward pains.'

Culinary: Hawthorn berries or flowers were used to make jellies, wines, liqueurs and sauces.

Miscellaneous: Legend says that Joseph of Arimathea, the owner of the tomb in which Christ was placed after the Crucifixion, brought the first hawthorn to England in about 63 AD. Planting his staff into the ground at Glastonbury, it rooted to produce a 'Holy Thorn', which thereafter always blossomed at Christmas. Because it was thought that the crown of thorns placed on Christ's head came from the hawthorn, taking the blossom into the house was said to invite disaster, or even death. Indeed some claimed that the plant actually smelled of death. In ancient Greece and Rome, however, the hawthorn was a symbol of hope and protection, and cuttings were brought into the home to ward off evil spirits. It was also associated with marriage and fertility. Pliny said that 'there are some who maintain that women who take the flower in drink conceive within forty days.' The tree, listed by Aelfric, was an important hedging plant, especially for protecting livestock.

HAY

Grass or other plants,
like Clover, grown for fodder

❖ 'Spring rains had brought a good hay crop, and June ideal conditions for gathering it.'

THE HERETIC'S APPRENTICE

Miscellaneous: In the meadows of medieval England there was an enormous diversity of flowering plants and seeding grasses. If left to itself, grassland would eventually revert to woodland; most, therefore, were managed: either by controlled grazing of animals; or by cutting the grass in summer for winter fodder. Traditionally, grassland was any area used for grazing animals; pasture, an enclosed flower-rich field for grazing animals; and meadow (derived from the Old English for to mow), an enclosed field grown specifically for hay, and in which the plants were allowed to flower, fruit and set seed. One ancient superstition encouraged young men and women to sleep in new haystacks to ensure that the hay would be sweet, and the girls would become pregnant.

✤ *'The hospice barn
was a commodious and even
comfortable place, warm
with the fragrance of the
summer's hay and the ripe scent
of stored apples.'*
THE POTTER'S FIELD

HAZEL

Corylus avellana

also known as Cobnut

Hazel grew in the hedges around the abbey enclosure at Shrewsbury. After peeling and soaking hazel withies in the shallows under the Welsh Bridge at Shrewsbury, Madog of the Dead-Boat wove them around the rim of a new coracle.

Ruling Planet: Mercury

USES

Medicinal: The leaves, bark and fruit of the hazel had various medicinal uses, including the treatment of varicose veins, circulatory disorders, menstrual problems, haemorrhoids and slow-healing wounds. Culpeper said the nuts, sprinkled with pepper, 'draws rheum from the head.'

Culinary: Hazel nuts or cobs were eaten raw, and used in cakes, bread, confectionery and liqueurs. Oil from the nuts was used in cooking.

Miscellaneous: A native of Britain and a major coppice tree, the hazel was listed by Aelfric. Since prehistoric times the long flexible twigs or 'withies' of the tree have been used to bind bundles, weave baskets, make hurdles and build coracles. In medieval times the twigs were used for the 'wattle' (or panels) in wattle and daub buildings. The hazel was considered sacred in Celtic mythology, and symbolized fertility and immortality. Because of its magical powers, the wood was used to make sorcerer's wands, together with the forked twigs favoured by dowsers and diviners. Hazel nuts were carried about the person to repel evil spirits, or ward off rheumatism. They were also associated with Hallowe'en, or 'Nutcrack Night'. Hazelnut oil was used for soap and cosmetics.

HEATHER

Calluna vulgaris

also known as Ling

CHRONICLES: VIII THE DEVIL'S NOVICE;
X THE PILGRIM OF HATE;
XVIII THE SUMMER OF THE DANES;
XIX THE HOLY THIEF;
XX BROTHER CADFAEL'S PENANCE

❖ 'Cadfael began to prowl uphill along the edge of the path, probing into the bushes, and then downhill again on the opposite side. Here and there the limestone that cropped out among the heather and rough grass on the ridge above broke through the grass and mould in stony patches, fretted away occasionally into small scattered boulders, bedded into the turf and moss.'

THE HOLY THIEF

Heather grew on outcrops in the Long Forest and on the limestone ridge near the track from Shrewsbury Abbey to the Longner ferry.

USES

Medicinal: Preparations of heather were mainly prescribed for urinary and kidney problems. It was also used to relieve rheumatic and arthritic pains, and as a mild sedative.

Culinary: The young shoots of heather were used to flavour beer.

Miscellaneous: A native to Britain, heather grows extensively on acid moorland and heathland. Its botanical name *Calluna* derives from the Greek for 'to brush', a reminder that bundles of heather twigs were used to make brushes and brooms. 'Ling' is derived from the Old English for fire, and refers to the plant's importance as a fuel in Anglo-Saxon times. Heather was used for thatching, bedding and to weave baskets. Most of the flowers are purple, but clumps of 'lucky' white heather can occasionally be found. Among the other species of heather growing wild in Britain are the bell heather (*Erica cinerea*) and the cross-leaved heath (*Erica tetralix*). The plant was used in tanning, and yields a yellow and orange dye. As the flowers are a rich source of nectar for honey, beekeepers often placed their hives amidst the heather moorland.

HEMLOCK

Conium maculatum

also known as Poison Parsley

CHRONICLES: III MONK'S-HOOD; XVII THE
POTTER'S FIELD

❖ "'I got what I wanted from a traveller . . . she
made for me what I wanted, one draught,
contained in so small a vial, my release from pain
and from the world. Tightly stoppered, she said it
would not lose its power. She told me its
properties, for in very small doses it is used against
pain when other things fail, but in this strength it
would end pain forever. The herb is hemlock."
"It has been known," said Cadfael bleakly, "to end
pain for ever even when the sufferer never meant
to surrender life. I do not use it. Its dangers are too
great. There is a lotion can be made to use against
ulcers and swellings and inflammations, but there
are other remedies safer.'" THE POTTER'S FIELD

Generys died after drinking a draught of wine
containing hemlock.

Ruling Planet: Saturn

USES

Medicinal: Although highly poisonous, hemlock
was valued for its sleep-inducing, antispasmodic
and pain-relieving properties. Greek and Arabian
physicians prescribed the plant for tumours, skin
diseases and pains in the joints. Pliny said that 'for
nosebleeds cicuta [hemlock] seed, beaten up into
water and inserted in the nostrils, is held to be
effective.' In the Middle Ages the plant was used
to treat epilepsy, nervous spasms, mania and St
Vitus's Dance. Externally, the leaves were used to
heal sores and ulcers, and to reduce inflammation,
swellings and haemorrhoids. Culpeper warned that
'hemlock is exceedingly cold, and very dangerous,
especially to be taken inwardly.'

Miscellaneous: In ancient Greece hemlock was
used for executing convicted criminals and
lawbreakers. After being condemned for impiety
and the corruption of the young, Socrates, the
Greek philosopher, chose to die by this fatal poison
in 199 BC. The botanical name *Conium* derives
from the Greek for to spin or to whirl, probably
because the first reaction after eating the plant is
giddiness. In folklore hemlock has long been
associated with the devil, and other evil
influences. It is said that the herb was an
ingredient in the ointment used by witches for
flying. The plant was listed by Aelfric.

HEMP

Cannabis sativa

also known as Cannabis or Indian Hemp

CHRONICLES: XVII THE POTTER'S FIELD

❖ 'A thin hand drew back the linen curtain as Cadfael stooped to the head of the litter. The shell was plaited from hemp, to be light of weight and give with the movement, and within it Donata [Blount] reclined in folded rugs and pillows. Thus she must have travelled a year or more ago, when she had made her last excursions into the world outside Longner.' THE POTTER'S FIELD

Fibres from the stem of hemp were plaited to form the shell of a litter for transporting the sick and wounded.

Ruling Planet: Saturn

USES

Medicinal: Long before the use or possession of hemp was made illegal in Britain, the herb was widely cultivated in monastic gardens as a drug for helping depression, easing pain, relieving muscle spasms and inducing sleep. Pliny said that 'its seed is reputed to make the genitals impotent. Its juice drives out of the ears the worms and any other creature that has entered them, but at the cost of a headache; so potent is its nature that when poured into water it is said to make it coagulate.' Culpeper noted that 'the decoction of the root eases the pains of the gout, the hard humours of knots in the joints, the pains and shrinkings of the sinews, and the pains of the hips.'

Miscellaneous: Possibly a native of Europe as well as parts of Asia, hemp was grown at least 5,000 years ago as a fibre plant, its stems being used to make rope, string, cordage, sacking and sail-cloth. Its use as a mind-affecting drug was, according to Herodotus, the Greek historian of the fifth century BC, known to the ancient Scythians, who got high by inhaling the fumes of the roasted seeds. In medieval England the stout cloth woven from the plant by cottagers in their homes was known as 'hempen home-spun'.

HERB OF GRACE

see Rue

HONEYSUCKLE

Lonicera periclymenum

also known as Woodbine

(Culpeper: *Lonicora caprifolium*)

CHRONICLES: XVI THE HERETIC'S APPRENTICE

❖ 'In the last gathering of the book the leaves reassumed their imperial purple, the final exultant psalms were again inscribed in gold, and the psalter ended with a painted page in which an empyrean of hovering angels, a paradise of haloed saints, and a transfigured earth of redeemed souls all together obeyed the psalmist, and praised God in the firmament of his power, with every instrument of music known to man. And all the quivering wings, all the haloes, all the trumpets and psalteries and harps, the stringed instruments and organs, the timbrels and the loud cymbals were of burnished gold, and the denizens of heaven and paradise and earth alike were as sinuous and ethereal as the tendrils of rose and honeysuckle and vine that intertwined with them, and the sky above them as blue as the irises and periwinkles under their feet, until the tips of the angels' wings melted into a zenith all blinding gold, in which the ultimate mystery vanished from sight.'

THE HERETIC'S APPRENTICE

Tendrils of honeysuckle were often represented in illuminated designs, carvings and engravings.

Ruling Planet: Mars

USES

Medicinal: The berries of the honeysuckle are extremely poisonous. Nevertheless, the plant was used for treating colds, asthma, constipation, skin infections and urinary complaints. In large doses it causes vomiting. Gerard said that 'the flowers steeped in oil, and set in the sun, are good to anoint the body that is benumbed, and grown very cold.'

Culinary: The fresh flowers were added to salads, or made into a substitute tea.

Miscellaneous: Although honeysuckle grew wild all over Britain, it was cultivated in gardens for its rich fragrance. Its common name 'woodbine' refers to the plant's climbing habit of entwining, or binding its tendrils around shrubs and trees. 'Honeysuckle' refers to the sweet juice, or nectar, of the flowers. Honeysuckle is an emblem of fidelity and affection. Tradition says that if the flowers are placed in a girl's bedroom, she will dream of love; and if brought into the home, there will soon be a wedding. The flowers were added to pot-pourri, and used for perfumes.

HOREHOUND

Marrubium vulgare

also known as White Horehound

CHRONICLES: III MONK'S-HOOD;
IX DEAD MAN'S RANSOM;
XII THE RAVEN IN THE FOREGATE;
XV THE CONFESSION OF BROTHER HALUIN;
XVII THE POTTER'S FIELD;
XIX THE HOLY THIEF

❖ 'Cadfael went back to his workshop in the herbarium, and blew up his brazier to boil a fresh elixir of horehound for the winter coughs and colds.'
DEAD MAN'S RANSOM

Horehound had a 'sharp, warm, steamy smell.' Cadfael used the herb in a medicinal preparation for rheum in the eyes or head, in an elixir for winter coughs and colds, and also in a linctus for sore throats.

Ruling Planet: Mercury

USES

Medicinal: Horehound has long been cultivated to treat various ailments, especially coughs, catarrh, asthma and respiratory complaints. The plant was especially valued by the Greeks and the Romans, as well as the ancient Egyptians. Pliny said that 'its seeds and leaves pounded together are good for the bites of serpents, pains in the chest and side, and chronic cough,' adding that, pounded with honey, it was 'remarkably good for maladies of the male genitals.' The herb was also used for heart, liver and digestive problems, for malaria and, according to Culpeper, to kill worms and heal dog-bites. Horehound candy was sold as cough sweets.

Culinary: The leaves of horehound were used to make liqueurs, ales and wine.

Miscellaneous: The ancient Egyptians dedicated horehound to Horus, the god of the sun and sky. A native to Britain, the herb was known to the Anglo-Saxons and listed by Aelfric. Said to be one of the bitter Passover herbs, its botanical name is derived from the Hebrew for bitter juice. The name is thought to come from the Old English for 'a downy plant'. Its leaves were used to clean milk pails and, soaked in fresh milk, to kill flies.

HOUND'S-TONGUE

Cynoglossum officinale

also known as Rats-and-Mice or Gypsy Flower

CHRONICLES: XVIII THE DEVIL'S NOVICE

❖ '"I've dressed his bite with a lotion of hound's-tongue, and anointed a few other cuts and grazes he has."'
THE DEVIL'S NOVICE

Cadfael applied a lotion containing the herb to the festered wound on the forearm of Harald, runaway villein and farrier.

Ruling Planet: Mercury

USES

Medicinal: Hound's-tongue was widely valued for its soothing, healing and painkilling properties, especially in the treatment of cuts, bruises, burns, sores and skin diseases. Culpeper recommended it for coughs and colds, as well as to cure the bite of mad dogs, baldness and venereal disease. The bruised leaves were rubbed on insect bites.

Miscellaneous: A native of Britain, hound's-tongue grew wild in grassland and on the edge of woodland throughout much of the country. Its botanical name *Cynoglossum* is derived from the Greek for dog's tongue, a reference to the shape and texture of the leaves. Ancient superstition held that dogs would be silenced and unable to bark at any person who placed a leaf of the herb under their big toe. Because of its pungent smell, hound's tongue was commonly known as 'rats-and-mice'.

HOUSELEEK

Sempervivum tectorum
also known as Live for Ever, Jupiter's Eye,
Thor's Beard or Sengren
CHRONICLES: III MONK'S-HOOD

❖ "'If you can make medicines from this plant,' said Prior Robert, with chill dislike, "so, surely, may others, and this may have come from some very different source, and not from any store of ours."
"That I doubt," said Cadfael sturdily, "since I know the odour of my own specific so well, and can detect here mustard and houseleek as well as monk's-hood. I have seen its effects, once taken, I know them again.'"   MONK'S-HOOD

Houseleek was used in an oil for rubbing into the skin to ease aching joints.

Ruling Planet: Jupiter

USES

Medicinal: Some 2,000 years ago Dioscorides prescribed houseleek for ulcers, burns, scalds and inflammations. It was also used to treat skin rashes, stings, insect bites, and to remove warts and corns. Chewing the fleshy leaves was said to relieve toothache.

Culinary: The young evergreen leaves of houseleek were added to salads, or eaten as a vegetable.

Miscellaneous: A native of mountainous areas of southern and central Europe, the houseleek may have been introduced into Britain by the Romans.

The Anglo-Saxon's knew it as *leac* or leek. Its botanical name *Sempervivum* derives from the Latin for always alive, a reference to the plant's ability to survive drought. It was traditionally believed that lightning would never strike a building with houseleeks growing on the roof. Indeed, not only was the plant grown on roofs in ancient Greece and Rome, it was also dedicated to two thunder-gods, the Roman Jupiter and the Scandinavian Thor. Charlemagne ordered that the plant be grown throughout his empire for its magical properties, which included keeping witches and evil spirits away.

Hyacinth
see Bluebell

Hyssop

Hyssopus officinalis
Chronicles: XV The Confession of
Brother Haluin

✤ "'I've known hyssop to kill. I was foolish to keep it among my stores, there are other herbs that could take its place. But in small doses, both herb and root, dried and powdered, are excellent for the yellow distemper, and useful with horehound against chest troubles, though the blue-flowered kind is milder and better for that. I've known women use it to procure abortion, in great doses that purge to the extreme. Small wonder if sometimes the poor girl dies.'"

The Confession of Brother Haluin

Both herb and root of hyssop, dried and powdered, was used for chest troubles and yellow distemper or jaundice. In large doses it could cause an abortion, or possibly death.

Ruling Planet: Jupiter (Hedge Hyssop: Mars)

USES

Medicinal: Hyssop was used to treat coughs, chest and lung complaints, urinary inflammations, and rheumatism. In ancient Greece the herb was burned with brimstone and inhaled to relieve sore throats. Pliny said that 'bruises disappear under applications of hyssop', and 'a handful of hyssop, boiled down to one third with salt, or pounded in oxymel and salt, both carries off phlegm and expels worms from the intestines.' Gerard said that 'a decoction of hyssop made with figs, water, honey, and rue, and drunken, helpeth the old cough.' Large doses of hyssop can be dangerous. It should not be taken during pregnancy.

Culinary: Hyssop flowers were added to salads, the leaves were included in soups, stews, stuffings, meat dishes and fruit pies, and the distilled oil was used to flavour liqueurs.

Miscellaneous: A native of Mediterranean lands, hyssop was probably introduced into England either by the Romans or by the Normans. Its botanical name is derived from the Greek for a holy herb, referring to its ancient use in purifying ceremonies, and in the cleansing of sacred temples. Botanical experts disagree as to whether or not the hyssop mentioned in the Bible was *Hyssopus officinalis*, as the name hyssop was given to a number of different plants in ancient times. Hyssop was one of the bitter herbs traditionally eaten by the Jews at the Passover. Strewn on the floor in churches and infirmaries, the herb was reputed to prevent the spread of infectious diseases. Bees and butterflies are particularly attracted to the flowers, and, grown near cabbages, it was said to lure away whiteflies. Hyssop was used in pot-pourri and perfumes.

IRIS, YELLOW FLAG

Iris pseudacorus

also known as Fleur-de-luce or
Fleur-de-lys; Orris or Florentine Iris:
Iris florentina or *Iris germanica*; Stinking or
Gladdon Iris: *Iris foetidissima*

❖ 'Irises were in tight, thrusting bud.'

THE PILGRIM OF HATE

An unnamed species of iris was found growing in the meadow outside the abbey enclosure at Shrewsbury. The flower was among those represented on the last page of Theofanu's priceless psalter. Fleur-de-luce was an ingredient in a draught meant to procure an abortion.

Ruling Planet: Moon

USES

Medicinal: Pliny said that 'the iris is valued only for its root, being grown for unguents and for medicine.' Dried, it was mainly used for chest complaints and as a powerful purgative. Culpeper noted that 'being stuffed up the nostrils, it purges the head, and clears the brain of thin serous phlegmatic humours.' Although the fresh root can cause violent and dangerous reactions, when dried it was often given to teething babies to chew on.

Culinary: Iris roots were used as a spice, or added to liqueurs and beers. The roasted seeds were used as a coffee substitute.

Miscellaneous: Because of their bright, multi-coloured flowers, all irises are named after Iris the Greek goddess of the rainbow, and the messenger of the gods. Pliny said that those who intend to dig the root up, must first offer 'a libation to please the earth. Then they draw three circles round it with the point of a sword, pull it up and raise it to the heavens. It is hot by nature, and when handled raises burn-like blisters. It is essential that those who gather it should be chaste.' The fleur-de-lys, probably a corruption of the French for flower of Louis (rather than flower of lily), was adopted as an emblem by King Louis VII of France in the Second Crusade against the Saracens. The violet-scented, powdered root of orris has been used in perfumery and cosmetics since ancient Egyptian times. It was also put in wardrobes to sweeten linen, used as a fixative in pot-pourri and used as a hair powder, or dry shampoo. The flowers of the flag iris yield a yellow dye; while the black dye from the roots was used as an ink. Hung about the doors of churches and houses, irises were reputed to ward off evil spirits. In medieval times the leaves were strewn on floors, and used to cover chairs and repair thatched roofs.

İVY, COMMON

Hedera helix
also known as Climbing Ivy
CHRONICLES: V THE LEPER OF SAINT GILES

❖ 'For Iveta [de Massard] needed to be delivered not only from this detestable match, but from the guardian who preyed on her and her inheritance like murderous ivy on an oak.'

THE LEPER OF SAINT GILES

Ivy grew at Huon de Domville's hunting lodge in the Long Forest.

Ruling Planet: Saturn

USES

Medicinal: Although all parts of ivy are poisonous, the berries were taken as a purgative. An infusion of the leaves was recommended for rheumatic pains, bronchial complaints, and whooping cough. Applied externally as a poultice, the leaves were used to treat burns, scalds, sores, wounds, painful swellings, bruises, neuralgia and sciatica. Culpeper said that 'the yellow berries are good against the jaundice, and a drunken surfeit.' He also said that they 'prevent and heal the plague.'

Miscellaneous: Ivy has been a sacred plant from at least Christian times. Pliny noted that it was used by 'the peoples of Thrace at solemn festivals to decorate the wands of the fertility god 'Father Liber' [Dionysus, or Bacchus], and also the worshippers' helmets and shields, although it is harmful to all trees and plants and destructive to tombs and walls, and very agreeable to chilly snakes, so that it is surprising that any honour has been paid to it.' During the Middle Ages the plant was reputed to be the enemy of the vine and would, therefore, prevent drunkenness, hence wine was often drunk out of ivy wood cups. Although ivy was believed to be a protective magical plant, in some areas of England it was considered unlucky to bring it into the house. It was also said that to lie down under an ivy tree could bring about a sleep from which there was no awakening.

Ivy, Ground

Glechoma hederacea

also known as Alehoof or
Gill-Go-Over-The-Ground

Chronicles: VIII The Devil's Novice

❖ 'Meriet [Aspley] ate his bread and cheese and onion, and drank his ale, and lay down flat as ground-ivy under the trees.' The Devil's Novice

Ruling Planet: Venus

USES

Medicinal: In the second century AD, Galen recommended the use of ground ivy to treat inflamed eyes and cure failing eyesight. An infusion made from the leaves was used for colds, chest complaints, digestive troubles, menstrual pains, and bladder and kidney infections. As a poultice ivy was used to heal boils, ulcers, wounds and skin irritations. 'Gill tea' was taken as a cough medicine. Culpeper said that 'the juice dropped into the ear doth wonderfully help the noise and singing of them, and helpeth the hearing which is decayed.' As an inhalant, ivy was reputed to relieve nasal congestion and headaches.

Culinary: Ground ivy was used in the making and clarifying of ale. The fresh shoots and leaves were added to salads, soups, and gruels, or cooked like spinach.

Miscellaneous: A native of Britain since prehistoric times, ground ivy was known to the ancient Greeks and Romans. Its use in the making of ale is reflected in the names 'alehoof' (ale herb) and 'gill-go-over-the-ground' ('gill' being derived from the French for to ferment ale). A varnish was made from the resin.

Jasmine, Common

Jasminum officinale

also known as Jessamine

Chronicles: V The Leper of Saint Giles

❖ 'For it certainly was not the old woman who had brought that faint, indefinable perfume into the room. Nor had the one who distilled it been gone from here very long, for such a fragrance would have faded away within a few days. Cadfael had a nose for floral essences, and recognised jasmine.' The Leper of Saint Giles

Ruling Planet: Jupiter in Cancer

USES

Medicinal: Jasmine flowers and their essential oil were used for depression, chest and respiratory complaints, nervous tension, menstrual problems and general tiredness. Culpeper said that 'it disperses crude humours, and is good for cold and catarrhous constitutions, but not for the hot.' The oil has long been considered an aphrodisiac, and a cure for frigidity. Jasmine tea was prescribed as a mild sedative, and a remedy for headache.

Miscellaneous: A native to south-west Asia, the earliest record that jasmine was cultivated in England dates from the sixteenth century. It was mainly grown in gardens for its sweet fragrance. Oil of jasmine was used in perfumery, while the flowers were added to pot-pourri.

JUNIPER

Juniperis communis
also known as Bastard Killer
CHRONICLES: IV SAINT PETER'S FAIR

❖ 'As for the matter of the flask of juniper spirits, what did it really signify? The man had been picked up too drunk to talk, no one had looked round for his bottle, it might well have been left lying, still more than half-full, if the stuff was as potent as Wat [Renold] said, and some scavenger by night might have picked it up and rejoiced in his luck.'
SAINT PETER'S FAIR

The oil from the berry-like cones of juniper was used to flavour a gin, known in England as juniper spirit, or in Holland, geneva.

USES

Medicinal: Pliny said that the juniper, 'even above all other remedies, is warming and alleviates symptoms.' Roman physicians prescribed it for pains in the stomach, chest and side, flatulence, coughs and colds, tumours and disorders of the uterus. Some even suggested smearing the body with an extract from the seeds as a protection against snake bites. Culpeper recommended the berries for a great variety of ailments, ranging from an antidote against poisons and a defence against the plague, to strengthening the brain and curing 'wind from any part of the body.' Its country name 'bastard killer' arose from the eating of the berries to procure an abortion. Juniper berries should not be taken during pregnancy, or by those with kidney problems.

Culinary: Oil of juniper, made from the sharp-tasting berries, was used to flavour liqueurs, notably gin, and added to marinades, stews, sauces, and certain meat dishes. The wood was burned to smoke preserved meats.

Miscellaneous: A native of Britain, appearing soon after the last Ice Age, juniper is one of the country's slowest-growing trees. In Biblical times the branches were burned as a purifying herb in temples. During more recent times in Britain, because the dry wood burns with very little smoke, it was favoured by those involved in the illicit distilling of spirits. The word gin is derived from the Dutch *geneva* (jenever), meaning juniper. In many areas of the country it was considered a powerful protection against witches, devils and evil spirits. Branches of juniper were strewn on floors to sweeten the smell of rooms, and burned to cleanse the air of disease and infection, especially during epidemics. The berries yield a brown dye.

KALE
see Colewort

LADY'S MANTLE

Alchemilla vulgaris
also known as Dewcup or Bear's Foot
CHRONICLES: III MONK'S-HOOD;
IV SAINT PETER'S FAIR

❖ 'Brother Mark ran to the herbarium to collect the paste of mulberry leaves and the unguent of Our Lady's mantle, known specifics for burns.'

SAINT PETER'S FAIR

Lady's mantle was used in a pot of salve for bed-sores, and also in an unguent, or ointment, for burns.

Ruling Planet: Venus

USES

Medicinal: Traditionally, lady's mantle (known as 'a woman's best friend') was used for treating female ailments, including vaginal discharges, itching and menstrual disorders. Culpeper said that 'it helps ruptures, and women who have over-flagging breasts, causing them to grow less and hard.' He also considered it to be one of 'the most singular wound-herbs,' highly praising it for 'all wounds, inward and outward.' In addition to being valued for its restorative and wound-healing properties, the herb was used to staunch bleeding, and to treat inflammation, bruises, boils, sores and burns. It was also taken as a digestive tonic, and for diarrhoea.

Culinary: The mildly-bitter leaves of lady's mantle were added to salads.

Miscellaneous: A native of mountainous areas of Europe, lady's mantle was reputed to possess magical powers, particularly as, unlike other herbs, its leaves produced big shining pearls of dew overnight. Collected at dawn, the dew, or 'celestial water', was used by medieval alchemists in their experiments to turn base metals into gold and silver. Indeed, its botanical name *Alchemilla* ('the little magical one') is thought to derive from the Arabic for 'alchemy'. Our Lady's mantle, however, refers to the Virgin Mary, to whom the herb is dedicated; while the shape of the leaves was supposed to resemble her cloak. Cows that graze on the herb were said to increase their milk production. It is also liked by horses and sheep. The leaves yield a green dye, and were also used in cosmetics.

L

LAUREL
see Bay

LAVENDER, COMMON OR ENGLISH

Lavandula augustifolia or
Lavandula officinalis

(Culpeper: *Lavandula spica*)

CHRONICLES: II ONE CORPSE TOO MANY;
V THE LEPER OF SAINT GILES;
VI THE VIRGIN IN THE ICE;
XVI THE HERETIC'S APPRENTICE;
XVII THE POTTER'S FIELD;
A RARE BENEDICTINE (THE PRICE OF LIGHT)

❖ "'And in this great sack – is it grain?' She plunged her hands wrist-deep inside the neck of it, and the hut was filled with sweetness. "Lavender? Such a great harvest of it? Do you, then, prepare perfumes for us women?'
"Lavender has other good properties," said Cadfael… "It is helpful for all disorders that trouble the head and spirit, and its scent is calming. I'll give you a little pillow filled with that and other herbs, that shall help to bring you sleep.'"

A RARE BENEDICTINE (THE PRICE OF LIGHT)

A fragrant plant grown in Cadfael's walled garden, the flowers or flowering-stems of lavender were harvested and dried, and used not only for their scent but also medicinally. Elfgiva hid the pair of candlesticks, made by Alard the silversmith, deep inside a sack of lavender in Cadfael's workshop.

Ruling Planet: Mercury

USES

Medicinal: A strong antiseptic with antibacterial properties, lavender oil was used to treat cuts, bites, stings, burns, coughs and colds, chest infections, rheumatic aches, giddiness and flatulence. As a soothing tonic for nervous and digestive disorders, the herb was prescribed to relieve tension, insomnia, and depression. William Turner, the 'father of English botany', said that 'the flowers of lavender, quilted in a cap, comfort the brain very well.' A sprig of lavender placed behind the ear was reputed to cure headaches. Culpeper warned that the oil 'is of a fierce and piercing quality, and ought to be carefully used, a very few drops being sufficient for inward or outward maladies.' The herb was also used in the form of lavender water, and tea.

Culinary: Lavender leaves were added to salads, and used to flavour jellies, jams, vinegars, pottages and stews. The flowers were also crystallized.

Miscellaneous: A native of the Mediterranean region, lavender was introduced into England by the Romans. Its botanical name *Lavandula* derives from the Latin for to wash, a reference to its use by the Romans as a scented additive to their bathwater. Grown in medieval monastic gardens, it was not only valued for its medicinal properties, but for its beauty and fragrance, and as a strewing herb, insect-repellant, and a mask for unpleasant smells. The dried flowers were added to pot-pourri, herb cushions and sachets for freshening and keeping moths away from linen. The oil was used in varnishes, perfumes, soaps and cosmetics.

LETTUCE

Lactuca sativa

also known as Garden Lettuce;
Wild, or Great Prickly Lettuce:
Lactuca virosa

CHRONICLES: I A MORBID TASTE FOR BONES;
XIII THE ROSE RENT

❖ 'On the open, sunlit expanse of the vegetable plots the ground dried out earlier, and the brothers on duty were busy sowing lettuces for succession, and hoeing and weeding.' THE ROSE RENT

Lettuces were grown in Cadfael's garden and along the Gaye in the vegetable plots of Shrewsbury Abbey.

Ruling Planet: Moon (Garden Lettuce); Mars (Wild Lettuce)

USES

Medicinal: The sedative properties of wild lettuce, which are most potent as the plant goes to seed, have been known since ancient times. Because it had a narcotic effect and helped to induce sleep, calm anxiety and ease pain, the milky sap or latex contained in the wild lettuce was known as 'poor man's opium'. The plant was also used to treat mania, nervous disorders, coughs, respiratory problems, aching muscles and joints, and liver and digestive complaints. Overdosage may cause poisoning.

Culinary: In medieval times the bitter, loose-leaved variety of lettuce was cooked as a vegetable, and added to porrays and soups. (The lettuce commonly used in salads nowadays has had both the bitterness and the medicinal virtues of its wild relative bred out of it.)

Miscellaneous: The ancient Greeks and Romans credited the lettuce with magical properties, believing it to be a protection against drunkenness, as well as an aphrodisiac. Dioscorides, however, prescribed it to diminish sexual desire, while the Pythagoreans called it 'eunuchs' plant'. In Greek mythology Aphrodite was reputed to have laid the dead body of her beloved Adonis on a bed of lettuce leaves. Pliny mentioned that there were a large variety of lettuce, but that all had a 'cooling quality', and 'relieved the stomach of distaste for food and promoted appetite.' He also mentioned that, during the months that they were out of season, the leaves were kept 'pickled in honey-vinegar.' The botanical name *Lactuca* is derived from the Latin for milk, a reference to the milky sap in the stems. When dried the latex was used to adulterate opium.

Lichen

plants composed of
fungus and algae in close combination

Lungwort: *Lobaria pulmonaria*

(Culpeper: *Pulmonaria officinalis**)

CHRONICLES: VIII THE DEVIL'S NOVICE;
XIII THE ROSE RENT; XIX THE HOLY THIEF

✤ 'They had gone no more than ten minutes deeper into the woodland, after their rest, when he checked to look about him, at the slant of the veiled sun between the trees, and the shape of the low, lichened outcrop of rocks on their right.'

THE DEVIL'S NOVICE

Lichens were found growing on rocky outcrops in the Long Forest. Godfrey Fuller produced from 'the lichens and madders' a variety of red, brown and yellow dyes for cloth.

Ruling Planet: Jupiter

USES

Medicinal: Lungwort (*Lobaria pulmonaria*) and the ancient scribbler (*Graphis scripta*) were among the lichens valued by old herbalists for their antibiotic properties. The dual organisms were mainly used for throat infections and lung (pulmonary) complaints, including tuberculosis. Culpeper said that lungwort* 'is of great use in diseases of the lungs, and for coughs, wheezings and shortness of breath, which it cures.' He also recommended it as a remedy for yellow jaundice, and to stop inward bleeding.

Miscellaneous: In Anglo-Saxon charters many trees were called *har* or 'hoar' trees, an adjective often used to describe old men's beards. According to Oliver Rackham, they were probably trees which had beard-like lichens growing on them, such as the *Usnea* and *Ramalina* species. In *The Last Forest* he reckoned that 109 species of lichen were found growing in Hatfield Forest between 1890 and 1969, 'of which 103 were on bark or wood'. This was despite the fact that the forest had suffered from acid rain, which is deadly to lichens (their abundance on trees indicates a clean atmosphere; while the absence of particular species is a measure of air and rain pollution). Some landmarks, notably in Wales and Cornwall were known as *Maen mellyn*, or yellow stone, referring to a rock covered with the yellow lichen *Xanthoria*. Experts can date, albeit approximately, the age of walls, tombstones and standings stones by their lichen encrustations (the organisms are so slow-growing that an area the size of a plate may be hundreds, if not thousands, of years old). Cudbear lichen (*Ochroelchia tartarea*), often found growing on birch trees, yields a crimson dye.

*The lungwort (*Pulmonaria officinalis*) referred to by Culpeper was 'a kind of moss that grows on oak and beech trees, with broad, greyish, rough leaves, diversely folded, crumpled, and gashed at the edges, some are spotted on the upper side. It never bears any stalk or flower.' This should not be confused with the common lungwort (*Pulmonaria officinalis*), which is a member of the borage family, and not a lichen.

LILAC

Syringa vulgaris

CHRONICLES: X THE PILGRIM OF HATE; XIV THE HERMIT OF EYTON FOREST

❖ 'The dawn was still fresh, dewy and cool, the light lying brightly across the roofs while the great court lay in lilac-tinted shadow. In the gardens every tree and bush cast a long band of shade, striping the flower beds like giant brush-strokes in some gilded illumination.' THE PILGRIM OF HATE

USES

Medicinal: Although rarely used in medicine, lilac was used in the treatment of fevers, particularly malaria, and to expel intestinal worms. In some parts of Europe it was made into an ointment for rheumatic pains in the joints. Inhaled deeply, the strong scent of the flowers can cause nausea.

Miscellaneous: A native of the eastern Europe and the Middle East, lilac was only introduced into Britain in the sixteenth century. In parts of the country the shrub, especially the white-flowered variety, was reputed to be unlucky, although, like the clover, those flowers with five petals were said to bestow luck on the finder. Lilac symbolized the first emotions in love. The flowers have long been used in perfumery.

Lily, Madonna

Lilium candidum

Lily of the Valley: *Convallaria majalis*

CHRONICLES: X The Pilgrim of Hate;
XII The Raven in the Foregate;
XV The Confession of Brother Haluin;
A Rare Benedictine (The Price of Light)

❖ 'Hamo FitzHamon and his party appeared at Vespers in full glory, to see the candlesticks reverently installed upon the altar in the Lady Chapel. Abbot, prior and brothers had no difficulty in sufficiently admiring the gift, for they were indeed things of beauty, two fluted stems ending in the twin cups of flowering lilies. Even the veins of the leaves showed delicate and perfect as in the living plant.'   A Rare Benedictine (The Price of Light)

Ruling Planet: Moon (Lily); Mercury (Lily of the Valley)

USES

Medicinal: Lilies were prescribed for bruises, boils, corns, burns, ulcers, inflammations, and for softening hard skin. Gerard said that 'the root of the garden lily stamped with honey glueth together sinews that be cut asunder.' Although potentially poisonous, lily of the valley was used to treat gout, sore eyes, poor memory, loss of speech, and heart disease. The dried and powdered root was used as a snuff to clear nasal mucous, and relieve headaches.

Culinary: The bulbs of the Madonna lily, not the poisonous lily of the valley, were cooked and eaten.

Miscellaneous: A favoured plant of the Greeks and Romans, the lily was sacred to Juno, wife and sister of Jupiter, and queen of the heaven. The lily was certainly known to the Anglo-Saxons, for St Etheldreda, the foundress of Ely abbey, was depicted holding the flower in a tenth-century illumination. The Madonna lily, however, is native to the Holy Land, and may have been brought to England by the Crusaders. The 'white and red' flowers of paradise mentioned in medieval literature, refer to the lily and the rose, both being useful as well as beautiful. The lily has long been associated with the Virgin Mary, or Madonna, its white flowers representing purity and innocence. 'Our Lady's tears', the alternative name for the lily of the valley, refers to the belief that it sprang up at the Cross where her tears were shed. In some parts of the country, the flowers were said to have been used as ladders by fairies. Although they were employed in spells to counter witchcraft and as a protection against evil, lilies were considered to be unlucky plants, especially if brought inside the house. Tradition held that anyone planting the lily of the valley in their garden would die within the year. Nevertheless, the plant has been cultivated in Britain since at least medieval times. The use of lilies at funerals symbolized the restored innocence of the soul after death. Lilies were used in perfumery and cosmetics.

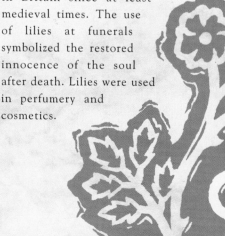

MADDER

Rubia tinctorum
also known as Dyer's Madder
CHRONICLES: XIII THE ROSE RENT

Madder was used to produce a red dye for cloth.

Ruling Planet: Mars

USES

Medicinal: Pliny recommended madder to cure jaundice, sciatica and paralysis, noting that he found in some authorities 'that jaundice is cured if this shrub is merely looked at while worn as an amulet.' In medieval times the roots were used externally for healing wounds and bruises, and internally for treating urinary problems, kidney and bladder complaints, constipation and the palsy.

Miscellaneous: A native to the Mediterranean and Middle East, madder was valued in both medicine and dyeing by the ancient Egyptians, as well as the Greeks and Romans. The red dye yielded by its roots (traditionally used to colour Turkish fezzes) is referred to in the plant's botanical name *Rubia*, derived from the Latin for red. A wide range of colours, however, can be obtained from the plant. It was listed by Aelfric.

MALLOW, MARSH

Althaea officinalis
also known as Mallards, or Cheeses;
Common Mallow: *Malva sylvestris*
CHRONICLES: XVI THE HERETIC'S APPRENTICE

The leaves and roots of marsh mallow were freshly prepared to soothe the surface soreness of a wound.

Ruling Planet: Venus

USES

Medicinal: The common and marsh mallow were used medicinally for many of the same ailments. Pliny said that one of the marvels of all mallows was that 'whoever swallows half a cyathus [wine-ladle] of the juice a day shall be immune to all diseases.' In England fresh mallow leaves were used as a poultice for wounds, bruises, sprains, inflammations, stings and insect bites. They were also used to treat coughs, chest and lung complaints, diarrhoea, insomnia, cystitis and gastric ulcers.

Culinary: Mallow leaves were eaten as a vegetable, and added to salads, soups and stews. The unripe seed capsules, known as 'cheeses', were eaten raw with salads. The modern sugary confectionery known as marshmallow, which contains no herbal extracts, originated from a soothing sweet recipe made from the powdered root of *Althaea officinalis*.

Miscellaneous: Native to Britain and Europe, the mallow was known to the Greeks, Romans, and Anglo-Saxons, and was listed by Aelfric. The botanical name *Althaea* comes from the Greek for to cure, while the common name mallow is derived

from the Greek for to soften, referring to its softening and soothing properties. From ancient times mallows were eaten to reduce sexual desire, especially as a countermeasure against aphrodisiacs and love-potions. They were also used in cosmetics.

MANDRAKE

Mandragora officinarum
also known as Devil's Apples
CHRONICLES: X THE PILGRIM OF HATE

In the preparation of a soothing ointment, Cadfael bruised the fresh leaves of mandrake in a mortar.

Ruling Planet: Mercury

USES

Medicinal: A powerful narcotic plant, reputed to cure sterility, mandrake was used in ancient times as an anaesthetic during operations. In medieval times it was prescribed for nervous disorders, as an emetic, purgative, sedative, pain-killer and aphrodisiac. Externally, the roots were used to treat ulcers. Anglo-Saxon herbalists believed that it could banish demons from those possessed. Mandrake is highly poisonous.

Miscellaneous: A native to southern Europe and the Mediterranean, mandrake has long been credited with all manner of magical powers, partly because of its narcotic and hallucinogenic properties, and partly because the forked root resembles the human form. The Hebrew word for mandrake means love-plant, and in Genesis both of Jacob's wives – unable to have children for different reasons – became pregnant after acquiring the herb. It has long been considered a powerful aphrodisiac: the ancient Egyptians called it the 'phallus of the field', and the Arabs 'Devil's apples' (the latter alluding to its apple-like fruit). As the plant was said to emit a terrible scream when anyone tried to dig it up (as well as striking them dead), the root was traditionally pulled out of the ground by tying a dog to it. Even Theophrastus, over 2,000 years ago, mentioned a precautionary root-gathering ritual: 'one should draw three circles round it with a sword, and cut it with one's face towards the west; and at the cutting of the second piece one should dance round the plant and say as many things as possible about the mysteries of love.' The plant, which was an ingredient in witches' brews, was listed by Aelfric. Gerard considered that 'there hath been many ridiculous tales brought up of this plant.'

MARJORAM, COMMON

Origanum vulgare
also known as Wild Marjoram or
Oregano; Sweet, or Knotted Marjoram:
Origanum marjorana
CHRONICLES: I A MORBID TASTE FOR BONES;
II ONE CORPSE TOO MANY

❖ "'Are you so eager to get rid of me?" she [Godith Adeney] said, offended. "And just when I'm getting to know sage from marjoram! What would you do without me?'" ONE CORPSE TOO MANY

Marjoram was one of the herbs grown in Cadfael's walled garden.

Ruling Planet: Mercury in Aries

USES

Medicinal: Valued as something of a cure-all, marjoram was prescribed for indigestion, insomnia, earache, loss of appetite, dropsy and many other ailments. The leaves and flowers were made into an aromatic tea to stimulate digestion, relieve flatulence, soothe nerves, cure colds and headaches, and promote menstruation. Dried and powdered, the leaves were used as a snuff to clear nasal congestion. Externally, marjoram was used to relieve pain, stings, bruises and rheumatic swellings. Gerard recommended the leaves boiled in water for 'such as are given to overmuch sighing.'

Culinary: A sweet and savoury pot-herb with a wide range of flavouring uses, marjoram was added to salads, soups, sauces, stuffings, stews and meat dishes. It was also used to flavour beer and other alcoholic drinks.

Miscellaneous: A native of Mediterranean regions, oregano was introduced into Britain by the Romans, who, like the Greeks, considered it to signify peace and happiness. As well as being worn by bridal couples, the herb was used to scent winding sheets, and was planted on graves to ensure that the dead rested in blessed peace. Its botanical name *Origanum* is derived from the Greek for 'joy of the mountain'. Medieval monks grew oregano in their gardens not only for its usefulness, but for its fragrance and decoration. Sweet marjoram was introduced into England during the Middle Ages. Valued as a preserving and disinfecting herb, marjoram was strewn on floors, and included in pot-pourri, cosmetics and perfumes. The scented leaves were used to polish furniture. The plant yields a reddish-purple dye, and is particularly favoured by bees.

MINT

Among the many different sorts of mint, cultivated or wild, are: Spearmint (*Mentha spicata*); Pennyroyal (*Mentha pulegium*); Peppermint (*Mentha piperita*); and Watermint (*Mentha aquatica*)

❖ 'He handed over the bunch of mint stems, their oval leaves still well formed and whole, for they had dried in honest summer heat, and had even a good shade of green left. "She'll need to rub it herself, but it keeps its flavour better so. If she wants more, and you let me know, I'll crumble it fine for her."'
MONK'S-HOOD

Mint, dried in bunches for storage, was grown in Cadfael's herb-garden. It was used in a mixture for coughs and colds, in a cordial to soothe the stomach of a baby with wind, and in a bottle of unspecified lotion. After dizziness or fainting, sniffing a little flask of mint and sorrel vinegar acted as a restorative.

Ruling Planet: Venus

USES

Medicinal: Mint, with its antiseptic, antibacterial, antispasmodic and anti-inflammatory properties, was prescribed for digestive problems, nervous headaches, fevers, colds, flatulence, colic,

and other ailments. Inhaled, it was used as a restorative. Gerard said that mint 'is marvellous wholesome for the stomach', and 'is good against watering eyes, and all manner of breakings out of the head, and against the infirmaries of the fundament [buttocks], it is a sure remedy for children's sore heads.' He also said, quoting Pliny, 'that it will not suffer milk to cruddle in the stomach.' The Romans believed that pennyroyal had the power to drive away fleas.

Culinary: Mint has been used for culinary flavouring since ancient times. Its many uses ranged from garnishing dishes to flavouring drinks, confectionery and sauces.

Miscellaneous: Mint was used by ancient physicians long before the Bible mentioned that the Pharisees collected tithes in mint, dill and cumin. Spearmint was probably introduced into England by the Romans. The mint, or *Mentha* family, is named after Minthe, a nymph in Greek mythology, who was changed into the herb by Persephone, the jealous wife of Hades. Pliny said that instead of 'mintha', the plant 'has begun to be called by a Greek word meaning sweet-scented', adding that it was 'agreeable for stuffing cushions, and at country feasts pervades the tables with its aroma.' It was also used as a strewing herb, an insect-repellant, and in perfumery. Listed by Aelfric, mint was grown in England in monastic gardens from at least the ninth century. Watermint was one of the three most sacred herbs of the Druids, the others being meadowsweet and vervain (*see* pp.196-7).

MISTLETOE

Viscum album

also known as Druid's Herb
(Culpeper: *Viscus quercus*)

CHRONICLES: VII THE SANCTUARY SPARROW

❖ 'Cadfael saw the spreading grey pallor round [Dame] Juliana [Aurifaber]'s mouth as soon as she relaxed her obstinate self-control and lay back against her cushions. He fetched water from the cooling jar, and shook out a dose of the powdered oak mistletoe for her to take.

THE SANCTUARY SPARROW

Powdered oak mistletoe, added to water, wine or milk, was to be drunk after a seizure.

Ruling Planet: Sun

USES

Medicinal: In addition to its own inherent medicinal properties, mistletoe was reputed to possess those of its host plant. Although poisonous, it was prescribed for heart diseases, high blood pressure, rheumatism, gout, nervous disorders, and tumours. Culpeper said that it was so highly esteemed by some that 'they have called it Lignum Sanctae Crucis, wood of the holy cross, believing it helps the falling sickness, apoplexy, and palsy, very speedily, not only to be inwardly taken, but to be hung at their neck.'

Miscellaneous: A native of Europe, mistletoe is an evergreen semi-parasitical plant which grows on a variety of deciduous trees, including apple, hawthorn and willow. Its Latin name *Viscum* means both mistletoe and birdlime (the latter referring to the sticky juice of the white berries which was used as a glue). The tradition of kissing under the mistletoe (and removing a berry with each kiss until none remain) dates back thousands of years to the use of the plant in fertility rituals. The Druids of Britain cut down oak mistletoe with a golden sickle, making sure that it did not fall to the ground, for contact with the earth would have drained its magical powers. Because the mistletoe remained green in winter, while the oak was bare, the Druids believed that it contained the life, or essence, of its sacred host (*see also* Oak). The plant was reputed to be the 'golden bough' of the legend of Aeneas, immortalised in Virgil's epic poem, the *Aeneid*. In Norse mythology Baldur, the god of light, was killed by a twig of mistletoe. The plant was listed by Aelfric.

MONEYWORT

Lysimachia nummularia

also known as Creeping Jenny, Herb
Twopence or String of Sovereigns

CHRONICLES: XI AN EXCELLENT MYSTERY

Found along the banks of the Meole brook and
around nearby meadows and hedgerows,
moneywort – a cleanser and an astringent – was
good for old, ulcerated wounds.

Ruling Planet: Venus

USES

Medicinal: Possessing astringent and antiseptic
properties, moneywort was highly valued by old
herbalists as a wound herb. Internally, it was
prescribed for stomach and intestinal disorders;
and externally, for slow-healing wounds, ulcers,
skin complaints, and rheumatic aches and pains.
Culpeper said 'it is good to stay all fluxes in man or
woman, whether they be laxes, bloody-fluxes, or
the flowing of women's courses; bleeding inward
and outwardly.'

Miscellaneous: A native to Britain, moneywort
grows in moist meadows, along riverbanks, and in
damp woodland clearings and hedgerows. The
rounded leaves of the plant, arranged in pairs
along the stems, explain the references to coins
and money in its various country names. Indeed
nummularia is derived from the Latin for coin-
money. Names like 'creeping Jenny', 'running
Jenny' and 'wandering sailor' refer to the way the
herb creeps rapidly along the ground.

MONK'S-HOOD

Aconitum napellus

also known as Aconite, Wolfsbane or
Blue Rocket

CHRONICLES: III MONK'S-HOOD

❖ '"It is an oil that I make for rubbing aching
joints, and it must have come either from the store
I keep in my workshop, or from some small
quantity taken from it, and I know of but one place
where that could be found, and that is our own
infirmary. The poison is monk's-hood – they call it
so from the shape of the flowers, though it is also
known as wolfsbane. Its roots make an excellent
rub to remove pain, but it is very potent if
swallowed.'"

MONK'S-HOOD

The ground root of monk's-hood, mixed with oils,
was used for rubbing deep into aching joints to
relieve pain. It is extremely poisonous.

Ruling Planet: Saturn

USES

Medicinal: Although extremely poisonous, monk's-hood was used internally and externally as a painkiller and sedative. It was also used to reduce fevers. Pliny said that 'it is in its nature to kill a human being unless in that being it finds something else to destroy.'

Miscellaneous: A native of the mountainous areas of Europe, monk's-hood was known to the Anglo-Saxons, and listed by Aelfric. Pliny said that of 'all poisons the quickest to act was aconite, and that death occurs on the same day if the genitals of a female creature are but touched by it.' Classical fable has it that the plant sprang out of the foam which dropped out of the mouths of the three-headed dog, Cerberus, when Hercules dragged him from the underworld. The plant's botanical name *Aconitum* is derived from the Greek for dart, a reference to the fact that extracts of the roots were once used to poison the tips of arrows. Aconite's resemblance to the cowl of a friar gave it the common name of monk's-hood. The plant was used by witches in their spells, and to give the sensation of flying. Gerard warned against trusting the appearance of a plant that 'beareth very fair and goodly blue flowers in shape like a helmet; which are so beautiful, that a man would think they were of some excellent virtue.'

MULBERRY, COMMON

Morus nigra
also known as Black Mulberry
CHRONICLES: IV SAINT PETER'S FAIR

Mulberry leaves were used in a paste for burns.

Ruling Planet: Mercury

USES

Medicinal: The leaves of the mulberry were prescribed for colds, fevers and headaches, and to staunch bleeding; the bark to kill intestinal worms; and the fruit for mouth ulcers, sore throats and constipation. Culpeper said that 'the juice of the leaves is a remedy against the bites of serpents, and for those that have taken aconite.'

Culinary: The fruit of the mulberry was eaten raw and cooked as a food. During the Middle Ages they were the main ingredient in a sweet and spicy pottage, known as 'murrey', often reinforced with pulped meat. Mulberries were also used to make jams, jellies, syrup, and wine. Unscrupulous innkeepers often sold English grape wine (doctored with mulberries to give it colour and a fuller taste) as Malmsey or French wine.

Miscellaneous: In the silk industry of ancient China the white mulberry (*Morus alba*) was cultivated as silkworm food. The secret of silk production was eventually discovered by the Greeks and Romans, the latter introducing the black mulberry to Britain for its fruit. Its botanical name *Morus* comes from the Latin for to delay, after the tree's habit of postponing the formation of buds in spring until after the cold weather has ended. Even then, as Pliny noted, 'it is one of the latest trees to blossom, but among the first to ripen.' The tree was listed by Aelfric.

MULLEIN, GREAT

Verbascum thapsus

also known as Aaron's Rod,
Hag's Taper or Bullock's Lungwort;
White mullein: *Verbascum lychnitis*;
Black Mullein: *Verbascum nigrum*

CHRONICLES: III MONK'S-HOOD;
XII THE RAVEN IN THE FOREGATE

✤ '"Even if you are desperate to have a fresh brew of cough syrup boiled up before tomorrow," said Brother Mark reasonably, coming out from Compline at Cadfael's side, "is there any reason why I should not do it for you? Is there any need for you, after the day you've had, to be stravaiging around the gardens all night, into the bargain? Or do you think I've forgotten where we keep mullein, and sweet cicely, and rue, and rosemary, and hedge mustard?" The recital of ingredients was part of the argument. This young man was developing a somewhat possessive sense of responsibility for his elder.'

MONK'S-HOOD

Mullein was used in an aromatic syrup for coughs and colds.

Ruling Planet: Saturn

USES

Medicinal: Although potentially poisonous, mullein was prescribed for coughs, respiratory disorders, and all inflammatory ailments. Externally, it was used to treat burns, wounds, ulcers, skin diseases, haemorrhoids, and rheumatic aches and pains. The smoke from the burning leaves was inhaled to relieve asthma. Mullein tea was taken as a sedative and pain-killer. Under the name of 'bullock's lungwort', the herb was used to treat cattle diseases, particularly those affecting the lungs. It is important that infusions or decoctions of mullein are finely strained to get rid of the irritant hairs, or down, which cover the plant.

Culinary: Mullein flowers were used to flavour liqueurs.

Miscellaneous: A native to Britain, mullein was valued by the Greeks and Romans who used it for many purposes, including wrapping figs in the leaves to prevent them from going bad; dipping the long, fibrous stems in wax or tallow, for use as candles; and mixing the infused flowers with lye, to produce a blonde hair dye. Some claim that mullein was the mythical herb *moly*, given to Ulysses by Hermes as a protection against the sorcery of Circe. The name hag's taper refers to the plant's use in the rites, potions and spells of witches. 'Aaron's rod' probably comes from its stiff, staff-like appearance. As a test of fidelity, a lover would bend the stem of a mullein plant in the direction of the partner's house: if the plant died then the latter was unfaithful; but if it resumed its upright position then there was no cause for concern. The plant was listed by Aelfric.

MUSHROOM, FIELD

Agaricus campestris

also known as Garden Mushroom;
Horse Mushroom: *Agaricus arvensis*;
Giant Puffball: *Lycoperdon giganteum*;
Fairy-Ring Champignon: *Maramius oreades*;
Oyster Mushroom: *Pleurotus ostreatus*;
Jew's Ear: *Auricularia auricula-judae*
CHRONICLES: I A MORBID TASTE FOR BONES;
II ONE CORPSE TOO MANY

❖ 'And here there were people moving from time to time about their legitimate business, a shepherd urging his flock towards home pasture, a woman coming home from the woods with mushrooms, two children driving geese.'   ONE CORPSE TOO MANY

Mushrooms were found growing in the woods and meadows beyond the Meole brook.

Ruling Planet: Mercury in Aries

USES

Medicinal: Gerard wrote that 'the fungous excrescence of the elder, commonly called Jew's Ear, is much used against the inflammations and all other soreness of the throat, being boiled in milk, steeped in beer, vinegar, or any other convenient liqueur.' Culpeper said of garden mushrooms: 'Roasted and applied in a poultice, or boiled with white lily roots, and linseed, in milk, they ripen boils and abscesses better than any preparation that can be made.'

Culinary: Edible mushrooms, such as those listed above, were cooked as a vegetable, and included in soups, sauces, pickles, and meat dishes. Some species were threaded on strings and hung up to dry for use over winter.

Miscellaneous: The hallucinogenic properties of certain mushrooms have been used in sacred ceremonies and rituals since ancient times, especially by holy men and warriors preparing for battle. It has been suggested that the juice of the toxic fly agaric (*Amanita muscaria*) was the principal ingredient of ambrosia, the food of the Olympian gods and the means by which they attained immortality. The Hebrews considered mushrooms to be holy and only priests, kings and other privileged people were allowed to eat them. The reference in Judges 15:4 to 'three hundred foxes' has been interpreted by some to mean a battalion of raiders made fearless by taking the fox-coloured juice of the fly agaric. (*see also* Fungus)

Mustard, Hedge

Sisymbrium officinale
also known as Singer's Plant;
Black Mustard: *Brassica nigra* or
Sinapis nigra; White Mustard: *Sinapis alba*,
Brassica alba or *Brassica hirta*;
Wild Mustard: *Sinapis arvensis*
Chronicles: I A Morbid Taste for Bones;
III Monk's-Hood;
V The Leper of Saint Giles;
XII The Raven in the Foregate

✤ 'He added the fruits of mustard, which belongs to Mars, but provides formidable pastes and poultices to fight malignant ulcers.'
The Leper of Saint Giles

The oil extracted from seeds of mustard – grown in Cadfael's herb-garden – was mixed with the ground root of monk's-hood and other plants to produce a rub for aching joints. An emetic mixture of mustard was swallowed to induce vomiting. Hedge mustard was used in a syrup for coughs and colds, and in a rubbing ointment for sore chests and throats.

Ruling Planet: Mars

USES

Medicinal: Mustard seeds were used to stimulate circulation, treat respiratory infections, and remedy stomach complaints. In large doses they acted as a powerful emetic. Added to baths they relieved muscular and rheumatic aches, and alleviated cold and flu symptoms. Used as a poultice, or plaster, they reduced inflammations and eased pain. The seeds were chewed for toothache. Powdered, they were used as a snuff to cure headaches. 'In short,' wrote Culpeper, 'whenever a strong stimulating medicine is wanted to act upon the nerves, and not excite heat, there is none preferable to mustard-seed.' The hedge mustard was known as the 'singer's mustard' because it was used to treat failing voices and improve vocal performance. Over use of mustard should be avoided; it may blister sensitive skins.

Culinary: Young mustard leaves and flowers were added to salads. The ground seeds were mixed with water, vinegar, wine, or verjuice, and used to make a variety of culinary mustards, the strongest being English (a mixture of white and black). As a pungent sauce, mustard was served with a variety of dishes, especially salt meats and fish. In medieval monasteries, mustard seeds were also valued as a food preservative, especially in pickles and chutneys. To produce the traditional 'mustard and cress' *Sinapis alba* was sown indoors in trays a few days after the slower-growing cress (*Lepidium sativum*).

Miscellaneous: A native of Mediterranean lands and much of Europe, mustard was cultivated by the ancient Greeks, Romans and Egyptians. Both black and white mustards were probably introduced into Britain by the Romans. The name derives from the Latin words *mustum* (unfermented grape juice) and *ardens* (burning or fiery), for the condiment was originally made by mixing the hot seeds with 'mustum'. In medieval times one of the main centres of mustard production was in the Vale of Gloucester. Indeed, Shakespeare mentions 'Tewkesbury mustard' in *Henry IV, Part II*. Traditionally, the ground seeds were made into balls for sale in shops and market-places. The plant, listed by Aelfric, was also grown for animal fodder, and as green manure.

NETTLE, COMMON OR STINGING

Urtica dioica
also known as Devil's Plaything;
Roman Nettle: *Urtica pilulifera*
(*see also* Archangel)
CHRONICLES: III MONK'S-HOOD;
XVII THE POTTER'S FIELD

❖ 'Nettle and groundsel had rooted and grown in the crevices of the flooring. It takes a very short time for earth to seal over the traces of humankind.'   THE POTTER'S FIELD

Common nettles were found growing in the crevices of the flooring at Ruald's derelict cottage.

Ruling Planet: Mars

USES

Medicinal: Pliny said 'What can be more hateful than the nettle? Yet this plant simply abounds in remedies.' Indeed, the Romans ate it in the 'devout belief that it will keep diseases away throughout the whole year.' They also believed that nettle stings would cure rheumatism. In medieval England, nettles were prescribed for all manner of ailments including gout, arthritis, anaemia, haemorrhages and skin diseases, such as eczema. Externally, they were used to treat wounds and ulcers, and staunch bleeding. Nettle tea was drunk to stimulate the circulation, and increase the flow of milk in nursing mothers. The plant was also said to prevent hair loss.

Culinary: Young nettle leaves, rich in vitamins and minerals, were cooked as a vegetable, and added to soups and stews. They were also used to produce nettle dumplings, nettle pudding, nettle porridge, nettle beer and nettle wine.

Miscellaneous: Culpeper said that 'nettles are so well known that they need no description; they may be found, by feeling, in the darkest night.' Native to Britain, nettles have been praised and cursed by mankind since prehistoric times. Their botanical name *Urtica* is derived from the Latin for to burn or to smart. Tradition says that the Romans brought the Roman nettle into England so that they could keep themselves warm by rubbing it on their bodies. Although now considered a weed, the nettle was one of the nine sacred herbs of the Anglo-Saxons. In various parts of Europe, it was believed that the plant was a protection against witches, demons, and being struck by lightning. Listed by Aelfric, its name is thought to come from the Old English for needle, referring either to its sting, or to the use of the stems in making fibre or thread. The stems were also woven into a coarse cloth, spun into rope, and used to flagellate the bare backs of medieval monks. The seeds were considered an aphrodisiac. Indeed, an old country method of getting hens to lay was to feed them with nettle seeds. The dye extracted from the leaves is green, and from the roots yellow.

OAK, ENGLISH

Quercus robur

also known as Pedunculate Oak

✤ 'The forest here was chiefly oak, and old, the ground cover light and low, and the deep layers of the leaves of many autumns made riding silent.'

THE HERMIT OF EYTON FOREST

Oak, an ancient tree, grew in woods and forests throughout England and Wales. The wood was used for boards, planks, carved panelling, reliquaries and coffins. It also provided the cleft heartwood for the spokes of wheels. Whatever hard labour Peredur was given as a penance, 'the result was likely to stand solid as oak and last for ever.'

Ruling Planet: Jupiter

USES

Medicinal: A decoction of bark was taken for diarrhoea, varicose veins, haemorrhoids and enteritis, and as a gargle for sore throats. Externally it was used to heal wounds and staunch bleeding. The oak gall (or oak apple) was also prescribed for haemorrhoids, as well as bleeding gums. Culpeper said that 'the water that is found in the hollow places of oaks, is very effectual against any foul or spreading scabs.'

Culinary: Acorns were eaten as food in times of famine. They were roasted and ground to make a substitute coffee.

Miscellaneous: Held sacred by many pre-Christian cultures, including the Greeks, Romans, Norse and Celts, the majestic, long-lived oak was considered the most powerful of all trees and many secret rites were performed under its spreading branches (*see* Mistletoe). Its association with gods of thunder like Zeus, Jupiter and Thor, probably arose from the fact that being a large tree it tended to be struck by lightning more than most. According to some experts, the word 'Druid' comes from an Indo-European root meaning 'men of oak' or 'oak knowledge'. Many early Christian churches were sited near Druidic oaks, despite (or probably because of) their pagan associations. As a symbol of inner as well as outer strength, the oak appears in many old customs and sayings. Even today, coupled with the saying 'great oaks from little acorns grow', it is often cited as the emblem of British strength. During the Middle Ages, oak timber was used to built furniture, houses, windmills, churches and ships, while the bark was extensively used in tanning leather. Pigs were turned out into the woods in autumn to forage on the fallen acorns. The tree was listed by Aelfric. Oak galls (ball-like growths caused by the egg-laying gall wasp), yield a black ink and hair dye.

OATS, CULTIVATED

Avena sativa

also known as Groats;
Wild Oats: *Avena fatua*

CHRONICLES: III MONK'S-HOOD;
IV SAINT PETER'S FAIR;
V THE LEPER OF SAINT GILES;
VI THE VIRGIN IN THE ICE;
VII THE SANCTUARY SPARROW;
VIII THE DEVIL'S NOVICE;
XIII THE ROSE RENT;
XVIII THE SUMMER OF THE DANES

✣ 'They tended his bodily needs, anointed his wounds and grazes, fed him a broth made from their austere stores of meat for the infirmary, with herbs and oatmeal, read the office with him before bed, and still, by the knotting of his brows, Brother Elyas pursued the memories that fled him and would not be snared.'　THE VIRGIN IN THE ICE

Oats were used in a bottle of unspecified lotion. The grain was ground to produce oatmeal, and also fed to horses. Susanna Aurifaber hid her stolen treasure in a big stone crock of oatmeal.

Ruling Planet: Venus

USES

Medicinal: Oats, an easily-digested and nutritious food, were prescribed for insomnia, depression, loss of appetite, nervous exhaustion, thyroid complaints and debility after illness. Externally, they were used to treat lumbago, stitches in the side, sciatica and skin problems. Culpeper said that as a poultice they 'help the itch and leprosy.' The roasted grains were used to make a laxative drink for haemorrhoids and constipation. Sleeping on oat-straw mattresses was reputed to ease rheumatic aches and pains.

Culinary: A staple food in monasteries, oats were made into gruel, oatcakes, oatmeal pastries and porridge.

Miscellaneous: A native of eastern and southern Europe, the wild oat (the ancestor of cultivated oat) was introduced into Britain during the Iron Age. Pliny reported, somewhat fancifully, that one tribe in the interior of Africa 'has the mouth closed up and has no nostrils, but only a single orifice through which they breath and suck in drink by means of oat straws, as well as grains of oat, which grows wild there, for food.' In medieval times a musical flute, known as an 'oaten pipe', was made from an oat-straw.

Onion, Common

Allium cepa

Ever-Useful Onion: *Allium cepa perutile*

CHRONICLES: III MONK'S-HOOD;
VIII THE DEVIL'S NOVICE;
XVII THE POTTER'S FIELD

✤ 'To judge by the aroma that wafted from the tray as it passed, beef boiled with onions, and served with a dish of beans.'   MONK'S-HOOD

A staple food for the monks, cooked or eaten raw, onions were grown in Cadfael's herb-garden, and dried in trays in his store-shed.

Ruling Planet: Mars

USES

Medicinal: The fresh bulb and the juice of the onion were valued for their antibiotic properties, and were eaten regularly to ward off coughs, colds and respiratory infections. They were also used for insomnia, indigestion and lethargy, and to strengthen the heart and restore sexual potency. A freshly sliced onion was prescribed to relieve insects stings, and promote hair growth. Culpeper said that 'onions are good for cold watery humours, but injurious to persons of bilious habit, affecting the head, eyes and stomach.'

Culinary: Like the leek and garlic (also of the *Allium* species), onions were extremely popular throughout the Middle Ages, being particularly valued for their appetising flavour and aroma. Onions were not only eaten raw or cooked as a vegetable, they were also used in salads, soups, stews, sauces and many other dishes. The bulbs were dried or pickled.

Miscellaneous: One of the earliest plants to be cultivated, onions were valued by many ancient civilizations, including the Indians, Chinese, Sumerians, Egyptians, Greeks and Romans. Today there are many varieties of onions, differing not only in colour and size, but also in pungency and smell. Although the origins of onions are obscure, some of their botanical names derive from the places where they were commonly grown: the shallot *Allium ascalonium*, for instance, comes from Ascalon in Palestine, from where it was brought to England by the Crusaders. The name is thought to be derived from the Latin for 'one large pearl'. In medieval times onions were reputed to have the power to ward off snakes and witches, as well as to absorb infection from the plague. Gerard said that they were 'good against the biting of a mad dog.' Those who placed an onion under their pillow were said to dream of their future partner. The skins of onions yield dyes ranging in colour from yellow to golden brown. The plant was listed by Aelfric.

ORCHIS

possibly Early Purple Orchid: *Orchis mascula*
or Spotted Bird's Orchis:
Orchis ornithophora folio maculoso
also known as Fox-Stones
Gerard lists sixteen kinds of Fox-Stones,
including the purple-flowered
Spotted Bird's Orchis
(Culpeper: *Satyrium*)
CHRONICLES: VII THE SANCTUARY SPARROW

❖ 'And something else, a sudden speck of colour. He picked it out and dipped it into the water to wash away the dirt that clouded it, and there it lay glistening in the palm of his hand, a mere scrap, two tiny florets, the tip of a head of flowers of a reddish purple colour, speckled at the tip with a darker purple and a torn remnant of one narrow leaf, just large enough to show a blackish spot on its green.

They had followed him out and gathered curiously to gaze. "Fox-stones, we call this," said Cadfael, "for the two swellings at its root like pebbles. The commonest of its kind, and the earliest, but I don't recall seeing it much here."'

THE SANCTUARY SPARROW

Fox-stones were found growing on the banks of the river Severn at Shrewsbury.

Ruling Planet: Venus

USES

Medicinal: Gerard said of fox-stones: 'There is no great use of these in physic, but they are chiefly regarded for the pleasure and beautiful flowers, wherewith Nature hath seemed to play and disport herself.' Culpeper, however, listed several uses, including killing worms in children, healing the 'king's-evil', strengthening the genital parts and helping conception.

Culinary: Culpeper said that a starchy preparation of orchis roots, known as 'salep', 'contains the greatest quantity of nourishment in the smallest bulk, and will support the system in privation and during famine, it is good for those who travel long distances and are compelled to endure exposure without food.'

Miscellaneous: 'Salep' is the same as the Arabic *sahlep*, a nutritious drink extracted from the tubers of various kinds of orchis. The best English salep, reputed to be an aphrodisiac as well as an energizing tonic, was made in Oxfordshire, with tubers imported from the East. It was sold in shops and markets throughout the country, including London. The name 'fox-stones' comes from the resemblance of the plant's two tubers to dog's, or fox's testicles. Pliny said that 'the larger, or, as some put it, the thinner, taken in water excites desire; the smaller or softer, taken in goat's milk checks it.' The name *Orchis* comes from the Greek for testicles.

Orpine

Sedum telephium

also known as Livelong, Midsummer
Men or *Herbe aux charpentiers*

Chronicles: A Rare Benedictine
(Eye Witness)

❖ 'Brother Ambrose, still voiceless, essayed speech and achieved only a painful wheeze, before Brother Cadfael, who was anointing his patient's throat afresh with goose-grease, and had a soothing syrup of orpine standing by, laid a palm over the sufferer's mouth and ordered silence.'

A Rare Benedictine (Eye Witness)

Orpine was used in a soothing syrup for a raging quinsy.

Ruling Planet: Moon

USES

Medicinal: Having astringent properties, orpine was used to produce salves and ointments for wounds, burns, scalds and haemorrhoids. It was also use to treat diarrhoea and internal ulcers. Made into a syrup with honey, the juice from the leaves was prescribed for sore throats and quinsy. The name *Herbe aux charpentiers* derives from its use in France for healing wounds made by carpenter's tools.

Miscellaneous: Although orpine can be found growing in the wild, it is not thought to be native to Britain. The sap from its fleshy leaves was said to be an aphrodisiac. The name is derived from the Old French for 'pigment of gold', even though the reddish-purple-flowered plant sports neither yellow nor gold. Its botanical name *telephium* comes from Telephus, the mythical son of Hercules, who was reputedly healed of a spear wound by the herb. Livelong refers to the plant's ability to survive, even if uprooted or picked, by drawing on water stored in its leaves. Hung up on the wall of a house on Midsummer's Eve, it was said to ward off both lightning and disease for as long as the leaves remained green. Two orpine plants, grown or placed side by side, one for each lover, were believed to predict whether they would marry: if the stems leaned towards each other the affair would blossom; if they leaned away it would wither and die.

Orris

see Iris

PARSLEY, CURLED

Petroselinum crispum
Culpeper: *Petroselinum sativum*
CHRONICLES: I A MORBID TASTE FOR BONES

Parsley was among the herbs grown in Cadfael's walled garden.

Ruling Planet: Mercury

USES

Medicinal: Parsley was prescribed for menstrual problems, urinary infections, gout, asthma, coughs, jaundice, dropsy and eye complaints. It was also used to stimulate appetite, and to encourage milk flow in nursing mothers. Chewed raw, the leaves were used as a breath-freshener, especially after eating garlic. As a poultice, they were applied to cuts, sprains, insect bites and swellings. Culpeper said that 'the distilled water is a familiar medicine with nurses to give children when troubled with wind in the stomach or belly . . . it is also greatly useful to grown persons.' The herb should not be taken during pregnancy

Culinary: Parsley leaves, freshly picked or dried, were added to sauces, salads, soups, pickles, pottages, and many other dishes. They were also used as a garnish. The roots were also grated raw, or boiled as a vegetable,

Miscellaneous: Possibly native to south-east Europe and the eastern Mediterranean, parsley was held sacred by the ancient Greeks and included in the wreathes used to crown victors of the Isthmian Games. Both the Greeks and the Romans used the herb in funeral rites and to decorate their graves. Indeed, it was commonly said of the dead: 'He has need now of nothing but a little parsley'. The herb was also associated with the devil, who was reputed to take a large proportion of the sown seeds, thereby accounting for their slow and erratic germination. Indeed, country folk claimed that only the wicked could grow parsley; and those that gave it away, or transplanted it, could expect misfortune. It was also said that when parsley grew well in a garden, it was the woman of the house who was the dominant partner. The herb's botanical name *Petroselinum* is derived from the Greek for rock-celery. It was listed by Aelfric. The stems yield a green dye.

PAYNIM POPPY

see Poppy, Opium

PEA

Pisum sativum

(also spelled Pease)

CHRONICLES: II ONE CORPSE TOO MANY;
III MONK'S-HOOD; V THE LEPER OF
SAINT GILES; VII THE SANCTUARY SPARROW;
X THE PILGRIM OF HATE;
XI AN EXCELLENT MYSTERY;
XII THE RAVEN IN THE FOREGATE;
XIII THE ROSE RENT;
XIV THE HERMIT OF EYTON FOREST;
XVI THE HERETIC'S APPRENTICE

❖ 'The earlier sown of the two pease fields that sloped down from the rim of the garden to the Meole Brook had already ripened and been harvested, ten days of sun bringing on the pods very quickly. Brother Winfrid, a hefty, blue-eyed young giant, was busy digging in the roots to feed the soil, while the haulms, cropped with sickles, lay piled at the edge of the field, drying for fodder and bedding.'   THE HERETIC'S APPRENTICE

Peas were grown in the abbey fields running down to the Meole brook and along the Gaye at Shrewsbury.

Ruling Planet: Jupiter in Aries

USES

Medicinal: The medicinal virtues of peas are similar to those of beans (*see* Bean). Gerard noted that they were 'not so windy as be the beans' and 'that they have not a cleansing faculty, and therefore they do more slowly descend through the belly.' Culpeper said they 'are good to sweeten the blood, and correct salt scorbutic illness.' Tradition said that drinking water in which peas had been boiled would cure measles.

Culinary: A staple food in medieval England, peas were used for soups, pottages, porreys and many other dishes. Dried they could be stored for over winter use. They were also used to fatten domestic pigs and pigeons.

Miscellaneous: Although the origins of the pea are uncertain, it is known that they were cultivated in England by at least Roman times. In folklore they were said to bring good fortune, especially if just one pea was found inside a pod. A pod with nine peas inside was used to cure warts, or to determine one's future marriage partner.

PEAR, COMMON

Pyrus communis

Wild Pear: *Pyrus pyraster*

(Culpeper: *Pyrus sativa*)

CHRONICLES: I A MORBID TASTE FOR BONES;
II ONE CORPSE TOO MANY;
III MONK'S-HOOD;
VII THE SANCTUARY SPARROW;
XIII THE ROSE RENT;
XIV THE HERMIT OF EYTON FOREST;
XVII THE POTTER'S FIELD

❖ 'Brother Oswin came into the porch to meet him, as large, cheerful and exuberant as ever, the wiry curls of his tonsure bristling from the low branches of the orchard trees, and a basket of the late, hard little pears on his arm, the kind that would keep until Christmas.'　　THE POTTER'S FIELD

Pear trees, sometimes plagued by the winter moths, were grown in the Gaye orchards at Shrewsbury. Cadfael made a wine from the fruit. Edwin Gurney fashioned a small reliquary out of pear-wood.

Ruling Planet: Venus

USES

Medicinal: Gerard said that the medicinal use of pears varied 'according to the differences of their tastes: for some pears are sweet, divers fat and unctuous, others sour, and most are harsh, especially the wild pears.' All, however, were taken to 'bind and stop the belly.' Culpeper said that wild pears, applied externally, were most effective for healing green [fresh] wounds and reducing inflammations.

Culinary: Most medieval pears were hard cooking pears. Depending on the variety, the fruit were either eaten raw, or cooked. They were also made into preserves, jams, puddings and sometimes comfits. Perry, a cider-like drink made from the fruit, may have been introduced into England by the Normans.

Miscellaneous: Originally from western Asia, the pear has been cultivated in Europe for thousands of years. Charcoal from the tree has even been discovered in Neolithic sites. The wild species (used as a root stock for grafting cultivated varieties) may not be native to Britain. According to some experts, it was an escapee from gardens and orchards. The pear appears in Anglo-Saxon charters, and was listed by Aelfric. To dream of a pear was considered a good omen. The hard, fine-grained wood was used for musical instruments, carving, turning and wood-engraving.

Peony, Common

Paeonia officinalis

also known as Roman Peony; Male Peony:
Paeonia mascula (Culpeper: *Paeonia*)

Chronicles: I A Morbid Taste for Bones;
X The Pilgrim of Hate;
XVII The Potter's Field

❖ 'In the walled shelter of Cadfael's herb-garden there were fat globes of peonies, too, just cracking their green sheaths. Cadfael had medicinal uses for the seeds, and Brother Petrus, the abbot's cook, used them as spices in the kitchen.'

The Pilgrim of Hate

Ruling Planet:
Sun in Leo

Uses

Medicinal: Peony roots were used for insomnia, kidney and bladder complaints, nervous diseases, epilepsy and madness. Pliny recommended red seeds to 'check menstrual discharge', and black for 'healing the uterus'. He also suggested that fifteen black grains taken in wine would prevent 'the mocking delusions that Fauns bring on us in our sleep.' The plant can be poisonous.

Culinary: In the Middle Ages peony seeds were used as a spice, and a substitute for hot pepper.

Miscellaneous: Said to be the oldest of all cultivated flowers, the peony was named after Paeon, physician to the Greek gods, and was considered a plant of the Moon. Pliny, who classified some peonies as male and others female, said that it should only be uprooted at night, 'because the woodpecker of Mars, should he see the act, will attack the eyes in its defence.' A string of beads, carved from dried peony roots, were once worn as a protective charm against evil. Peonies were grown in medieval monastic gardens as a herb, as well as for their beauty. Although the common peony, a native of southern Europe, was listed by Aelfric, it is not known how or when it was introduced into England. The *Paeonia mascula*, however, appears to have been brought across the Channel by the Augustinians, who established a priory on Steep Holm island, in the Bristol Channel, in the late twelfth or early thirteenth century. It was the only place in Britain where the plant grew (and still grows) in the wild. The dried petals were added to pot-pourri.

PERIWINKLE, GREATER

Vinca major

also known as Sorcerer's Violet or
Flower of Death;
Lesser Periwinkle: *Vinca minor*

CHRONICLES: VII THE SANCTUARY SPARROW;
IX DEAD MAN'S RANSOM;
XI AN EXCELLENT MYSTERY;
XV THE CONFESSION OF BROTHER HALUIN;
XVI THE HERETIC'S APPRENTICE

❖ '[Liliwin's eyes] were hollow and evasive, and one of them half-closed and swelling, but in the light of the candles they flared darkly and brilliantly blue as periwinkle flowers.'

THE SANCTUARY SPARROW

A trailing plant, periwinkle was often represented in illuminated designs and engravings.

Ruling Planet: Venus

USES

Medicinal: Periwinkle was used to check internal bleeding, heal sores, wounds and ulcers, soothe inflammations, relieve cramps, and reduce blood pressure and nervous tension. Culpeper said 'it is a great binder, and stays bleeding at the mouth and nose, if it be chewed.' It was also taken for diabetes and constipation. The plant can be poisonous.

Miscellaneous: The periwinkle was known in Britain by at least Anglo-Saxon times, and was listed by Aelfric. As a symbol of immortality, it was traditionally linked with death, and sometimes worn by those about to be executed. Culpeper said 'that the leaves eaten by man and wife together, cause love between them.'

PINE, SCOTS

Pinus sylvestris

CHRONICLES: VI THE VIRGIN IN THE ICE

❖ 'The porter had set fresh pine torches in the shelter of the arched gateway to provide a beacon glow homeward, for fear some of the searchers should themselves go astray and be lost.'

THE VIRGIN IN THE ICE

A resinous wood, pine was used for making torches.

Ruling Planet: Mars

USES

Medicinal: Pine resin was used in ointments and plasters for wounds, skin irritations and muscular aches and pains. Other pine extracts were prescribed for urinary disorders, respiratory infections and gall bladder problems. Inhaling steam from the boiling shoots was said to relieve colds and bronchitis. Oil added to bath-water was supposed to relieve aches and pains.

Culinary: The ground inner bark of Scot's pine was used to make bread, or mixed with oats to make griddle cakes. The cones were used to flavour beer and wine.

Miscellaneous: A native of Britain, the Scots pine appeared on the ravaged surface of the land not long after the glaciers retreated at the end of the last Ice Age. It was listed by Aelfric. The wood, soft yet strong, was used for construction purposes, joinery, waterwheels and ships' masts. It was also a valuable source of turpentine, resin and tar. Pine oil was used in soaps and perfumery. The cones yield a reddish-yellow dye.

PLUM

Prunus domestica

CHRONICLES: II ONE CORPSE TOO MANY;
V THE LEPER OF SAINT GILES;
XI AN EXCELLENT MYSTERY; XIII THE ROSE RENT;
XVI THE HERETIC'S APPRENTICE

❖ 'They gathered the purple-black Lammas plums next day, for they were just on the right edge of ripeness. Some would be eaten at once, fresh as they were, some Brother Petrus would boil down into a preserve thick and dark as cakes of poppy-seed, and some would be laid out on racks in the drying house to wrinkle and crystallize into gummy sweetness. Cadfael had a few trees in a small orchard within the enclave, though most of the fruit-trees were in the main garden of the Gaye, the lush meadow-land along the riverside. The novices and younger brothers picked the fruit, and the oblates and schoolboys were allowed to help; and if everyone knew that a few handfuls went into the breasts of tunics rather than into the baskets, provided the deprecations were reasonable Cadfael turned a blind eye.'

AN EXCELLENT MYSTERY

Ruling Planet: Venus

USES

Medicinal: Dried plums (prunes) were prescribed for constipation, to stimulate digestion and to strengthen the stomach. Culpeper said that 'the gum of the tree is good to break the stone. The gum or leaves boiled in vinegar, and applied, kills tetters [skin disease] and ringworms.'

Culinary: Plums were eaten raw, cooked, pulped into a 'murrey', or made into jams and preserves. Prunes were used in stews, stuffings, sauces, desserts and cakes. They were also preserved in brandy or vinegar.

Miscellaneous: The plum, a native of Mediterranean lands, was introduced into England by the Romans. Pliny listed 'a vast crowd of plums'. He also said that they were grafted on to other fruit stock, thereby producing 'nut-plums', 'apple-plums' and 'almond-plums'. Listed by Aelfric, plums were plentiful in the wild, and, therefore, seldom grown in gardens. (*see* Damson)

POND-WEED
see Water-Weed

POPPY, FIELD

Papaver rhoeas

also known as Corn Rose

CHRONICLES: XIII THE ROSE RENT;
XVII THE POTTER'S FIELD

Poppies were found growing wild amongst the unreaped grass in the Potter's Field.

Ruling Planet: Moon

USES

Medicinal: A syrup made from poppy seeds and flowers was taken for coughs, throat infections, chest complaints, insomnia and whooping-cough. Externally, the plant was used to cool inflammations, ease pains and relieve migraines.

Culinary: Ripe poppy seeds were sprinkled on bread and cakes. Oil from the seeds was also used in cooking. The flowers were used to colour wines.

Miscellaneous: Among the seeds of various species of poppy discovered in an Egyptian tomb dating from 2,500 BC, were those of the field poppy. From ancient times until well into the twentieth century the flowers were commonly found in cornfields. Indeed, the poppy was sacred to Ceres, the Roman goddess of corn, who was often depicted wearing a wreath of the flowers. In addition to being a symbol of remembrance (the colour of its flowers representing the blood of dead warriors), the poppy has long been associated with fertility. Magical potions containing poppies were reputed to be an antidote for those bewitched into love. The plant was listed by Aelfric,

POPPY, OPIUM

Papaver somniferum

also known as Paynim Poppy or
Oriental Poppy

CHRONICLES: I A MORBID TASTE FOR BONES;
IV SAINT PETER'S FAIR;
V THE LEPER OF SAINT GILES;
IX DEAD MAN'S RANSOM;
X THE PILGRIM OF HATE;
XI AN EXCELLENT MYSTERY;
XII THE RAVEN IN THE FOREGATE;
XV THE CONFESSION OF BROTHER HALUIN;
XVII THE POTTER'S FIELD; A RARE
BENEDICTINE (THE PRICE OF LIGHT)

✤ 'But behind their shrinking ranks rose others taller and more clamorous, banks of peonies grown for their spiced seeds, and lofty, pale-leaved, budding poppies, as yet barely showing the white or purple-black petals through their close armour. They stood as tall as a short man, and their home was the eastern part of the middle sea, and from that far place Cadfael had brought their ancestors in the seed long ago, and raised and cross-bred them in his own garden, before ever he brought the perfected progeny here with him to make medicines against pain, the chief enemy of man. Pain, and the absence of sleep, which is the most beneficent remedy for pain.' A MORBID TASTE FOR BONES

The 'poppies of Lethe' were originally brought as seed from the east, cross-bred and perfected, before Cadfael grew them in his herb garden. Poppy-juice was used in a mixture for coughs and colds, and to make a sweet syrup to dull pain and induce deep sleep. The seeds were harvested from the heads for the following year's crop, and were also used in cakes.

Ruling Planet: Moon

USES

Medicinal: Opium (the milky juice extracted from unripe poppy heads) was used to make various drugs, including morphine, codeine and heroin. Since ancient times it has been taken to kill pain and induce sleep. Culpeper said that 'it relaxes the nerves, abates cramps, and spasmodic complaints; but it increases paralytic disorders, and such as proceed from weakness of the nervous system.' Gerard warned that 'it mitigateth all kinds of pains: but it leaveth behind it oftentimes a mischief worse than the disease itself.'

Culinary: Fully ripe poppy seeds (which do not contain opium) were used to make poppy-seed cakes, and fillings for pastries. They were also used in bread and confectionery.

Miscellaneous: The narcotic properties of opium were known to many ancient civilizations, including the Sumerians, the Egyptians, the Greeks and the Romans. Because of the effect the juice can have on the mind, the plants were known as the 'poppies of Lethe'. Lethe, in Greek mythology, is the river of forgetfulness, for once its waters have been tasted by the souls of the dead they cease to remember their past life. Pliny mentioned various ways of testing whether opium was pure or unadulterated, the chief test being the smell, 'that of pure opium being unbearable.' Another 'especially wonderful' way was by using the summer sun: 'for pure opium sweats and melts until it becomes like freshly gathered juice.' The poppy was listed by Aelfric.

Primrose

Primula vulgaris

also known as Early Rose or
First Rose

Chronicles: I A Morbid Taste for Bones;
V The Leper of Saint Giles;
VI The Virgin in the Ice;
IX Dead Man's Ransom;
XI An Excellent Mystery;
XVII The Potter's Field;
XVIII The Summer of the Danes;
XIX The Holy Thief;
XX Brother Cadfael's Penance

❖ 'March had come in more lamb than lion, there were windflowers in the woods, and the first primroses, unburned by frost, undashed and unmired by further rain, were just opening.'

THE HOLY THIEF

Ruling Planet: Venus

USES

Medicinal: Primroses were prescribed for bronchitis, insomnia, inflammations, nervous tension, rheumatism, gout and to purify the blood. As an infusion the herb relieved coughs and sore throats, and acted as a mild sedative, and antispasmodic. Externally it soothed minor wounds and eased paints in the joints. The leaves, rubbed on the skin, were reputed to get rid of blemishes. Gerard said that 'the roots of primrose stamped and strained, and the juice sniffed into the nose with a quill or such like, purgeth the brain, and qualifieth the pain of the migraine.'

Culinary: The flowers and young leaves of primroses were added to salads, while the leaves were boiled as a vegetable. Desserts, like primrose pottage, were made from the flowers, which were also crystallized, or made into jams and wine.

Miscellaneous: A native of Britain and Europe, the primrose – being early flowering – was long considered a herald of spring. Indeed, the name is derived from the Latin for first rose. In folklore it was said that by eating the flowers children could see fairies. Primroses were also included in love potions, and in charms to protect against evil. As most flowers had five petals, those with six were believed to be lucky, especially in matters relating to love and marriage. Although it was lucky to bring thirteen primroses into the house, a single flower would bring misfortune. The powdered roots were added to pot-pourri, while the flowers were used in cosmetics.

PULSE

Lens esculenta
also known as Lentils
(Culpeper: *Ervum lens*)
CHRONICLES: III MONK'S-HOOD

P

❖ 'The conventual fare of pulse, beans, fish, and occasional and meagre meat, benefited by sudden gifts of flesh and fowl to provide treats for the monks of St Peter's. Honey-baked cakes appeared, and dried fruits, and chickens, and even, sometimes, a haunch of venison, all devoted to the pittances that turned a devotional sacrament into a rare indulgence, a holy day into a holiday.'
MONK'S-HOOD

Pulse, a staple food of the monks at Shrewsbury Abbey, was grown in the fields running down to the Meole brook.

Ruling Planet: Venus

USES

Medicinal: Lentils checked loose bowels, healed ulcers and soothed abscesses. Culpeper noted that 'eaten with their skins they bind the body, and stop looseness, but the liquid they are boiled in loosens the belly.'

Culinary: One of the staple foods of medieval England, lentils were added, fresh or dried, to soups, stews, pottages and many other dishes.

Miscellaneous: Although pulse was a common term for lentils, the name also embraced peas, beans and other leguminous plants (see Bean and Pea). Pliny said that the ship which brought an obelisk from Egypt to Rome for the Emperor Gaius (Caligula), 'carried 120 bushels of lentils for ballast.' He also said that 'a lentil diet leads to an equable temper.'

RADISH, GARDEN

Raphanus sativus

Wild Radish: *Raphanus raphanistrum*

CHRONICLES: XIII THE ROSE RENT

❖ 'The first radishes will be fibrous and shrunken as old leather.'

THE ROSE RENT

Cadfael grew radishes in his walled garden.

Ruling Planet: Mars

USES

Medicinal: Radishes were used to treat coughs, bronchitis, asthma, rheumatism, gout, respiratory complaints and digestive disorders. Culpeper said that 'it provokes urine and is good for the stone and gravel.'

Culinary: The hot, pungent roots of radish were eaten raw or put in pottages, sauces and stews. The leaves were added to porrays, and the young seed pods included in salads.

Miscellaneous: Several varieties of radish were grown by the ancient Egyptian, Greeks and Romans. Pliny recommended oil of radish to 'smooth roughness of the skin on the face.' The plant was used by the Anglo-Saxons, and listed by Aelfric. Because they were plentiful in the wild and had similar properties, radishes were seldom cultivated in medieval gardens in England.

RAGWORT

Senecio jacobaea

also known as St James Wort, Ragweed, Stinking Nanny, Staggerwort or Cankerwort;

Oxford Ragwort: *Senecia squalidus*

CHRONICLES: XI AN EXCELLENT MYSTERY

A cleanser and astringent, good for old, ulcerated wounds, ragwort was found along the banks of the Meole brook and in hedgerows and meadows nearby.

Ruling Planet: Venus

USES

Medicinal: The astringent juice of ragwort was used for wounds, ulcers, sores, burns and inflammations. Its country name 'cankerwort' refers to its use in the treatment of cancerous ulcers. As a poultice the herb was used for aching joints, swellings, rheumatic pains, sciatica and gout.

Miscellaneous: Ragwort's botanical name *jacobaea* is derived from St James the Greater, whose feast day, the 25 July, is said to be time when the herb starts flowering. 'Ragwort' comes from the ragged appearance of the foliage. When bruised, the leaves give off an unpleasant odour, hence the names 'stinking Nanny' and 'stinking Billy'. Staggerwort arose from the mistaken belief that the plant had the power to cure horses of staggers, a disease of the brain and spinal cord. The plant can be harmful to cattle, even if included amongst the dried hay crop. The Oxford ragwort, an introduced species, escaped into the wild from the city's Botanical Garden in the nineteenth century.

REED, COMMON

Phragmites communis or
Phragmites australis

CHRONICLES: XI AN EXCELLENT MYSTERY;
XII THE RAVEN IN THE FOREGATE; XIII THE ROSE RENT;
XVI THE HERETIC'S APPRENTICE;
XVII THE POTTER'S FIELD

❖ 'Rimy grass overhung the high bank, undercut here by the strength of the tail-race . . . The frost had done no more than form a thin frill of ice in the shallows, where the reed beds thickened and helped to hold it.' THE RAVEN IN THE FOREGATE

Reed-beds were found in the shallows around the abbey mill pond and along the banks of the river Severn. Reeds were used as building material for huts.

USES

Medicinal: Despite Gerard's assertion that 'as for their natures and virtues we do not find any great use of them worth setting down,' the roots and rhizomes of reeds were used to treat fevers, coughs, phlegm, lung complaints, urinary problems, nausea and arthritis.

Culinary: The roots, shoots and seeds of the common reed were eaten in times of famine. The stems yield a sweet, edible sap.

Miscellaneous: Reeds grow in sediment at the edges of rivers, lakes, and brackish waters throughout Britain. Although their long creeping roots help combat erosion on riverbanks, they also choke waterways and, once established in thick carpets, or beds, are hard to get rid of. The botanical name *Phragmites* is derived from the Greek for screen or fence. The long, sturdy stems (and leaf blades) were harvested and used for thatching, especially in East Anglia. They were also used for matting, pipes and fuel. The plant was listed by Aelfric.

ROSE

Rosa

Apothecary's Rose or Red Rose of
Lancaster: *Rosa gallica officinalis*;
White Rose: *Rosa alba semi-plena*;
Damask Rose: *Rosa damascena*

CHRONICLES: I A MORBID TASTE FOR BONES;
II ONE CORPSE TOO MANY;
IV SAINT PETER'S FAIR; V THE LEPER OF
SAINT GILES; VIII THE DEVIL'S NOVICE;
X THE PILGRIM OF HATE;
XI AN EXCELLENT MYSTERY;
XII THE RAVEN IN THE FOREGATE;
XIII THE ROSE RENT;
XIV THE HERMIT OF EYTON FOREST;
XVI THE HERETIC'S APPRENTICE;
XIX THE HOLY THIEF;
XX BROTHER CADFAEL'S PENANCE

❖ 'The roses were coming into full bloom, and their scent hung in the warm air like a benediction.'　　　THE PILGRIM OF HATE

Roses, used as a fragrant ingredient in perfumed oils for altar lamps, were grown in the abbot's own garden at Shrewsbury, as well as in the cloister garth, Cadfael's walled garden and the rose garden. White scented roses grew on the bush in Judith Perle's old garden in the Abbey Foregate. Climbing roses were often represented in illuminated designs.

Ruling Planet: Moon (White Rose); Jupiter (Red Rose); Venus (Damask Rose)

USES

Medicinal: Rose petals were used to treat diarrhoea, bronchial infections, coughs and colds, chest complaints, nervous tension and lethargy. The distilled water was prescribed for eye inflammations, to refresh the spirits and to strengthen the heart. Rose oil was applied to chapped skins. Gerard said that roses 'staunch bleedings in any part of the body.'

Culinary: Rose petals, in addition to being added to salads, were crystallized and made into syrup, jams, preserves, and vinegars. Rose water was used to flavour confectionery, jellies, sauces, and sweet and savoury dishes.

Miscellaneous: Roses have been cultivated for their fragrant beauty and medicinal properties for thousands of years. The oldest cultivated rose is thought to be the red *Rosa gallica*, the ancestor of all medieval roses in Europe. Possibly introduced into Britain by the Romans, it was known to the Anglo-Saxons and listed by Aelfric. During the Middle Ages the noble house of York adopted the white rose as its emblem and the house of Lancaster the red: the fifteenth-century conflict between them being the Wars of the Roses. In addition to being the emblem of England, the rose is a symbol of love, and of secrecy (things spoken of under a rose carved on the ceiling of dining-rooms were *sub rosa*, 'under the rose', and in strict confidence). The damask rose, one of the most fragrant of roses, was introduced into medieval England from Persia by returning Crusaders. Its petals produced the oil, attar of roses, used for flavouring and perfumes. Rose petals were also used in soaps, cosmetics and pot-pourri (*see also* Briar and Eglantine).

ROSE, DOG, OR WILD
see Briar

ROSEMARY

Rosmarinus officinalis

CHRONICLES: I A MORBID TASTE FOR BONES;
II ONE CORPSE TOO MANY;
III MONK'S-HOOD; V THE LEPER OF
SAINT GILES; A RARE BENEDICTINE
(THE PRICE OF LIGHT)

❖ 'Rosemary and lavender, mint and thyme, all manner of herbs filled the walled garden with aromatic odours, grown a little rank now with autumn, ready to sink into their winter sleep very soon. The best of their summer was already harvested.'   THE LEPER OF SAINT GILES

Grown in Cadfael's herb-garden, rosemary was used in a cough syrup, and in a medicinal preparation for rheum in the eyes or head. The needles were dried and stored.

Ruling Planet: Sun

USES

Medicinal: Rosemary was prescribed to relieve pain, nervous tension, headaches and flatulence, and to promote liver function, improve blood circulation, and increase the flow of bile. Externally, it was used for rheumatism, ulcers, eczema, sores and wounds, and also as a hair tonic and antiseptic. Rosemary tea was recommended for digestive complaints. The virtues of the herb were considered so marvellous that even a garland worn around the neck was reputed to cure stuffy heads. Gerard said that the herb 'comforteth the cold, weak and feeble brain in a most wonderful manner.' *Banckes's Herbal* even suggested: 'Make thee a box of the wood of rosemary and smell to it and it shall preserve thy youth.' In extremely large doses the herb is poisonous.

Culinary: A strong aromatic herb, rosemary was valued for flavouring many dishes, including soups, stews, fish, meats, eggs and vegetables. The flowers and leaves were added to salads, and the sprigs used in stuffings. The herb was also used in jams, jellies, biscuits, cordials, vinegars and wines.

Miscellaneous: A native of the Mediterranean region, rosemary was worn by the ancient Greeks to improve memory, especially by students studying for examinations. Introduced into Britain by the Romans and known to the Anglo-Saxons, the herb, it seems, was then lost and reintroduced in the fourteenth century. Its botanical name *Rosmarinus* is derived from the old Latin for 'dew of the sea', a reference to its pale blue dew-like flowers and its habit of growing near the coast. Long considered a symbol of remembrance and friendship, rosemary was carried by wedding couples as a sign of love and fidelity. Placed under a pillow at night, it was reputed to ward off evil spirits and bad dreams. Tradition says that the plant will grow for thirty-three years, until it reaches the same height as Christ when he was crucified, then die. It was strewn on floors to mask bad smells, and put in wardrobes to discourage insects and moths. The wood was used to make lutes and similar musical instruments. It was also burnt instead of incense. The essential oil was included in perfumes, cosmetics, disinfectants and herbal shampoos.

Rue, Garden

Ruta graveolens
also known as Herb of Grace or Herbygrass
Chronicles: I A Morbid Taste for Bones;
III Monk's-Hood;
XII The Raven in the Foregate

'Cadfael had returned to the church after Prime to replenish the perfumed oil in the lamp on Saint Winifred's altar. The inquisitive skills which might have been frowned upon if they had been employed to make scents for women's vanity became permissible and even praiseworthy when used as an act of worship, and he took pleasure in trying out all manner of fragrant herbs and flowers in many different combinations, plying the sweets of rose and lily, violet and clover against the searching aromatic riches of rue and sage and wormwood.'

The Raven in the Foregate

Grown in Cadfael's herb-garden, rue was used in a cough syrup, and in perfumed oils for altar lamps.

Ruling Planet: Sun in Leo

USES

Medicinal: Rue was used to treat headaches, strained eyes, colic, indigestion, flatulence, heart palpitations and menstrual problems. Rue tea expelled intestinal worms. Externally, the herb was applied to sprains, bruises, rheumatic pains, gout, chilblains and skin diseases. Pliny said it was one the Roman's chief medicinal plants, and 'an antidote for all poisons'. He also said that it was eaten, with bread and cress, by engravers and painters to improve their vision. In large doses the herb is poisonous. Even handling the leaves can cause blisters. It should not be taken during pregnancy.

Culinary: Rue, a strong aromatic herb, was used to give a bitter flavour to foods and alcoholic drinks, especially grappa. It was also added to salads.

Miscellaneous: A native of southern Europe and the Mediterranean, rue was introduced into England by the Romans, who not only believed that it improved eyesight, but that it had the power to bestow second sight on those who consumed it regularly. Indeed, it was for these vision-enhancing powers that Leonardo da Vinci and Michelangelo claimed to have taken the herb. The name is derived from the Greek for to set free, a reference to its efficacy as an antidote, or release from poisons. As a symbol of sorrow and repentance, rue was known as 'herb of grace' (for to Christians true repentance leads to God-given grace). Brushes of rue were used to sprinkle holy water in exorcisms and before a Mass. For Moslems the plant has a special significance, in that it is the only herb said to have been blessed by Muhammad. The phrase 'rue the day' comes from the custom of throwing a bunch of rue in the face of one's enemy, while cursing them. The herb was also worn for luck, and as a protection against witchcraft, the 'evil eye' and the plague. In medieval times, rue was placed near magistrates to protect them against gaol fever brought into court by prisoners. It was also hung inside houses to repel insects. Listed by Aelfric, the plant was used in perfumes and cosmetics.

Rush, Common

Juncus conglomeratus
Soft Rush: *Juncus effusus* ;
Common Bulrush: *Scirpus lacustris*

Chronicles: II One Corpse Too Many;
III Monk's-Hood; IX Dead Man's Ransom; XII
The Raven in the Foregate;
XIII The Rose Rent;
XIV The Hermit of Eyton Forest;
XV The Confession of Brother Haluin; XVIII
The Summer of the Danes

✣ 'There was a small rush-light burning somewhere within the house, a tiny broken beam showed through the pales.' One Corpse Too Many

Rushes were used for rush lights or rush candles, for bedding and for covering floors. The stems were woven into baskets.

Ruling Planet: Saturn

USES

Medicinal: Pliny noted that 'some foreign people' inhale the smoke of rushes to ensure, 'even from day to day, increased briskness and greater strength.' Culpeper said that the seed of the soft rush, 'if drunk in wine and water, stays laxes and women's courses, when they come down abundantly.' It was also recommended for coughs. Gerard, however, warned that the 'seed of the bulrush is most soporiferous, and therefore the greater care must be had in the administration thereof, lest in provoking sleep you induce a drowsiness or dead sleep.'

Miscellaneous: Rushes have been used since ancient times for matting, baskets and wicker-work. Indeed, the name is derived from the German for to bind or to plait. Strewn on the stone floors of churches, castles and houses, rushes not only helped soften the tread, but freshened the air and provided protection against the cold. 'Rush-bearing Sunday' referred to the ceremony of renewing the rushes on a church floor, which was usually carried out on the Sunday nearest the festival of its special saint. The pith inside the stems was made into wicks for candles and lamps. Dipped into animal fat, rushes were an economical source of domestic lighting. In medieval times the plants were made into crosses and hung over doorways as a protection against evil. Rushes were listed by Aelfric.

SAFFRON

Crocus sativus

also known as Saffron Crocus;
Meadow Saffron: *Colchicum autumnale*;
False Saffron: *Carthamus tinctorius*

CHRONICLES: X THE PILGRIM OF HATE

❖ 'Above him, in the deep, soft summer night that now bore only a saffron thread along the west, an answering hail shrilled, startled and merry, and there were confused sounds of brief, breathless struggle.'
THE PILGRIM OF HATE

Ruling Planet: Sun in Leo (Meadow Saffron: Saturn)

USES

Medicinal: Saffron was used to reduce fevers, increase perspiration, relieve cramps, calm nerves, lift depression, aid digestion, remedy menstrual disorders and, because of its colour, cure yellow jaundice. Externally, it was used for bruises, rheumatism and neuralgia. English saffron was reputed to make people happy: 'Some', according to Culpeper, 'have fallen into an immoderate convulsive laughter, which ended in death.' Turner said that 'if any person use saffron measurably it maketh in them a good colour, but if they use it out of measure it maketh him look pale, and maketh the head ache and hurteth the appetite.' Large doses of saffron can be dangerous. Meadow saffron belongs to an entirely different plant family and, although used medicinally, is extremely poisonous.

Culinary: Saffron flower stigmas were used to colour and flavour a wide variety of dishes, as well as cakes, bread, confectionery and liqueurs.

Miscellaneous: A native of the Middle East, saffron was held in high esteem by many ancient civilizations, so much so that it was almost worth its own weight in gold. It is estimated that it took over 4,000 flowers to produce one ounce of the spice. As it was so expensive 'false saffron' proved to be a useful substitute. Pliny, who included aphrodisiac properties among the plant's many virtues, said that 'nothing is adulterated as much as saffron.' In Europe severe penalties, such as being buried alive, were administered to those who sold the adulterated product. The name is an Anglicized form of the Arabic word for yellow. Tradition says that it was introduced into medieval England from the Holy Land, either by the Knights of St John or by a pilgrim, who, at the risk of being punished by death if caught, stole a bulb from the Arabs and hid it in the head of his staff. The plant was grown commercially in England from at least the fourteenth century, especially in the area around the Essex town of Walden (now called Saffron Walden). The thread-like stigmas yield a yellow dye. Saffron was also used in cosmetics and perfumes.

SAGE, COMMON

Salvia officinalis

also known as Garden Sage or
Sawge; Purple Sage: *Salvia officinalis*
'purpurascens'

CHRONICLES: I A MORBID TASTE FOR BONES;
II ONE CORPSE TOO MANY;
III MONK'S-HOOD; X THE PILGRIM OF HATE; XII
THE RAVEN IN THE FOREGATE

S

❖ "'She [Richildis Bonel] asks for some sage, and some basil, if you have such. She brought a dish with her to warm for the evening," said Aelfric, thawing a little, "and has it on a hob there, but it wants for sage.'"

MONK'S-HOOD

A fragrant culinary herb, sage was grown in Cadfael's walled garden. It was also used as an aromatic ingredient in perfumed oils for altar lamps.

Ruling Planet: Jupiter

USES

Medicinal: Possessing antiseptic and astringent properties, sage was prescribed for coughs, colds, headaches, epilepsy, lethargy, palsy, menstruation problems and liver complaints. It was also used as a hair conditioner, to soothe nerves, to stimulate the digestive system and to cleanse the blood. Sage tea was used to treat sore throats, laryngitis, tonsillitis, mouth ulcers and infected gums. In medieval times sage was chewed to whiten yellowing teeth. Gerard said that Agrippa 'called it the Holy-herb, because women with child if they be like to come before their time, and are troubled with abortments, do eat thereof to their great

good; for it closeth the matrix, and maketh them fruitful, it retaineth the birth, and giveth it life.' Large doses of the herb can be dangerous.

Culinary: Sage, a strong aromatic herb, was used in salads, stuffings, pottages, soups, pickles, cheeses, desserts, jellies, vinegars, wines, liqueurs, and ales. It was also eaten to make fatty meats, like pork and duck, more digestible.

Miscellaneous: A native of Mediterranean regions, sage was considered sacred by the ancient Greeks and Romans, the latter gathering the herb in a special ceremony that involved the use of a knife not made of iron (because sage reacts with iron salts). Its botanical name Salvia derives from the Latin for to be saved, or to be well. Introduced into England by the Romans, the herb was known to the Anglo-Saxons, and was listed by Aelfric. In addition to being a 'cure-all', sage was reputed to possess the power of longevity. An Arabian proverb asked: 'How can a man die who has sage in his garden.' While in England it was said: 'He that would live for aye, must eat sage in May.' Folklore maintained that when sage flourished in a garden the owner's business would prosper, but when it withered their business would fail. The herb was used in soaps, perfumes, cosmetics and pot-pourri.

St John's Wort, Common

Hypericum perforatum

also known as Perforate St John's Wort

Chronicles: XI An Excellent Mystery; XIV The Hermit of Eyton Forest

✣ 'Cadfael had also brought a draught to soothe the pain, a syrup of woundwort and Saint John's wort in wine, with a little of the poppy syrup added.'
                                        An Excellent Mystery

Used in an ointment for wounds, St John's wort was also added to wine, together with a little poppy and woundwort syrup, to soothe pain.

Ruling Planet: Sun in Leo

USES

Medicinal: St John's wort was used for nervous exhaustion, epilepsy, depression, insomnia, bronchial catarrh, stomach complaints and madness. Externally, it was used for wounds (particularly deep sword cuts), sores, burns, bruises, inflammations, sprains, haemorrhoids and nerve pains, such as neuralgia and sciatica.

Culinary: The fresh leaves of St John's wort were added to salads.

Miscellaneous: A native of Britain, St John's Wort was reputed to possess healing and protective powers derived from John the Baptist: the red spots on its leaves (said to appear on 29 August, the anniversary of his death) representing the blood spilled when the saint was beheaded. When crushed, the yellow flowers also release a red juice. Alternatively, some authorities claim that the herb takes its name from the Knights of St John, who used it to treat those wounded in the Crusades. The glandular dots or 'perforations' around the edges of the leaves were said to have been caused by the devil in a vain attempt to destroy the plant with a needle. As a protection against evil, the herb was once known as *Fuga daemonium*, or the 'devil's flight', because its scent was said to be so abhorrent to the devil that he was forced to keep well away. Its botanical name *Hypericum* is thought to be derived from the Greek for 'over a picture', a reference to the flowers being placed above a religious image to ward off evil. Superstition claimed that those treading on the plant after sunset would be carried away by a fairy-horse on a wild journey that would last the entire night. The herb yields a yellow dye with alum and a violet-red dye with alcohol.

SANICLE

Sanicula europoea
also known as Wood Sanicle
CHRONICLES: XI AN EXCELLENT MYSTERY;
XIV THE HERMIT OF EYTON FOREST

S

❖ 'Cadfael bathed away the encrusted exudations and cleaned the gash with a lotion of water betony and sanicle.' THE HERMIT OF EYTON FOREST

A cleanser and astringent, good for old, ulcerated wounds, sanicle was found along the banks of the Meole brook and in the hedgerows and meadows nearby. It was an ingredient in a lotion for cleaning gashes and grazes.

Ruling Planet: Mars

USES

Medicinal: In medieval England sanicle was valued as one of the great wound herbs. Gerard said that it was used in 'vulnerary potions, or wound drinks, which maketh whole and found all inward wounds and outward hurts: it also helpeth the ulcerations of the kidneys, ruptures, or burstings.' It was also prescribed for diarrhoea, dysentery, coughs, catarrh, chest complaints, and urinary and liver disorders. Externally, it was used in a gargle for sore throats, and to treat various skin diseases.

Miscellaneous: A native of Europe, sanicle was once held to be a panacea. So powerful were its healing properties, that it was said: 'He that hath sanicle, needeth no surgeon.' Although the name is said to come from the Latin for sound or healthy, it may be a derivation of St Nicholas, (Santa Claus) the patron saint of apothecaries. The plant was listed by Aelfric.

SAVORY, GARDEN OR SUMMER

Satureja hortensis
Winter or Mountain Savory:
Satureja montana
CHRONICLES: I A MORBID TASTE FOR BONES

Savoury [sic] was grown in Cadfael's herb-garden.

Ruling Planet: Mercury

USES

Medicinal: Both winter and summer savory possess similar medicinal properties (the former, however, being less effective). The herbs were mainly used for stomach and bowel complaints, intestinal disorders and flatulence. They were also used to relieve tired eyes and insect stings. Infused as a tea, savory stimulated the appetite, eased indigestion, and served as a gargle for sore throats. The plant should not be taken during pregnancy.

Culinary: A hot peppery-flavoured herb, savory was added to salads, sauces, stews, soups, stuffings, meats, vegetables, syrups, conserves, vinegars and liqueurs. Because it helped prevent flatulence, savory was widely used in bean dishes.

Miscellaneous: A native of southern Europe and the Mediterranean, savory was valued by the Romans who classed it as a spice, and also introduced it into Britain. The plant was known to the Anglo-Saxons, and was listed by Aelfric. Its botanical name *Satureja* is thought to be derived from the Latin for satyr, a term referring to the herb's aphrodisiacal reputation for encouraging sexual indulgence. It was also used in perfumes, and as a strewing herb.

Saxifrage

Pimpinella saxifraga

also known as Burnet Saxifrage;
Greater Burnet Saxifrage: *Pimpinella major*

Chronicles: III Monk's-Hood

✣ "'What is it?' asked Brother Edmund curiously. Many of Brother Cadfael's preparations he already knew, but there were constantly new developments. Sometimes he wondered if Cadfael tried them all out on himself.
"There's rosemary, and horehound, and saxifrage, mashed into a little oil pressed from flax seeds, and the body is a red wine I made from cherries and their stones. You'll find they'll do well on it, any that have the rheum in their eyes or heads, and even for the cough it serves too.'" Monk's-Hood

Ruling Planet: Moon

USES

Medicinal: Held in high esteem by ancient herbalists, saxifrage was used to stimulate digestion, ease respiratory infections, treat kidney and urinary complaints, cure flatulence and protect against the plague. Externally, it was used to treat slow-healing wounds, and as a gargle for sore throats. Chewing the fresh root was said to remedy toothache and paralysis of the tongue.

Culinary: Saxifrage was added to salads, cakes, sauces, soups, and fish and vegetable dishes. The herb was also used to flavour alcoholic drinks.

Miscellaneous: A native of Britain, burnet saxifrage is a member of the *Umbelliferae* (parsley) family, and therefore neither a burnet nor a saxifrage.

Selfheal

Prunella vulgaris

also known as Carpenter's Herb,
Hook-heal, or Sicklewort

Chronicles: V The Leper of Saint Giles

Selfheal grew among the white stones of a wall near Huon de Domville's hunting lodge in the Long Forest.

Ruling Planet: Venus

USES

Medicinal: Although selfheal had various medicinal uses, including being a traditional cure for sore throats, in medieval England it was primarily regarded as a wound herb. Culpeper said that it 'is a special remedy for inward wounds; for outward wounds in unguents and plasters.' He also recommended its external use for headaches.

Culinary: The young leaves of selfheal were added to salads and cooked as a vegetable.

Miscellaneous: A native of Europe, selfheal flourished in grassland, pastures and open woodland throughout Britain. Although there is doubt as to whether it was listed by Aelfric, the plant was certainly known to the Anglo-Saxons. Its common names, sicklewort and hook-heal, come from the resemblance of the upper part of the flower to a billhook or sickle (this, according to the 'Doctrine of Signatures', was an outward sign of the plant's use as a healer of accidental wounds). As the throat was also discerned in the shape of the flower, selfheal was also used to treat diseases of the throat. Indeed, its botanical name *Prunella* is derived from the German for quinsy.

SNOWDROP

Galanthus nivalis

also known as Fair Maids of
February or Bulbous Violet

❖ 'The hand with which she re-coiled the yarn
was languid and translucent, and the eyelids half-
lowered over her hollow eyes were marble-white,
and veined like the petals of a snowdrop.'

THE POTTER'S FIELD

USES

Medicinal: The snowdrop was used to promote
menstrual discharge and ease digestive disorders.
The crushed bulbs were applied as a poultice to
frostbite. The plant is poisonous.

Miscellaneous: A native of central and southern
Europe, snowdrops were rarely mentioned in
herbals. Gerard said: 'Touching the faculties of
these bulbous violets we have nothing to say,
seeing that nothing is set down hereof by the
ancient writers, nor anything observed by the
moderns, only they are maintained and cherished
in gardens for the beauty and rareness of the
flowers, and sweetness of their smell." Being
among the first plants to flower, the snowdrop
represented the passing of winter and the arrival of
spring. It was also considered to be a symbol of
purity and hope. Folklore warned that it was
extremely unlucky to bring a snowdrop into the
home, for a death in the household was sure to
follow. One explanation for this tradition was that
the flower resembled a corpse in a white shroud.
Its botanical name *Galanthus* is derived from the
Greek for milk-flower, clearly a reference to its
milk-white colour.

SORREL, COMMON OR GARDEN

Rumex acetosa

also known as Green Sauce, Sour Leaves
or Cuckoo's Meat

A little flask of mint and sorrel vinegar was sniffed
as a restorative after dizziness and fainting.

Ruling Planet: Venus

USES

Medicinal: Sorrel was used to cleanse blood, ease
constipation, reduce fever, treat jaundice, and
remedy urinary, kidney and liver disorders. As a
poultice it was used for infected wounds, boils,
ulcers and various skin complaints. Pliny said that
the root was used to 'treat lichen and leprous
sores', and chewed, it 'strengthens loose teeth.'
Large doses of sorrel can be poisonous.

Culinary: In medieval times sorrel was an
important vinegar and pot vegetable. The young
leaves were used in salads, sauces, porrays, soups,
stews and other dishes. Because of its acid taste,
the herb was also added to verjuice.

Miscellaneous: A native of Britain, sorrel has been valued for its culinary and medicinal properties since ancient times. The name comes from the old French for sour. Rumex is derived from the Latin for to suck, a reference to the use of the leaves by Roman soldiers to relieve thirst, and *acetosa* comes from the Latin for vinegar. Folklore said that the cuckoo ate the plant to lubricate its vocal chords, hence the name cuckoo's meat. The plant was also used to remove stains from linen, and as a substitute for rennet in curdling milk. It yields a yellow or green dye.

SOW-THISTLE, SMOOTH

Sonchus oleraceus

also known as Hare's Lettuce;
Prickly Sow-thistle: *Sonchus asper*

CHRONICLES: XIII THE ROSE RENT

❖ 'Cadfael . . . plucked out a leggy sow-thistle from among his mint. "How is it that weeds grow three times faster than the plants we nurse so tenderly? Three days ago that was not even there. If the kale shot up like that I should be pricking the plants out by tomorrow."'   THE ROSE RENT

Ruling Planet: Venus

USES

Medicinal: Sow-thistle was prescribed for fevers, urinary disorders, stomach complaints, stones, deafness, inflammation, swelling and haemorrhoids. Gerard said that 'the juice of these herbs doth cool

and temper the heat of the fundament and privy parts.' It was also recommended for those that were short-winded and troubled by wheezing.

Culinary: The leaves of sow-thistle were eaten raw in salads, and cooked in soups or as a vegetable.

Miscellaneous: A native of Britain, sow-thistle was a common weed of waysides, and waste and cultivated ground. Listed by Aelfric, it was believed to possess various magical properties, including the power to repel witches, and increase strength and stamina. Probably with the latter in mind, Pliny mentioned that sow-thistle was eaten by Theseus, the mythical Greek hero who slew the Minotaur. The plant was also a principal ingredient in an ointment reputed to make those who smeared it on their body invisible. The name arose because the juice in its hollow stems was said to have been eaten by nursing sows to increase their milk. As the weed was a favourite food of hares (and, indeed, rabbits), it came to be known as 'hare's lettuce' or 'hare's thistle'. The milky juice was used as a cosmetic.

SPIKENARD

Nardostachys grandiflora
or *Nardostachys jatamansi*
also known as Nard
CHRONICLES: A RARE BENEDICTINE
(THE PRICE OF LIGHT)

❖ '"Beware of the sin of those apostles who cried out with the same complaint against the woman who brought the pot of spikenard, and poured it over the Saviour's feet. Remember Our Lord's reproof of them, that they should let her alone, for she had done well!"'

A RARE BENEDICTINE (THE PRICE OF LIGHT)

USES

Medicinal: Oil of spikenard was taken to relieve nervous headaches, indigestion, insomnia and depression. Externally, it was used to treat skin rashes and inflammations. Gerard said that 'it provoketh urine, helps gnawing pains of the stomach, dries up the defluxions that trouble the belly and entrails, as also those that molest the head and breast. It stays the fluxes of the belly, and those of the womb, being used in a pessary, and in a bath it helps the inflammation thereof.'

Miscellaneous: A native of Asia, spikenard was mentioned in the Bible, and used to anoint the feet of Jesus at the Last Supper. The perfume extracted from the root was held in high esteem by the Romans. Pliny said that the Indian 'nard' held 'a foremost place among perfumes,' adding that in Rome 'the next most highly praised kind is the Syrian, then that from Gaul, and in the third place is the Cretan.' The plant's botanical name *Nardostachys* is derived from the Greek for spike, or ear of corn.

STOCK
see Clove-Pink

STONECROP, COMMON OR BITING

Sedum acre
also known as Wall-pepper
CHRONICLES: V THE LEPER OF SAINT GILES

Stonecrop was found growing among the white stones of a wall near Huon de Domville's hunting lodge in the Long Forest.

Ruling Planet: Moon

USES

Medicinal: Stonecrop was used to stem bleeding, heal ulcers and sores, treat scurvy, cure scrofula or the 'king's evil', resist fevers, expel poisons, treat haemorrhoids and kill intestinal worms. It was also prescribed to remove warts and corns. Culpeper said that 'the juice taken inwardly excites vomiting.' The plant is potentially poisonous. Even external use can cause blisters or skin irritation.

Culinary: The dried and powdered leaves of stonecrop were used as a substitute for pepper.

Miscellaneous: A native of Britain, stonecrop grew wild on roofs, rocks, walls, sand dunes and dry grassy slopes. Its botanical name *Sedum* is thought to be derived from the Latin for to calm or to settle, a reference to its soothing properties. *Acre*, like 'wall-pepper', alludes to the acrid, bitter taste of the fresh leaves. Among its reputed magical properties, the plant was said to repel witches and protect houses from fire and lightning.

S

STRAWBERRY, WILD

Fragaria vesca
also known as Wood Strawberry;
Alpine Strawberry:
Fragaria vesca 'semperflorens'
CHRONICLES: XIII THE ROSE RENT

❖ 'The twentieth of June dawned in a series of sparkling showers, settling by mid-morning into a fine, warm day. There was plenty of work waiting to be done in the orchards of the Gaye, but because of the morning rain it was necessary to wait for the midday heat before tackling them. The sweet cherries were ready for picking, but needed to be gathered dry, and there were also the first strawberries to pick, and there it was equally desirable to let the sun dry off the early moisture.'

THE ROSE RENT

Ruling Planet: Venus

USES

Medicinal: Strawberries were used for wounds, stomach and urinary disorders, dysentery, diarrhoea, liver complaints and digestive upsets. Strawberry leaf tea was taken as a tonic after illness, and for anaemia and bad nerves. According to the 'Doctrine of Signatures' the colour and shape of the fruit suggested that it was a cure for heart disease. Gerard said 'the distilled water drunk with white wine is good against the passion of the heart, reviving the spirits, and making the heart merry.' The crushed fruits were used to lighten the complexion, remove freckles, soothe sunburn and whiten discoloured teeth.

Culinary: Strawberries were eaten raw, made into sauces, desserts, jams and syrups, or used to flavour liqueurs, cordials and cooked meat.

Miscellaneous: A native of Britain, wild strawberries were known to the ancient Britons, the Romans and the Anglo-Saxons. The plant was listed by Aelfric. The name comes from the Old English for to strew, and refers to the spreading of the plant's creepers over the ground, and not from the much later practice of putting straw under the berries. Some authorities, however, suggest that the name may come from the scattering of pips over the surface of the fruit. As a symbol of perfection and righteousness, the strawberry was dedicated to the Virgin Mary. In medieval art and literature it also represented sensuality and earthly desire. The fruit was used in cosmetics, and the dried leaves were added to pot-pourri.

SWEET CICELY

Myrrhis odorata

also known as Sweet Chervil,
the Roman Plant or British Myrrh
(Culpeper: *Scandix odorata*)

CHRONICLES: III MONK'S-HOOD

Ruling Planet: Jupiter

USES

Medicinal: Sweet cicely was prescribed for flatulence, digestive complaints, epilepsy, rheumatism, coughs, pleurisy and to give protection against the plague. It was also applied as a compress for bruises and swellings. As an ointment it was used to treat green wounds, sores, ulcers and gout. Gerard said that the roots were 'very good for old people that are dull and without courage; it rejoiceth and comforteth the heart, and increaseth their lust and strength.'

Culinary: The aniseed-flavoured leaves of sweet cicely were included in fruit and vegetable salads, or cooked as a pot-herb. Added to acid fruits, they reduced the amount of sugar required in cooking. Gerard said: 'The seeds eaten as a salad whilst they are yet green, with oil, vinegar, and pepper, exceed all other salads by many degrees, both in pleasantness of taste, sweetness of smell, and wholesomeness for the cold and feeble stomach.' The seeds were also used to flavour certain liqueurs, while the roots were cooked, or grated raw into salads.

Miscellaneous: A native of the mountainous parts of southern Europe, sweet cicely was probably introduced into Britain by the Romans. Its botanical name *Myrrhis odorata* means 'the fragrant perfume of myrrh'. Cicely comes from *sesili* or *seselis*, the ancient Greek name for the plant. The flowers, among the first to appear in spring, were a favourite source of nectar for bees. The seeds were used to scent and polish furniture.

TANSY

Tanacetum vulgare or
Chrysanthemum vulgare

also known as Golden Buttons;
Garden Tansy: *Tanacetum hortis*

CHRONICLES: I A MORBID TASTE FOR BONES

Tansy was grown Cadfael's herb-garden.

Ruling Planet: Venus

USES

Medicinal: Tansy was used to expel worms, aid digestion, relieve flatulence, treat gout, dissolve concealed blood and promote menstruation. Externally, the herb was applied to swellings, sprains, bruises and varicose veins. Tansy tea was prescribed as a general tonic, and to stimulate appetite, treat jaundice, reduce blood pressure and strengthen the heart. Of the garden tansy Culpeper said 'Let those women that desire children love this herb, it is their best companion, the husband excepted.' The herb should not be taken during pregnancy. An overdose can be poisonous.

Culinary: The bitter, aromatic leaves of tansy, used sparingly, were stewed with rhubarb, and added to sauces, salads, cakes, creams, omelettes, possets and custards. In medieval England they were made into tansy pancakes, traditionally eaten to mark the end of the Lenten fast; being bitter, they also served as a reminder of Christ's suffering. Tansy was also used as a substitute for spices like nutmeg and cinnamon. The leaves, wrapped around meat, were said to act as a preservative and fly-repellant.

Miscellaneous: A native of Britain, tansy was known to the Anglo-Saxons, and listed by Aelfric. The botanical name *Tanacetum* is derived from the Greek for immortality, referring to the long-lasting appearance of the flowers when dried, or to the ancient use of the plant in embalming or preserving corpses. In Greek mythology Ganymede, cup-bearer of Zeus, was made immortal by drinking the juice of tansy. During the Middle Ages the plant was a popular disinfecting herb for strewing, and an insect-repellant. As a remembrance of the bitter Passover herbs, it featured in various Easter rituals. The flowers yield a yellow-orange dye, and were added to pot-pourri.

Tare, Hairy

Vicia hirsuta
Smooth Tare: *Vicia tetrasperma*
CHRONICLES: XVI THE HERETIC'S APPRENTICE

Tares were found growing like weeds in wheatfields.

Ruling Planet: Moon

USES

Medicinal: Culpeper said: 'Tares are rarely used in medicines, though the vulgar boil them in milk, and give the decoction to drive out the small-pox and measles.'

Miscellaneous: The hairy tare, common on cultivated ground and grassland throughout Britain, is a member of the pea family. Despite improving the fertility of poor soils, it reduced the crop-yield in cornfields, and made harvesting more difficult. The tare referred to in the Biblical parable is thought to be the bearded darnel (*Lolium temulentum*), the commonest of the four species of tares to be found in the Holy Land.

Thyme, Common

Thymus vulgaris
also known as Garden Thyme;
Wild Thyme or Mother of Thyme:
Thymus praecox or *Thymus serpyllum*
CHRONICLES: I A MORBID TASTE FOR BONES;
II ONE CORPSE TOO MANY;
V THE LEPER OF SAINT GILES;
X THE PILGRIM OF HATE;
XII THE RAVEN IN THE FOREGATE;
XVI THE HERETIC'S APPRENTICE;
XVII THE POTTER'S FIELD

✣ 'Beyond lay his herb garden, walled and silent, all its small, square beds already falling asleep, naked spears of mint left standing stiff as wire, cushions of thyme flattened to the ground, crouching to protect their remaining leaves, yet over all a faint surviving fragrance of the summer's spices.'
THE RAVEN IN THE FOREGATE

Cadfael grew thyme in his herb-garden. In Father Eadmer the elder's undulating garden, 'a short bench of earth' had been 'turfed over with wild thyme, for a seat.'

Ruling Planet: Venus

USES

Medicinal: Possessing antiseptic and disinfectant qualities, thyme was used for indigestion, flatulence, gastric upsets, bronchial troubles, coughs, colds, laryngitis, colic, rheumatism and menstrual disorders. Thyme tea was prescribed for hangovers, flu, and mouth, gum and throat infections. Sleeping on a pillow stuffed with thyme was recommended for giddiness and nightmares.

Pliny said that thyme cured melancholy, 'troubles of hypochondria' and 'aberrations of the mind', adding that it was 'also administered to epileptics, who when attacked by a fit are revived by its smell.' Thyme should not be taken during pregnancy.

Culinary: A pot-herb, thyme stimulated the appetite and helped the digestion of fatty meats, such as mutton and pork. It was used in salads, stews, soups, stuffings, vegetables, pickles, sauces, cheeses, omelettes, and various other dishes. The herb was also used to flavour liqueurs. Thyme honey was especially valued.

Miscellaneous: A native of the Mediterranean region, thyme was employed by the ancient Etruscans and Egyptians for embalming their dead. As a herb traditionally associated with death, the flowers were said to provide a resting-place for the souls of those who had died. It was also said that the scent of thyme could be detected in places where murders had been committed. The plant's botanical name *Thymus* is derived from either the Greek for courage or to fumigate, the latter referring to its use as incense in temples. The herb was introduced into Britain by the Romans, and listed by Aelfric. As an emblem of courage, thyme was added to soups and beer to cure shyness. During the Middle Ages ladies presented their 'bold and brave' knights with 'favours' embroidered with a sprig of thyme. In addition to being carried by judges to ward off gaol fever, bunches of thyme were strewn on floors, and burned to fumigate houses and repel insects. It was also put in wardrobes to keep moths away from linen. Being a favourite flower of the fairies, thyme was reputed to possess the power to make them visible to humans. The herb was used in soaps, cosmetics, perfumes and pot-pourri.

TOADFLAX, COMMON

Linaria vulgaris
also known as Flaxweed,
Lion's Mouth or Devil's Head
CHRONICLES: V THE LEPER OF SAINT GILES

❖ 'Among the rough white stones of the wall there were all manner of wild herbs growing, toadflax and ivy, stonecrop and selfheal, known by their leaves even now that hardly any flowers remained.'
THE LEPER OF SAINT GILES

Ruling Planet: Mars

USES

Medicinal: Toadflax was prescribed for constipation, dropsy, kidney complaints, liver diseases, scrofula, enteritis, hepatitis and gall bladder problems. Externally, the herb was used for cuts, haemorrhoids, sores, malignant ulcers, skin rashes and conjunctivitis. The herb should not be taken during pregnancy.

Miscellaneous: A native of Britain, toadflax flourished in hedges, banks, meadows, waste ground and roadsides. The botanical name *Linaria* comes from the Greek for flax, a reference to the herb's flax-like leaves. 'Toadflax' may derive from the similarity of the oddly-shaped flowers to little toads. However, T. F. Thiselton Dyer in *The Folk-Lore of Plants* claimed that the prefix 'toad' meant 'spurious', in the sense that toadflax 'before it comes into flower, bears a tolerably close resemblance to a plant of the true flax.' Because the mouth of the flower opened when its sides were squeezed, the plant was also called 'lion's mouth', 'devil's head', and so on. During the Middle Ages it was used for laundry starch, and, boiled in milk, as a fly poison.

Toadstool
see Fungus

Trefoil, Heart

Trifolium cordatis

Chronicles: VII The Sanctuary Sparrow

❖ '"Now here I'm leaving you this flask – it's the decoction of heart trefoil, the best thing I know to strengthen the heart."'   The Sanctuary Sparrow

Cadfael gave Dame Juliana Aurifaber a decoction of heart trefoil after a seizure.

Ruling Planet: Sun

USES

Medicinal: Culpeper said that heart trefoil 'is a great strengthener of the heart, and cherisher of the spirits, relieving those who faint and swoon; it is a remedy against poison and pestilence, and defends the heart against the noisome vapours of the spleen.'

Miscellaneous: Gerard took the heart trefoil to be *Medicago arabica* (spotted medick), 'which grows wild in many places with us, having the leaves a little dented at the ends, so that they resemble the vulgar figure of a heart; and each leaf is marked with a blackish, or red spot: the flowers be small and yellow.' (*see* Clover)

Vetch, Common

Vicia sativa

Tufted Vetch: *Vicia cracca*

Chronicles: II One Corpse Too Many; XI An Excellent Mystery

❖ 'Then she [Godith Adeney] sat down in the grass and vetches and moth-pasture of the bank to wait.'   One Corpse Too Many

Tendrils of vetch were often represented in illuminated designs and engravings.

Ruling Planet: Moon

USES

Medicinal: Gerard, quoting Galen, said that although eaten in times of famine, vetch 'is hard of digestion, and bindeth the belly. Therefore seeing it is of this kind of nature, it is manifest that the nourishment which comes thereof hath in it no good juice at all, but ingendereth a thick blood, and apt to become melancholy.'

Miscellaneous: Despite its name, common vetch is less common that the tufted vetch. Although distributed in the wild throughout Britain, the plant is only really common in south-eastern England. It was probably introduced into the country by the Romans, and was listed by Aelfric. During the Middle Ages vetch was grown for silage and fodder, and the seeds fed to domestic pigeons. As it disliked being trampled by cattle, the plant was more likely to be found in hay meadows than on grazing land (*see* Hay). It was also grown in monastic gardens to add colour to hedges. The characteristic feature of vetches is their habit of climbing ladder-like up neighbouring plants by means of branched tendrils. Tufted vetch is a close relative of the hairy tare (*see* Tare).

VINE
see Grapevine

VIOLET, SWEET

Viola odorata
Dog Violet: *Viola riviniana*
CHRONICLES: XII THE RAVEN IN
THE FOREGATE;
XVI THE HERETIC'S APPRENTICE

❖ '"See the violets, and how true their colour is!"
THE HERETIC'S APPRENTICE

Violets, used as a fragrant ingredient in perfumed oils for altar lamps, were sometimes represented in illuminated designs.

Ruling Planet: Venus

USES

Medicinal: Sweet violets were used as a mild laxative, and to relieve respiratory disorders, hot swellings, coughs, colds, mouth and throat infections, catarrh, headaches, insomnia, quinsy, pleurisy, epilepsy and many other ailments. Gerard said 'the leaves of violets are used in cooling plasters, oils, and comfortable cataplasms, or poultices; and are of greater efficacy among other herbs, as Mercury, Mallows, and such like.'

Culinary: Violet petals were added to salads, crystallized for cake and pudding decorations, and made into a sweet syrup for flavouring custards and omelettes. They were also used to flavour wine.

Miscellaneous: A native of Europe, North Africa and the Middle East, sweet violets have been cultivated for their perfume and healing properties for over 2,000 years. Pliny said that 'placed on the head in chaplets, or even smelt, they disperse the after-effects of drinking and its headaches.' The ancient Greeks held the flower in such high esteem that they made it the emblem of Athens. It was also the flower of Aphrodite (Venus), the goddess of love, and as such was often included in love-potions. As a symbol of purity and humility, it was associated with the Virgin Mary. The plant was known to the Anglo-Saxons, and listed by Aelfric. Folklore says that violets blooming in autumn foretell the arrival of some kind of epidemic in the following year. Although there are about nine British violets, most country folk recognized only two: the sweet violet (the only one to have scented flowers) and the dog violet (the prefix being a derogatory term for a plant that was in some way inferior to its relative – that is, it had no perfume). Gerard highly praised violets, 'for they admonish and stir up a man to that which is comely and honest; for flowers through their beauty, variety of colour, and exquisite form, do bring to a liberal and gentlemanly mind, the remembrance of honesty, comeliness, and all kinds of virtues.' Violets yield a purple dye. The flowers were used in perfumes, floral waters and pot-pourri.

WALNUT, ENGLISH

Juglans regia

also known as Persian Walnut
or Jupiter's Nuts

CHRONICLES: XIII THE ROSE RENT

Two big walnut trees grew in the orchards of the Gaye at Shrewsbury Abbey.

Ruling Planet: Sun

USES

Medicinal: The leaves or fruit of the walnut were used to treat stomach complaints, kidney and urinary stones, flatulence, intestinal worms, hair loss and the bite of a mad dog or man! Walnut leaf tea was prescribed as a tonic, and to stimulate the appetite. Externally, it was used for rheumatism, gout, swellings, scrofula and various skin complaints, including eczema and herpes. Pliny said oil of walnuts 'is useful for mange, and is injected into the ears for hardness of hearing.' The shelled nut's resemblance to the human brain led to the medieval belief that it could cure mental disorders.

Culinary: Walnuts were eaten raw, pickled, preserved in syrup, and added to cakes, stuffings, salads and sauces. They were also included in fruit pies, nut comfits, nut jam, and sweet and sour meat dishes. The leaves and green husks were used to make cordials, liqueurs and wine. The nuts were a valuable source of cooking oil.

Miscellaneous: A native of south-eastern Europe and the Middle East, the walnut was introduced into Britain by the Romans. Its botanical name *Juglans regia*, is derived from the Latin for the 'royal nut of Jove' (hence also 'Jupiter's nuts'). Walnut, or 'walsh nut' is said to come from the German for foreign. Pliny said that walnuts 'received their name in Greek [meaning 'torpor'] from the heaviness of the head which they cause; the trees themselves, in fact, and their leaves give out a poison that penetrates to the brain.' The plant was listed by Aelfric. In folklore the tree was reputed to ward off lightning. Its nuts were said to promote fertility, reveal the face of one's true love, and, if placed under a witch's chair, rob her of all power of mobility. The custom of giving the tree a sound whipping to improve its fruit, is referred to in the old saying: 'A spaniel, a woman, and a walnut-tree, the more they're beaten, the better they be.' The leaves were used in the home to repel flies, insects and moths. Certain parts of the tree yield a brown dye, once used to colour hair. The wood was used to make furniture, cabinets and interior panelling. Walnut oil was used in lamps, wood polish, and artists' paints.

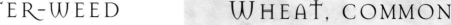

WATER-WEED

Curled Pondweed: *Potamogeton crispus*;
Broad-leaved Pondweed: *Potamogeton natans*
CHRONICLES: V THE LEPER OF SAINT GILES;
IX DEAD MAN'S RANSOM

❖ 'Elis [ap Cynan] waded into the water, and selected a place for one of his stakes, hidden among the water-weed with its point sharply inclined to impale anyone crossing in unwary haste.'
DEAD MAN'S RANSOM

Ruling Planet: Moon

USES

Medicinal: Gerard said that pondweed 'is good against the itch, and consuming or eating ulcers', and 'also it is good being applied to the inflammation of the legs'. Quoting Galen, he also suggested the plant 'doth bind and cool'.

Miscellaneous: Broad-leaved and curled pondweed – two of some twenty-four water-weeds found in Britain – thrive in the mud at the bottom of ponds, lakes, canals, ditches and slow-moving rivers. In some parts of England, country folk believed that the floating leaves of broad-leaved pondweed gave birth to young pike, hence its common names, 'fish-leaves' and 'pickerel-weed'. The botanical name *Potamogeton* is derived from the Greek for river and neighbour, a reference to its aquatic habitat. Canadian pondweed (*Elodea canadensis*), a native of North America, was introduced into England in the early nineteenth century and spread so rapidly that it blocked rivers and drains, causing navigational problems and severe flooding.

WHEAT, COMMON

Triticum vulgare
also known as Corn
CHRONICLES: II ONE CORPSE TOO MANY;
IV SAINT PETER'S FAIR;
V THE LEPER OF SAINT GILES;
VII THE SANCTUARY SPARROW;
X THE PILGRIM OF HATE;
XI AN EXCELLENT MYSTERY;
XII THE RAVEN IN THE FOREGATE;
XIII THE ROSE RENT;
XV THE CONFESSION OF BROTHER HALUIN;
XVI THE HERETIC'S APPRENTICE;
XVII THE POTTER'S FIELD;
XVIII THE SUMMER OF THE DANES;
XX BROTHER CADFAEL'S PENANCE

❖ 'The reapers came back in time for Vespers, sun-reddened, weary and sweat-stained, but with the corn all cut and stacked for carrying.'

ONE CORPSE TOO MANY

Summer and winter wheat was grown in the fields beyond the Gaye, almost opposite Shrewsbury castle. After the crop had been harvested and stored in the barns the sheep and cattle were allowed to graze the stubble. The corn was ground in the abbey mill.

Ruling Planet: Venus

USES

Medicinal: Wheat was used for inflammations, swellings, eczema, ringworm, painful joints, wounds and ulcers. Gerard said 'the fine flour mixed with the yolk of an egg, honey, and a little saffron, doth draw and heal boils and such like sores, in children and in old people, very well and quickly.' Pliny mentioned that a man seized with the pains of gout buried himself in wheat up to his knees, and 'he was relived of the pain, and the water in his feet dried up in a wonderful way.'

Culinary: Grains of wheat, ground into flour, were used in cooking, especially for bread, cakes and pastries. The wheat germ, extracted before milling, was also a valued food.

Miscellaneous: Wheat, one of the oldest and most important of cereal crops, has been cultivated in Britain since prehistoric times. Archaeological research has established that a form of the grass grew in the Holy Land some 9,000 years ago. Grains of wheat have been discovered in ancient Egyptian tombs. In medieval times a corn dolly, plaited from the straw of the last sheaf of wheat to be harvested, was stored over winter and ploughed into the ground the following spring. It was believed to contain the Harvest Spirit, whose survival was essential to ensure the success of the crop that followed. The reed straw was also used for thatching.

WILLOW, WHITE

Salix alba

Crack Willow: *Salix fragilis*;
Common Osier: *Salix viminalis*;
Pussy Willow: *Salix caprea*

❖ 'Even the willow leaves hung motionless here, sheltered from the faint breeze that stirred the grasses along the river bank.' ONE CORPSE TOO MANY

❖ 'A freckled boy of about seventeen was stooped over his jointer, busy bevelling a barrel stave, and another a year or two younger was carefully paring long bands of willow for binding the staves together when the barrel was set up in its truss hoop.' AN EXCELLENT MYSTERY

A source for withies, willows grew along the banks of the river Severn and around the abbey millpond at Shrewsbury. Many of the trees were pollarded (the practice of cutting back the top branches to produce a dense crop of new shoots for fencing, and so on). Long bands of willow were used for binding the staves of a barrel together.

Ruling Planet: Moon

USES

Medicinal: The bark of willow was used to alleviate pain, relieve headaches, and reduce fevers. It was also used for rheumatism, arthritis, internal bleeding, inflammations, gout, heartburn, colds, nervous insomnia, digestive problems and stomach complaints. Externally, it was applied for burns, sores, cuts and skin rashes. Culpeper said: 'The leaves bruised and boiled in wine, and drank, stays the heat of lust in man or woman, and quite extinguishes it, if it be long used.'

Miscellaneous: Willows were among the earliest trees to recolonize the landscape after the Ice Age. Although there are over twenty different species of willow, those listed above are native to Britain. Their botanical name *Salix* is said to be derived from the Celtic for near water. 'Crack willow' comes from the fact that the brittle twigs tend to snap off easily. As some of the broken twigs take root when washed ashore, crack willows tend to form lines along river banks. In addition to making baskets, fish-traps, fences and coracles, willow was used in tanning, as fodder, to attract bees, to make artists' charcoal, to produce a purple dye, and to prevent erosion along the banks of rivers and ditches. The downy covering of the seeds was used as mattress stuffing. In folklore the willow was associated with sorrow and lost love. Sprigs were sometimes worn as a sign of mourning; or by those who had been forsaken in love, hence the saying 'to wear the willow'. Some sorcerers and enchanters favoured wands made of willow. The plant was listed by Aelfric.

WILLOWHERB, ROSEBAY

Epilobium angustifolium
also known as Fireweed;
Broad-Leaved Willowherb:
Epilobium montanum;
Great Hairy Willowherb:
Epilobium hirsutum

CHRONICLES: II ONE CORPSE TOO MANY

❖ '"I am not finding it at all dull, these days," said Cadfael, plucking out willowherb from among the thyme. "And as for enemies, the devil makes his way in everywhere, even into the cloister, and church, and herbarium."' ONE CORPSE TOO MANY

Ruling Planet: Saturn

USES

Medicinal: According to Culpeper: 'All the species of willowherbs have the same virtues,' the 'most powerful' being the yellow willowherb (*Epilobium lysimachia*). The plants were prescribed for haemorrhages, migraine, dropsy, stomach and urinary disorders, asthma and whooping cough. As an ointment, they were used to treat skin inflammations and infections.

Culinary: Rosebay willowherb shoots were boiled and eaten like asparagus, and the leaves used as a tea substitute.

Miscellaneous: Found in the wild throughout Britain, willowherbs were so named because of the resemblance of their leaves to those of the willow. As the rosebay willowherb often colonized ground that had been cleared by fire, it was commonly known as 'fireweed'. Gerard said that 'the fume or smoke of the herb burned, doth drive away flies and gnats, and all manner of venomous beasts.'

WINDFLOWER
see Anemone

Woad

Isatis tinctoria

Chronicles: XIII The Rose Rent

❖ 'As heiress to the clothier's business for want of a brother, she had learned all the skills involved, from teasing and carding to the loom and the final cutting of garments, though she found herself much out of practice now at the distaff. The sheaf of carded wool before her was russet-red. Even the dye-stuffs came seasonally, and last summer's crop of woad for the blues was generally used up by April or May, to be followed be these variations on reds and browns and yellows, which Godfrey Fuller produced from the lichens and madders. He knew his craft. The lengths of cloth he would finally get back for fulling had a clear, fast colour, and fetched good prices.'

THE ROSE RENT

Ruling Planet: Saturn

USES

Medicinal: The leaves of woad were strongly astringent and helped stem the flow of blood, which is probably why the Celts, or ancient Britons, painted themselves with woad before going into battle. Externally, as an ointment or plaster, the herb was used to staunch bleeding, and heal wounds, ulcers, and inflammations. Gerard said: 'The decoction of woad drunken is good for such as have any stopping or hardness in the milt or spleen.' However, internal use is not advisable, as the herb is poisonous.

Miscellaneous: A native of south-eastern Europe, woad – valued for the blue dye extracted from its leaves – arrived in Britain several thousand years ago. Pliny said that 'with it the wives of the Britons, and their daughters-in-law, stain all the body, and at certain religious ceremonies march along naked.' The plant was listed by Aelfric. During the Middle Ages woad was extensively cultivated as a wool and cloth dye. Gerard's comment that it was 'profitable to some few, and hurtful to many', is probably a reference to the fact that the herb robbed the soil of nourishment and made it necessary to move the crop to another plot of land every two years. This led to a shortage of fertile land for food production, resulting in hardship for large numbers of common folk. Parkinson reported another harmful and equally serious effect of woad: 'Some have sown it but they have found it to be the cause of the destruction of their bees, for it hath been observed that they have died as it were of a Flix, that have tasted thereof.'

WOLFSBANE
see Monk's-Hood

WORMWOOD, COMMON

Artemisia absinthium

also known as Absinthe or Green Ginger;
Roman Wormwood: *Artemisia pontica*;
Sea Wormwood: *Artemisia maritima*

CHRONICLES: XII THE RAVEN IN THE FOREGATE

Wormwood was used as an aromatic ingredient in perfumed oils for altar lamps.

Ruling Planet: Mars

USES

Medicinal: Wormwood was traditionally used in childbirth. The herb was also prescribed for stimulating the appetite, aiding digestion, treating jaundice, constipation and kidney disorders, reducing fevers, expelling intestinal worms, remedying liver and gall bladder complaints, curing flatulence and improving blood circulation.

Externally, it was applied to sprains, bruises, inflammation, rheumatism and lumbago. Pillows stuffed with wormwood were recommended for insomnia. An overdose can be dangerous. It should not be taken by pregnant or breast-feeding women.

Culinary: Sparsely employed in cooking because of its extreme bitterness, wormwood was used to flavour alcoholic drinks, especially vermouth, and the dangerously potent absinthe.

Miscellaneous: A native of Britain, Europe and Asia, wormwood was highly esteemed by many ancient civilizations, including the Egyptians, Greeks and Romans. Pliny said that a draught of the herb was offered to the winner of a ritual, four-horsed chariot race on the Capitoline Hill at Rome, 'our ancestors thinking, I believe, that health was a very grand prize to give.' Its botanical name *Artemisia* comes from the Greek Artemis (known to the Romans as Diana), goddess of chastity. *Absinthium* is derived from the Greek for without sweetness, or undrinkable. 'Wormwood' refers to the medicinal use of the herb as a vermifuge. Legend says that it sprang up in the tracks of the serpent as it was leaving the Garden of Eden. In medieval England bunches of the herb were hung up in rooms to repel moths, fleas and insects, prevent infection, and ward off evil spirits. It was also used as a strewing herb and hair dye. Added to ink, it discouraged mice from eating the writing material.

WOUNDWORT
see Betony

Yew

Taxus baccata

also known as English Yew

Chronicles: X The Pilgrim of Hate

❖ "'There he checked, rounding the corner of the yew hedge into the rose garden.'"

The Pilgrim of Hate

Ruling Planet: Saturn

Uses

Medicinal: Yew was used as a purgative, and to treat heart and liver diseases, gout, rheumatism, arthritis and urinary infections. Culpeper said 'though it is sometimes given usefully in obstructions of the liver and bilious complaints, those experiments seem too few to recommend it to be used without the greatest caution.' The plant is poisonous.

Miscellaneous: A native of Britain, the yew has long been revered as a sacred tree, and as a potent protection against evil. Since prehistoric times, and certainly during the Middle Ages, the wood has been highly prized for making longbows and axe-handles. A yew spear found near Clacton-on-Sea in Essex has been estimated to be some 150,000 years old. The botanical name *Taxus* is derived from the Greek for arrow. Indeed, the crushed seeds were once used as an arrow poison. Pliny said that the tree was so toxic that 'even wine-flasks for travellers made of its wood in Gaul are known to have caused death.' Although Gerard claimed that the yew in England was not poisonous, he said that 'in most countries, it hath such a malign quality, that it is not safe to sleep, or long to rest under the shadow thereof.' In folklore the tree, being evergreen and long-lived, was a symbol of immortality, or life after death. As such, it was often planted in graveyards. In some places, the trees are reputed to be so old that they may have existed before the early Christians built their churches. To bring cuttings of yew into the home was said to lead to a death in the family. Even damaging the tree was considered to bring bad luck. Smoke from the burning leaves was supposed to repel gnat and mosquitoes, as well as kill rats and mice. The tree was listed by Aelfric.

Select List of
Additional Medieval Plants and Herbs

Agrimony (*Agrimonia eupatoria*)
Mainly used to treat wounds and staunch bleeding.*

Alecost (*Chrysanthemum balsamita* or *Tanacetum balsamita*)
Used to flavour ale, treat liver diseases and clear urine.*

Balm, Lemon (*Melissa officinalis*)
Known as the bee plant, it was rubbed on hives to attract swarms.*

Bedstraw, Lady's (*Galium verum*)
Mixed with other herbs, the dried plant was used for stuffing mattresses.

Buttercup, Meadow (*Ranunculus acris*)
Used externally to soothe and relieve pain, but can cause blistering.

Catmint (*Nepeta cataria*) also known as Nep
Used to induce perspiration in fevers, season meat and attract bees.*

Celandine, Greater (*Chelidonium majus*)
The juice, mixed with honey, was used to treat eye infections.

Celery, Wild (*Apium graveolens*)
The leaves were used to relieve indigestion and purify the blood. The ground seeds were an ingredient of celery salt.*

Chamomile (*Chamaemelum nobile*)
Highly valued as a soothing and mildly sedative tonic for nervous complaints and restlessness.*

Chives (*Allium schoenoprasum*)
Used for flavouring, and to soothe inflammation and insect bites.

Coriander (*Coriandrum sativum*)
Mentioned in ancient Sanskrit texts and in the Bible, the herb was used in cooking, and was reputed to be an aphrodisiac.*

Corncockle (*Agrostemma githago*)
Once a common cornfield weed. Unless removed from the crop, its poisonous seeds ruined flour.

Cranesbill, Meadow (*Geranium pratense*)
Astringent and antiseptic, the herb was used for haemorrhages, wounds and excessive menstruation.

Cress, Garden (*Lepidium sativum*) also known as Dittander
One of the Anglo-Saxon 'hot' medicinal herbs, possessing natural antibiotic properties. Added to salads, sauces and 'porrays'.*

Cumin (*Cuminum cyminum*)
A popular medieval condiment. Prescribed as a tonic and as a stimulant. Now mainly used in veterinary medicine and Indian cooking.*

Daffodil, Wild (*Narcissus pseudonarcissus*) also known as Lenten Lily
The bulbs were used as a narcotic, purgative and emetic.

Elecampane (*Inula helenium*) also known as Horseheal
The candied root was made into lozenges for throat infections. The leaves were applied as a poultice for sciatica and various skin diseases.*

Elder (*Sambucus nigra*)
Fruits and flowers were used to make wines and jams.

Euphorbia (*Euphorbia hortense*) also known as Garden Spurge; Greater Spurge: *Euphorbia major*
Applied externally, the milky, acrid and poisonous juice was used to remove warts, calloses and carbuncles.

Feverfew (*Chrysanthemum parthenium*, or *Tanacetum parthenium*)
Mainly used to reduce fevers and cure migraine.*

Foxglove, Purple (*Digitalis purpurea*) also known as Witches' Gloves, Dead Men's Bells and Fairy Thimbles
Valued in the treatment of heart disease and dropsy. Poisonous.

Garlic (*Allium sativum*)
Used for culinary and medicinal purposes since ancient times.*

Germander, Wall (*Teucrium chamaedrys*)
Used to lower fevers and stimulate digestion. Externally, it was used for skin problems and snakebites.

Greenweed, Dyer's (*Genista tinctoria*)
Yellow dye plant. Combined with woad it made an excellent green.

Hart's Tongue Fern (*Phyllitis scolopendrium*)
A shade-loving plant, used to treat liver and spleen disorders.

Hellebore, Green (*Helleborus viridis*)
Used as a purgative, and for skin problems, epilepsy and depression. Poisonous.

Hellebore, Black (*Helleborus niger*) also known as Christmas Rose
A purgative and heart stimulant, also applied as a poultice for leprosy. Poisonous.

Henbane (*Hyoscyanus niger*) also known as Hog's Bean
Used as a sedative and painkiller for nervous conditions and toothache, and as a poultice for gout. Poisonous.*

Holly (*Ilex aquifolium*)
Believed to possess magical protective powers. Infused leaves were used for coughs and colds. The berries are poisonous.

Hollyhock (*Althea rosea*)
Grown for ornamental value and soothing medicinal properties. Used for coughs and certain chest complaints.

Leek (*Allium porrum*)
Extremely popular vegetable with the Celts, Anglo-Saxons and Normans.*

Liquorice (*Glycyrrhiza glabra*)
Used since ancient times for coughs, colds and throat infections. Probably cultivated in England from the fourteenth century, previously imported.

Lovage (*Levisticum officinale* or *Ligisticum levisticum*) also known as Love Parsley
An 'all-healing plant', mainly used to treat digestive complaints and urinary problems. A medieval pot-herb.*

Marigold, Corn (*Chrysanthemum segetum*)
Valued for all kinds of fevers, and to promote sweating.

Marigold, Pot (*Calendula officinalis*)
A medieval emblem of enduring love. Flowers used to relieve wasp and bee stings.*

Mayweed (*Anthemis cotula*) Scentless Mayweed: *Matricaria maritima*
Used to treat female complaints. The name is derived from the Old English for maiden.*

Meadowsweet (*Filipendula ulmaria*)
One of the three most sacred herbs of the Druids (*see* Mint p.139). Used in medieval times as a strewing herb, and for flavouring mead and beer.*

Medlar (*Mespilus germanica*)
A tree traditionally planted in herb gardens. The fruit was made into preserves, and used medicinally to staunch bleeding and for diarrhoea.*

Mugwort (*Artemisia vulgaris*)
One of the nine sacred herbs of the Anglo-Saxons. Reputed to have magical powers, especially against witchcraft. Used for nervous disorders and female complaints, and as a poultice for ulcers and swellings.*

Nightshade, Black (*Solanum nigrum*) also known as Poisonberry
Used in painkilling ointments, and as a poultice for inflammation. Poisonous.*

Pansy, Wild (*Viola tricolor*) also known as Heartsease
Used to stimulate the immune system, cleanse blood and treat skin complaints. Associated with love and remembrance.

Plantain, Great (*Plantago major*) also known as Waybroad or Waybread; Ribwort Plantain: *Plantago lanceolata*
One of the nine sacred herbs of the Anglo-Saxons. The leaves were used as a poultice to heal wounds, blisters and bites. Internally, it was used for gastric ulcers, catarrh and sinus problems.*

Rocket (*Eruca sativa*)
A popular salad herb in ancient times. Also reputed to be an aphrodisiac. Used to promote urine.

Savin (*Juniperus sabina*)
Used externally only, for spreading ulcers, sores, carbuncles and ringworm. Poisonous.

Soapwort (*Saponaria officinalis*) also known as Fuller's Herb
Crushed and boiled in water the herb produced a mild soapy liquid, ideal for washing delicate fabrics. Fullers used it for cleaning cloth. Also used to treat skin conditions.

Solomon's Seal (*Polygonatum officinale* or *Polygonatum odoratum*)
Cultivated for ornament and medicine. Gerard said the root 'taketh away in one night, or two at the most, any bruise, black or blue spots gotten by falls or women's wilfulness, in stumbling upon their hasty husband's fists, or such like.'

Southernwood (*Artemisia abrotanum*) also known as Lad's Love
Prescribed to stimulate digestion, destroy intestinal worms and promote menstruation. Culpeper said that 'the ashes mingled with old salad oil, helps those that are bald, causing the hair to grow on the head or beard.'*

Sweet Rocket (*Hesperis matronalis*)
A sweet-smelling herb, grown for its fragrance.

Teasel, Common (*Dipsacus fullonum*)
Fuller's Teasel: *Dipsacus fullonum* 'sativus'; also known as Brushes and Combs
Water collected in the stems was reputed to possess soothing, healing properties. The hooked spines on the ends of the bracts of fuller's teasels were used for fluffing up cloth.*

Valerian (*Valeriana officinalis*)
The dried roots were used in medieval times as a spice and perfume. Reputed to be an aphrodisiac. The juice was used for calming nerves, epilepsy and hysterical complaints.

Vervain (*Verbena officinalis*)
One of the three most sacred herbs of the Druids. Used to ward off evil, and included in love potions and aphrodisiacs. Believed to protect against the plague. Prescribed for jaundice, sore throats, headaches and, as a poultice, to heal wounds.*

Wallflower (*Cheiranthus cheiri*)
Cultivated for scent and beauty.

Water-lily, White (*Nymphaea alba*)
A poetic symbol of purity of heart. Used to reduce sexual desire.

Woodruff, Sweet (*Galium odoratum* or *Asperula odorata*)
A strewing herb. Gerard said 'being made up into garlands or bunches, and hanged up in houses in the heat of summer, doth very well attemper the air, cool and make fresh the place, to the delight and comfort of such that are therein.'*

Yarrow (*Achillea millefolium*) also known as Bloodwort, Soldier's Woundwort or Nosebleed
Valued for healing wounds, staunching bleeding and reducing fevers. Used as a digestive and cleansing tonic. The stems were used for divination.*

THE SHREWSBURY QUEST

Many of the plants and herbs listed in this book can be found growing in the gardens of The Shrewsbury Quest: a medieval heritage centre that not only celebrates the colourful world of Brother Cadfael, but offers visitors a fascinating re-creation of monastic life in the twelfth century.

Located opposite the Abbey of St Peter and St Paul at Shrewsbury – and incorporating renovated parts of the monastic buildings, demolished after the Dissolution – The Quest officially opened its gates to the public on 23 June 1994. Among its various attractions are: Ellis Peters' study, containing books and memorabilia associated with the best-selling author; the scriptorium, where visitors can learn about the medieval art of calligraphy and create their own illuminations; a restaurant, which serves food inspired by medieval recipes; and, for would-be sleuths of all ages, intriguing mysteries with clues to solve.

Yet probably the most popular of all The Quest's attractions are the unique twelfth-century gardens, complete with cloistered walkway, fish-pond and tunnel arbour. Inspired by a rare surviving plan of a monastic garden at the cathedral priory of Christ Church, Canterbury, dating from about 1165, the gardens were designed in authentic medieval style by Sylvia Landsberg, the garden historian, and creatively laid out by Graham Cox, The Quest's head gardener. Covering a quarter of an acre, the site consists of the Cellarer's Beds, the Green Court, the Abbot's Herber and Cadfael's Herb and Private Gardens.

The plants and herbs, some common and others quite rare, are all known to have been cultivated in England during the period in which *The Chronicles of Brother Cadfael* are set. The wide and varied collection was carefully selected from the list of plants compiled by John Harvey, the renowned historian of medieval architecture and gardens.

Among the medieval garden tools in practical use is a simple and ingenious watering thumb-pot. Once the pot is full, the water is prevented from spraying out of the perforations in the base by placing the thumb over the hole in the top. When the thumb is released, the water flows; replace it and the water stops.

Within the walls of the great Benedictine monastery of Christ Church, Canterbury, was a large green area, similar in function to a village green. As space at The Quest is restricted, this area is represented by the Green Court, its central feature being a turf seat, symbolically planted with a Glastonbury Thorn (*Crataegus monogyna biflora*). The Abbot's Herber has been laid out as a small, ornamental pleasure garden, for use by the abbot as his private retreat. The Cellarer's Beds contain vegetables and herbs for use either in the infirmary or in the kitchen. Cadfael's Herb or Physic Garden, although full of medicinal herbs, has been designed to give a feeling of intimacy and personal pride, in keeping with descriptions in the *Chronicles*. Germander, hyssop and certain other plants, although not native to Britain, have been included by Landsberg as 'examples of plants that informed travellers such as Cadfael could have brought into the country.' Cadfael's Private Garden demonstrates the frequent custom of growing rare or poisonous plants, such as monk's-hood and henbane, in a partitioned or 'locked' section of the physic garden.

Adjacent to his 'herbal kingdom', and without which the gardens would not be complete, is a painstakingly detailed replica of Cadfael's Workshop, that 'dim, timber-scented, herb-rustling miniature world where he spent so much of his time, and did his best thinking.'

From the doorway, the visitor can look out over the gardens of Cadfael's herbarium, and across the roof of the cloister walk to the tower and battlements of the abbey church. Despite the massive changes that have taken place over intervening centuries, it is not difficult to imagine oneself transported back to that medieval, monastic world created by Ellis Peters in *The Chronicles of Brother Cadfael*, and described so vividly, so accurately and so entertainingly.

In a letter to the Ellis Peters Appreciation Society in the USA, Cadfael's author wrote of The Shrewsbury Quest: 'I am a wholehearted supporter, and urge all who come to Shrewsbury to regard it as my enterprise no less than the town's, and to visit it and enjoy it.'

Given her thrill and enthusiasm for The Quest, it can be assumed that the fictional monk-detective himself would have been delighted to give it his full and generous blessing. Especially the gardens.

❖ 'IN THE SWEET-SCENTED TWILIGHT
CADFAEL WENT TO PAY HIS USUAL
NIGHTLY VISIT TO HIS WORKSHOP,
TO MAKE SURE ALL WAS WELL THERE, AND
STIR A BREW HE HAD STANDING TO COOL
OVERNIGHT. SOMETIMES, WHEN THE
NIGHTS WERE SO FRESH AFTER THE HEAT
OF THE DAY, THE SKIES SO FULL OF
STARS AND SO INFINITELY LOFTY, AND
EVERY FLOWER AND LEAF SUDDENLY SO
IMBUED WITH ITS OWN LAMBENT COLOUR
AND LIGHT IN SPITE OF THE LIGHT'S
DEPARTURE, HE FELT IT TO BE A GREAT
WASTE OF THE GIFTS OF GOD TO
BE GOING TO BED AND SHUTTING HIS
EYES TO THEM.'

AN EXCELLENT MYSTERY

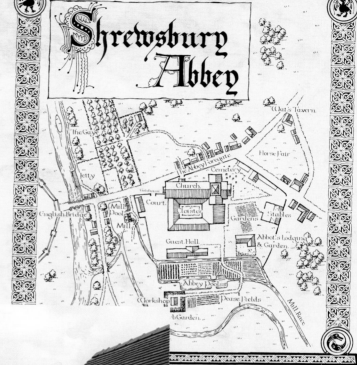

Brother
CADFAEL

BIBLIOGRAPHY

Black, Maggie, *Food and Cooking in Medieval Britain: History and Recipes*, H.M.B.C.E., London, 1985

Blunt, Wilfrid, & Raphael, Sandra, *The Illustrated Herbal*, Frances Lincoln, London, 1979

Boyd, Anne, *Life in a Medieval Monastery*, Cambridge University Press, Cambridge, 1975

Brock, A.J. (trans.), *Galen: On the Natural Faculties*, Harvard University Press, London, 1916

Culpeper, Nicholas, *Culpeper's Complete Herbal*, Foulsham, London, n.d. (1st pub. 1653)

Culpeper, Nicholas, *Culpeper's Complete Herbal & English Physician*, Gleave, Manchester, 1829

Desmond, Ray, *Wonders of Creation: Natural History Drawings in the British Library*, British Library, 1986

Dyer, T.F. Thiselton, *The Folk-Lore of Plants*, London, 1889

Fleming, Laurence, & Gore, Alan, *The English Garden*, Michael Joseph, London, 1979

Garland, Sarah, *The Herb Garden*, Frances Lincoln, London, 1984

Gerard, John, *The Herbal or General History of Plants*, (enlarged and amended by Thomas Johnson), London 1633 (1st pub. 1597)

Gordon, Lesley, *A Country Herbal*, Webb & Bower, Exeter, 1980

Grieve, Mrs M., *A Modern Herbal*, Cape, London, 1931

Handford, S.A. (trans.), *Caesar: The Conquest of Gaul*, Guild, London, 1951 (rev. 1982)

Harvey, John, *Mediaeval Gardens*, Batsford, London, 1981

Hort, Arthur, (trans.), *Theophrastus: Enquiry Into Plants* (2 vols.), Harvard University Press, London, 1916

Hunt, Tony, *Plant Names of Medieval England*, Brewer, Cambridge, 1989

Jones, W.H.S. (trans.), *Hippocrates* (2 vols.), Heinemann, New York, 1923

Landsberg, Sylvia, *The Medieval Garden*, British Museum Press, London, 1996

Law, Donald, The Concise Herbal Encyclopedia, Bartholomew, Edinbugh, 1973

Loewenfeld, Claire, & Back, Philippa, *Herbs for Health and Cookery*, Pan, London, 1965

McLean, Teresa, *Medieval English Gardens*, Collins, London, 1981

McVicar, Jekka, *Jekka's Complete Herb Book*, Kyle Cathie, London, 1994

Michael, Pamela, *A Country Harvest*, Exeter Books, New York, 1987 (1st pub. in GB 1980)

Milner, J. Edward, *The Tree Book*, Collins & Brown, London, 1992

Minter, Sue, *The Healing Garden*, Headline, London, 1993

Ody, Penelope, *The Herb Society's Complete Medicinal Herbal*, Dorling Kindersley, London, 1993

Owen, H. and Blakeway, J.B., *A History of Shrewsbury* (2 vols.), Harding, Lepard and Co., 1825

Page, T.E. (ed.), Eichholz, D.E. (trans.), *Pliny: Natural History* (10 vols.), Loeb Classical Library, Heinemann, London, 1962

Palaiseul, Jean, (trans. Pamela Swinglehurst), *Grandmother's Secrets: Her Green Guide to Health from Plants*, Barrie & Jenkins, London, 1973

Rackham, Oliver, *The History of the Countryside*, Dent, London, 1986

Rackham, Oliver, *The Last Forest*, Dent, London, 1989

Rohde, Eleanour Sinclair, *The Old English Herbals*, Dover, New York, 1971 (1st pub. 1922)

Sanecki, Kay N., *History of the English Herb Garden*, Ward Lock, London, 1992

Spencer, William David, Mysterium and Mystery: The Clerical Crime Novel, Southern Illinois University Press, Carbondale, USA, 1992 (1st pub. 1989)

Strange, Richard le, *A History of Herbal Plants*, Angus and Robertson, London, 1977

Stuart, Malcolm, (ed.), *The Encyclopedia of Herbs and Herbalism*, Macdonald, London, 1979

OTHER BOOKS BY TALBOT & WHITEMAN

The Cotswolds, The English Lakes, Shakespeare's Avon, Cadfael Country, The Yorkshire Moors & Dales, The Heart of England, The West Country, Wessex, The Garden of England, English Landscapes, East Anglia & the Fens.
Photographs by Talbot:
Shakespeare Country, The Lakeland Poets, Cotswold Villages.
Text by Whiteman:
The Cadfael Companion.

ACKNOWLEDGEMENTS

Robin Whiteman and Rob Talbot would like to acknowledge: Arthur Fielder, Beringar Limited (exclusive licensing agents for Brother Cadfael on behalf of Ellis Peters and Carlton UK Television) for permission to use copyright material relating to Brother Cadfael; The Shrewsbury Quest for permission to take photographs of their monastic exhibitions and gardens; and David Austin Roses for the use of the photograph of their 'Brother Cadfael' rose on page 167. (It should be noted that, with the permission of Beringar Ltd, David Austin Roses named a new and improved variety of English rose 'Brother Cadfael' *Rosa ausglobe*.) The quote from William David Spencer's *Mysterium and Mystery: The Clerical Crime Novel* (Carbondale, Illinois, USA: Southern Illinois University Press, 1989, 1992; reprint of London: UMI Research Press, 1989) is used with the kind permission of the author.